Essays and Studies 2022

Series Editor: Ceri Sullivan

The English Association

The English Association is a membership body for individuals and organisations passionate about the English language and its literatures. Our membership includes teachers, students, authors, and readers and is made up of people and institutions from around the world.

Our aim is to further the knowledge, understanding, and enjoyment of English studies and to foster good practice in their teaching and learning at all levels, by

- encouraging the study of English language and literature in the community at large
- working toward a fuller recognition of English as core to education
- fostering discussion about methods of teaching English at all levels
- supporting conferences, lectures, and publications
- responding to national consultations and policy decisions about the subject

More information about the Association is on our website: http://bit.ly/join-the-EA

Publications

The Year's Work in English Studies – published annually, *The Year's Work in English Studies* is a qualitative narrative bibliographical review of scholarly work that year about the English language or literatures in English, from Old English to contemporary criticism.

The Year's Work in Critical and Cultural Theory – a companion volume in the field of critical and cultural theory, recording significant debates in a broad field of research in the humanities and social sciences.

Essays and Studies – published since 1910, *Essays and Studies* is an annual collection of essays on topical issues in English, edited by a different distinguished academic each year. The volumes cover a range of subjects and authors, from medieval to modern.

English – published quarterly, *English* is a forum for people who think hard and passionately about literature and who want to communicate those thoughts to a wide audience. It includes scholarly essays and reviews on all periods of literary history and new work by contemporary poets.

English 4 to 11 – published three times a year, this magazine contains material produced by and for the classroom leader. It is a reader-friendly magazine, backed by sound pedagogy, offering ideas for developing classroom practice.
The Use of English – published three times per year, this journal's articles and reviews are designed to encourage teachers to further their own interest and expertise in the subject.
Newsletter – produced three times per year, the *Newsletter* contains topical articles, news items, and interviews about English studies and updates about The English Association's activities.

Benefits of Membership

Unity and voice – members join others with a wealth of experience, knowledge, and passion for English to foster the discussion of teaching methods and respond to national issues.
Resources – members can access high quality resources on the Association's website, and in its volumes, journals, magazines, and newsletters.
Networking – members can network with colleagues and leading practitioners, including joining national special interest groups and their local Regional Group. Members are also given reduced rates for the Association's conferences and other events.

Essays and Studies 2022

The Waste Land after One Hundred Years

Edited by
Steven Matthews

for the English Association

D. S. BREWER

ESSAYS AND STUDIES
IS VOLUME SEVENTY-FIVE IN THE NEW SERIES
OF ESSAYS AND STUDIES COLLECTED ON BEHALF OF
THE ENGLISH ASSOCIATION
ISSN 0071-1357

First published 2022
D. S. Brewer, Cambridge

D. S. Brewer is an imprint of Boydell & Brewer Ltd
PO Box 9, Woodbridge, Suffolk IP12 3DF, UK
and of Boydell & Brewer Inc.
668 Mt Hope Avenue, Rochester, NY 14620-2731, USA
website: www.boydellandbrewer.com

ISBN 978-1-84384-636-9

A CIP catalogue record for this book is available
from the British Library

Printed and bound in Great Britain by
TJ Books Limited, Padstow, Cornwall

Contents

Notes on Contributors

Rebecca Beasley is Professor of Modernist Studies at the University of Oxford. She is the author of *Ezra Pound and the Visual Culture of Modernism* (Cambridge University Press, 2007), *Theorists of Modernist Poetry: Ezra Pound, T.S. Eliot and T.E. Hulme* (Routledge Critical Thinkers, 2007), and *Russomania: Russian Culture and the Creation of British Modernism, 1881–1922* (Oxford University Press, 2020). She is editor, with Philip Ross Bullock, of *Russia in Britain: From Melodrama to Modernism* (Oxford University Press, 2013) and, with Tim Armstrong, co-editor of the Edinburgh University Press book series Edinburgh Critical Studies in Modernist Culture. She is a former Chair of the British Association for Modernist Studies.

Rosinka Chaudhuri is Director and Professor of Cultural Studies at the Centre for Studies in Social Sciences, Calcutta (CSSSC). She was inaugural Mellon Professor of the Global South at Oxford University, 2017–18, and has held visiting positions at St Hugh's College, Oxford, King's College, London, Delhi University, Cambridge University and Columbia University. Her books include *Gentlemen Poets in Colonial Bengal: Emergent Nationalism and the Orientalist Project* (Seagull, 2002), *Freedom and Beef-Steaks: Colonial Calcutta Culture* (Orient Blackswan, 2012) and *The Literary Thing: History, Poetry and the Making of a Modern Cultural Sphere* (Oxford University Press, 2013, Peter Lang, 2014). She has edited *Derozio, Poet of India: A Definitive Edition* (Oxford University Press, 2008), *The Indian Postcolonial* (with Elleke Boehmer, Routledge UK, 2010), *A History of Indian Poetry in English* (Cambridge University Press, 2016), *An Acre of Green Grass and Other English Writings of Buddhadeva Bose* (Oxford University Press, 2018), and a series titled *Social Science Across Disciplines* (co-edited with Partha Chatterjee, Oxford University Press, 2019). Most recently, she has edited, annotated and introduced George Orwell's *Burmese Days* for Oxford World's Classics (2021). Her translation of Rabindranath Tagore's letters, *Letters from a Young Poet (1887–94)* (Penguin Modern Classics, 2014) received an Honorable Mention at the A.K. Ramanujan Prize for Translation (S. Asia) 2016.

William Davies is an independent scholar, teacher, writer and editor. His research interests include twentieth-century British and Irish poetry, modern war writing and modernism and its legacies. He has recently completed a series of publications on the work of Samuel Beckett, including the monograph *Samuel Beckett and the Second World War* (Bloomsbury, 2020) and the essay volumes *Beckett and Politics* (with Helen Bailey, Palgrave, 2021) and *Samuel Beckett's Poetry* (with James Brophy, Cambridge University Press, 2022). He is also the author of essays on the works of Donald Davie, Harold Pinter and Thomas MacGreevy, among others. He is an English editor for *LONGITŪDINĒS*, an art and translation magazine. He is currently writing a book about Harold Pinter's work beyond the stage.

Hugh Haughton was born in Cork and is Emeritus Professor of Modern Literature at the University of York. He is the author of *The Poetry of Derek Mahon* (Oxford University Press, 2007), and the editor of *The Chatto Book of Nonsense Poetry* (1988), *The Letters of T.S. Eliot*, Volumes 1 and 2 (Faber, 2009), *Second World War Poems* (Faber, 2005), and Freud, *The Uncanny* (Penguin, 2005). He has written numerous essays on twentieth-century British and Irish poetry, including recently on Yeats, Eiléan Ni Chuilleanáin, T.S. Eliot and Marianne Moore, as well as on Queer Nonsense.

Steven Matthews is Professor of Modernist and Beckett Studies, and Director of the Samuel Beckett Research Centre at Reading University. His books include *Irish Poetry: Politics, History, Negotiation* (Macmillan, 1997); *Yeats as Precursor* (Macmillan, 2000); and *Les Murray* (Manchester University Press, 2001). *T.S. Eliot and Early Modern Literature* appeared with Oxford University Press in 2013 and *Ceaseless Music*, a critical-creative reflection on Wordsworth's *The Prelude*, with Bloomsbury in 2017. Collaboration with The Wordsworth Trust, Grasmere, on aspects of the project led to a two-month exhibition, 'Sounds of Wordsworth', at the Wordsworth Museum, Grasmere, co-curated with the composer Paul Whitty. Archived at https://wordsworth.org.uk/blog/2017/07/26/sounds-of-wordsworth/. His edition of Samuel Beckett's *Philosophy Notes*, with Matthew Feldman, was published by Oxford University Press in 2020. Matthews was an inaugural poet-in-residence at the Natural History Museum, Oxford in 2016. *Guests of Time*, an anthology which includes poems from the residency, appeared with Valley Press in 2017. He has published two poetry collections – *Skying* (Waterloo Press, 2012) and *On Magnetism* (Two Rivers, 2017). A third collection, *Some Other Where*, is scheduled for 2023.

Marjorie Perloff was Sadie D. Patek Professor of Humanities Emerita at Stanford University until her retirement in 2002. She is also Florence Scott Professor Emerita of English at the University of Southern California. Perloff is the author of many books with the University of Chicago Press, including,

Frank O'Hara: Poet among Painters (1977), *The Poetics of Indeterminacy: Rimbaud to Cage* (1981), *The Futurist Moment: Avant-Garde, Avant-Guerre, and the Language of Rupture* (1986, new edition, 1994), *Radical Artifice: Writing Poetry in the Age of Media* (1992), *Wittgenstein's Ladder: Poetic Language and the Strangeness of the Ordinary* (1996), *21st Century Modernism* (2002), and *Unoriginal Genius: Writing by Other Means in the New Century* (2011). *The Edge of Irony: Modernism in the Shadow of the Habsburg Empire* (2016) enlarges on the theme of her 2004 memoir *The Vienna Paradox* (New Directions Press). *Circling the Canon: The Collected Book Reviews of Marjorie Perloff, 1969–2016* was published in two volumes by the University of New Mexico Press in 2019 and her most recent book, *Infrathin: An Experiment in Micropoetics,* has just been published by the University of Chicago Press. Perloff's first English translation/edition of Wittgenstein's *Private Notebooks 1914–16,* is forthcoming from Liveright in Winter 2022.

Andrew Michael Roberts is Professor of Modern Literature in the School of Humanities at the University of Dundee and Co-Director of the Centre for Poetic Innovation at the Universities of Dundee and St Andrews. His research interests are in modernist fiction and poetry, contemporary British and Irish poetry, digital poetry, literature and science, and literature and visual culture. He was Principal Investigator for two AHRC-funded interdisciplinary research projects: 'Poetry Beyond Text: Vision, Text and Cognition' (2009–11), leading a team of researchers in Literature, Psychology, and Fine Art from the Universities of Dundee and Kent; and 'The Archive of Reading' (2011), in collaboration with the Scottish Poetry Library (www.poetrybeyondtext.org). His books include *Conrad and Masculinity* (Palgrave, 2000), *Poetry and Contemporary Culture: The Question of Value* (edited with Jonathan Allison; Edinburgh University Press, 2002), *Geoffrey Hill* (Northcote House, 2004), and *Strangeness and Power: Essays on the Poetry of Geoffrey Hill* (edited collection, Shearsman, 2020). He is currently completing a book on *Poetry & Ethics* for Liverpool University Press.

Peter Robinson is Professor of English and American Literature at the University of Reading. The poetry editor for Two Rivers Press and author of many books of poetry, translations, prose fiction, and literary criticism, he has been awarded the Cheltenham Prize, the John Florio Prize, and two Poetry Book Society Recommendations. His *Collected Poems 1976–2016* was published by Shearsman Books in 2017. Recent publications include *The Sound Sense of Poetry* (Cambridge University Press, 2018), *Bonjour Mr Inshaw* (Two Rivers Press, 2020), *Poetry & Money: A Speculation* (Liverpool University Press, 2020), *The Personal Art: Essays, Reviews & Memoirs*

(Shearsman Books, 2021), and a second, revised edition of *English Nettles and Other Poems* (Two Rivers Press, 2022).

Michael Wood is Professor Emeritus of English at Princeton University. He is a Fellow of the Royal Society of Literature and a member of the British Academy, the American Academy of Arts and Letters, and the American Philosophical Society. He writes regularly in literary publications such as *The New York Review of Books* and the *London Review of Books,* where he is also an editorial board member. His books include *The Magician's Doubts: Nabokov and the Risks of Fiction* (Chatto and Windus, 1994), *Children of Silence: on Contemporary Fiction* (Columbia University Press, 1998), *The Road to Delphi: the Life and Afterlife of Oracles* (Farrar Straus and Giroux, 2003), *Literature and the Taste of Knowledge* (Cambridge University Press, 2005), *Yeats and Violence* (Oxford University Press, 2010), *Alfred Hitchcock: The Man Who Knew Too Much* (Houghton Mifflin Harcourt, 2015), and *On Empson* (Princeton University Press, 2017).

Introduction

STEVEN MATTHEWS

This special issue of *Essays and Studies* both celebrates and reflects upon the centenary of the publication of T.S. Eliot's *The Waste Land*. After a well-attested period of editorial consideration where suggestions and cuts were made by Eliot's wife, Vivien, and by Ezra Pound, and after a relatively difficult process of negotiation around its time and place of publication, the sequence appeared in the first number of the journal Eliot edited in London, the *Criterion*, on 16 October 1922. This version of the work arrived without the Notes which Eliot later added to the end of the sequence – as did the edition which introduced *The Waste Land* to US readers, in the November 1922 issue of the *Dial*. The complete text as we now know it, both poetry and Notes, was first published as a book in the US by Boni and Liveright on 1 December 1922. The first UK publication of the poetry plus the Notes in book form came on 12 September 1923, when *The Waste Land* appeared from Leonard and Virginia Woolf's Hogarth Press.

Interestingly, the work was initially massively more successful in the US than in Britain; the Boni and Liveright book had already sold 1,000 copies by February 1923, sales which rapidly rose to 5,000. In contrast, the 443 copies printed by the Woolfs did not sell out totally until February 1925. The work received forty-six reviews in North America, and only twelve in the UK, of which ten were negative.[1] A return to some of those immediate responses to the poem a hundred years after its first publication, however, reveals several threads that continue through the whole century of critical responses, including in some of the essays gathered here.

For example, the *Times Literary Supplement*, in which an anonymous reviewer considered the whole first issue of the *Criterion* where the poem appeared, compared *The Waste Land* to the translation of 'Dostoevsky's

---

[1]   These dates and figures are given by Lawrence Rainey in his edition *The Annotated Waste Land with Eliot's Contemporary Prose* (New Haven, CT: Yale University Press, 2005), 32, 36. Rainey provides a narrative of the writing of the sequence, including the editorial work by Pound and Vivien; his account and dating is contentious, however, and should be cross-checked against the Commentary on the poem in *The Poems of T.S. Eliot: The Annotated Text*, Volume 1, edited by Christopher Ricks and Jim McCue (London: Faber, 2015).

"Plan for a Novel"', also printed in that issue. The Russian novelist must have found composition 'difficult', the reviewer avers; there are 'hints' of 'spiritual discoveries', but these are not 'fully revealed', and there actually seems to be no 'orderly planning' in this 'Plan'. Eliot's poem 'is also a collection of flashes ... there is no effect of heterogeneity'. Yet the poem is declared both 'beautiful' and revealing of the 'inextricable tangle of the sordid and the beautiful that make up life.' Ultimately the poem is 'purgatorial'.[2] After an elaborate delineation of sources, the American critic Edmund Wilson considered the poem to 'lack structural unity', but nonetheless argued that to move from moment to moment as readers we progress 'simply from one triumph to another'. Again from the States, important negative commentary came from Louis Untermeyer, who claimed that the poem showed 'authenticity' as a rendition of modern 'dissolution', but failed in its duty to 'give form to formlessness'; it is mere 'documentary', not poetry.

Even Eliot's friend, Conrad Aiken, found himself forced to admit that 'the poem is not, in any formal sense, coherent'. But it is from this point that he makes defence of Eliot's practice as 'a brilliant and kaleidoscopic confusion ... a series of sharp, discrete, slightly related perceptions and feelings, dramatically and lyrically presented ... an intimately modern, intensely literary consciousness'. The typically disgruntled but equally telling English response might be represented here by F.L. Lucas's *New Statesman* review, which spoke of the 'philosophy of the poem, if such it be', and of Eliot's method as one of parodies which are 'cheap', and of imitations which are 'inferior' to their original sources.[3]

All of these views are gathered from ephemeral responses to *The Waste Land*, often in the first few months after its publication. They illustrate that these first readers felt that the key questions about the sequence were largely what they remain one hundred years later. Do the moments and immediate experience of passages of the poem predominate over its ultimate design or, in terms of meaning ('philosophy'), over its coherence? Does the poem merely reflect what was already, by late 1922, perceived as an agreed version of and attitude towards 'modern life' – one which it showed little inclination to 'redeem' (that key word in Eliot's later *Ash-Wednesday* (1928))? With its welter of reference and citation, is the work too exclusive, 'intellectual', 'liter-

---

[2]   *T.S. Eliot: The Critical Heritage*, Volume 1, edited by Michael Grant (London: Routledge and Kegan Paul, 1982), 134–5. Notable here is the use of 'heterogeneity', immediately criticising Eliot's poem in terms redolent of Samuel Johnson's famous dismissal of 'the metaphysicals' in his 'Life of Cowley'. For more on this inheritance in Eliot see Steven Matthews, *T.S. Eliot and Early Modern Literature* (Oxford: Oxford University Press, 2013).

[3]   *T.S. Eliot: The Critical Heritage*, vol. 1, 143; 151–3; 158, 160; 198–9.

ary'? That the poem displays a lack of personal response to those seemingly-obviously confusing and dire contemporary circumstances, and particularly a lack of direct emotion, flitters across these reviews, including Aiken's anxious justification. This doubt about a lack of personal emotion or sensitivity in the poem was particularly evident in Elinor Wylie's review from January 1923, as it runs into that other question surrounding the poem for these early as for later readers, that of authenticity: 'When he says *Shantih* three times ... you may not think he means it'. Wylie makes clear that she thinks Eliot does mean it; but that this question of faith in the poem and its speaker is a matter of whether you feel any 'passion', as she does, in the poem's 'tortured pity for ugly and ignoble things'.[4]

All of these issues seemed to be further exacerbated and dramatized with the publication which brought significant renewed attention to the poem as it neared its half-century in 1971, when Faber published *The Waste Land: a facsimile and transcript of the Original Drafts including the Annotations of Ezra Pound*, edited by Valerie Eliot. For the first time, it was possible to consider Eliot's mature drafts towards the poem. The editorial work, not just by Pound but by Vivien Eliot, in making *The Waste Land* perhaps the epochal poem of the twentieth century, was put on show. It was also possible to see more clearly, through these and other means, as several contributors to this special issue consider, the uncertain relation between the poem as a form of displaced personal expression, and its by then well-established status as a kind of document encapsulating particular facets of early twentieth-century consciousness in the cities of Europe in the wake of the First World War. These issues coalesce perhaps further when reading a more recent re-presentation of the poem in the 'Editorial Composite' of all the drafts which is included by Christopher Ricks and Jim McCue in their two-volume Annotated Text edition of *The Poems of T.S. Eliot* (2015). Bewilderment, and uncanny questions of referentiality, are immediately experienced when reading the opening two lines of the (late addition) to the start of the poem in this 'Composite', with their mention of 'Tom's place' and a drunken 'old Tom', lines adopting the abbreviation which Eliot's friends across his life made to his Christian name.

Eliot himself, on the indication of some of his mid-to-late writing, would not have appreciated the isolation of one of his works, as is enacted in the essays in this volume, for particular consideration. In 1930, when introducing a critical work on Shakespeare, Eliot notably emphasised that the dramas must not be considered singly, but as part of a career-long development; what he calls the 'pattern' underlying Shakespeare's writing only becomes visible

---

[4]   Ibid., 156.

once all of the elements are taken together.[5] This is a view about reading and understanding an author's work that he reiterates in various contexts to the end of his critical writings, as for example in the slim book on George Herbert from 1962.[6] Individual publications are, as it were, simply stepping stones across a career, the distinctive features of which are only evident after the author's death. In its turn, this insistence has permeated the ways in which Eliot's poetry, including *The Waste Land*, has been viewed. Indeed, some of the most telling criticism of Eliot's writing has taken this injunction of his from 1930 to heart, establishing the dialogues and thematic developments which are discernible when Eliot's works are read successively, early to late.[7]

In contrast, other critics, with *The Waste Land* firmly in mind, have warned against what, in the approach outlined above, are seen to become 'riskily retrospective' readings of Eliot. Gareth Reeves, whose words these are, considers in his book *T.S. Eliot: A Virgilian Poet* the 'triangular relationship between Eliot, Dante and Virgil' which impels key parts of the work. But Reeves notes that 'retrospect' presents a 'misleading unity' where none existed at the time of a poem's creation: indeed, it specifically 'violates' the nature of the poetry in *The Waste Land*, which Reeves describes as 'exploratory, indeterministic and open-ended'.[8] What is needed in such a various career as Eliot's, Reeves implies, is a criticism which accounts for the unpredictable adjustments and realignments that took place as Eliot set out on each new poem. Rather than seeking some version of coherence which might have become available as Eliot, as it were, caught up with himself through criticism or commentary, we need an approach which recognises the *in*coherence, the *in*completeness of what, at each stage, he undertook.

Something of these tensions around our reading of *The Waste Land* are inevitably re-echoed in the nature of the essays included in this special issue. Some contributors have decided to celebrate Eliot's poem by catching it on the wing, to see the poem as though it had not been read before. Others decided to think about the poem within its textual history; within the history of the sequence's own emergence in its major forms from 1922–23, then 1971, then 2015. Others still decided to see the poem *within* history – either

[5]   T.S. Eliot, 'Introduction' to G. Wilson Knight, *The Wheel of Fire* (London: Oxford University Press, 1930), xv.

[6]   T.S. Eliot, *George Herbert* (Plymouth: Northcote House, 1994), 22.

[7]   See, for example, Christopher Ricks's reading of the redemptive potentiality in *Ash-Wednesday* as deriving from its attention to Eliot's previous work, 'The Hollow Men'. *T.S. Eliot and Prejudice* (London: Faber, 1994), 223.

[8]   Gareth Reeves, *T.S. Eliot: A Virgilian Poet* (London: Macmillan, 1989), 29.

the cultural moment into which it originally emerged, or that history which it has created through responses made to it by later critics and poets.

The sheer range of responses made by our contributors shows how unsettled and unsettling *The Waste Land* remains. It is a poem of perhaps uniquely uncertain and complex standing, one 'fed' by a panoply of seemingly incompatible influences, a poem whose status, as Aiken originally suggested, derives from the strikingly 'modern' nature of its irresolvability. This Introduction will now spend some time sketching some of these original uncertainties as a means of contextualising the essays in the volume. In order to consider *The Waste Land* in this centenary moment against perspectives from 1921, during its drafting, through to its publication in 1922, this Introduction will resist, as Reeves suggests, any 'retrospective' consideration on the basis of Eliot's later criticism or reflections; instead, it will seek to capture some of the conflicting ideas which lay behind, and to an extent instigated, the work at its outset. Certainly, when looked at from the privileged position of the 1971 *Facsimile and Transcript*, Eliot was, at the moment of working on *The Waste Land*, notably conflicted about what he was doing, and, even more notably perhaps, caught between various poetic moods and modes. It is this uncertainty, but also this generic doubt, from which Pound's excisions, at least partly, created the poem as we now know it.

*   *   *

The most extensive cuts made on Pound's advice in the first three sections of the work annul a tendency in Eliot's drafts towards satire, a version of the poem which turned it for significant stretches into a dated and weary commentary on contemporary affairs in the beau monde and on the streets of London. The deletion of that late additional section right at the start of Eliot's draft, in which a 'Tom', gets 'blind' with drink (unlike the final poem's Tiresias, blinded for his violation of the gods' secrets), is followed up when Pound's red pen crossed through a long 'Popean' passage about Fresca, a society woman's levée in Part III, 'The Fire Sermon'.[9] Then, the decision, presumably on Pound's advice, entirely to leave out a section from the loose leaves bundled with the manuscript headed 'The Death of the Duchess', further erodes the notion that one prominent scene for the poem is fashionable 'Hampstead' – the poem as first published is as a result firmly centred in the financial district, the 'City' where Eliot worked for Lloyd's Bank. Other,

---

[9]   This latter passage was given an afterlife when, substantially rewritten, it appeared in a satiric sketch that Vivien Eliot contributed to the April 1924 number of the *Criterion*. See Ann Pasternak Slater, *The Fall of a Sparrow: Vivien Eliot's Life and Writings* (London: Faber, 2020), 522.

shorter passages where Eliot's writing seemed to be lapsing towards satire on modern times, such as mention of the 'swarming life' of London in the drafts towards 'The Fire Sermon', received a similarly robust response from Pound, again in red: 'B—ll—S'.[10]

We can see, therefore, that in its final draft version – the version that Eliot showed to Pound for comment, initially in January 1922 – *The Waste Land* was deeply unsettled in its perspective upon the contemporary world. In a prose piece published when he was working on the early sections of the poem, the 'London Letter' published in the *Dial* in May 1921, Eliot registered, via Baudelaire intriguingly, his appreciation for the 'violence' of English caricature in the journalism of H.M Bateman, and also in the work of his friend Wyndham Lewis, especially when it approaches 'the border of satire and caricature'.[11] Further, he displays his knowledge of this English tradition, from Rowlandson and Cruikshank to Hogarth.[12] In one late version of the poem as it existed in Eliot's mind (as it had from at least as far back as 5 November 1919[13]), the work as we now know it was punctuated by a scabrous and misogynist look at the modern city and its inhabitants – partly deriving from similar passages in earlier work, such as the opening of 'The Love Song of J. Alfred Prufrock', 'Hysteria', and the 'Preludes'. Yet the context behind this (largely deleted) strain in the drafts towards *The Waste Land* reconfirms how much of the eventual poem derives from the proximity between Eliot's critical engagements across this period and the process of poetic creation.[14]

Punctuating this contemporary prose, and indeed often driving it, is a sense of the 'dullness' (or *Dunciad*-like 'dulness') of the cultural, and thence, the social scene, both in England and in America. The 'London Letter' of

---

[10]   T.S. Eliot, *The Waste Land: a facsimile and transcript*, edited by Valerie Eliot (London: Faber, 1971), 4, 26, 104, 30.

[11]   Reprinted in Rainey, *The Annotated Waste Land*, 169.

[12]   In a letter from October 1921, Eliot sees the thought of writing a book on Hogarth as 'fun'. *The Letters of T.S. Eliot*, Volume 1: 1898–1922, edited by Valerie Eliot and Hugh Haughton, revised edition (London: Faber, 2009), 587.

[13]   *The Waste Land: a facsimile and transcript*, xvii–xviii.

[14]   Just two instances: Eliot signed off the short piece 'The Lesson of Baudelaire', written in March 1921, with the phrase '*Vous, hypocrite lecteur ...*' (his italics); although Andrew Marvell's 'To his Coy Mistress' had been glancingly alluded to in 'The Love Song of J. Alfred Prufrock', the poem receives extended discussion in his 31 March 1921 *TLS* contribution on the poet, where he mentions its pertinent modern qualities of 'high speed' and 'surprise'. Marvell's poem then gets taken into the echo-chamber of the second verse paragraph of 'The Fire Sermon'. See Rainey, *The Annotated Waste Land*, 145, 149–50.

March 1921, indeed, enquires where the 'centre of gravity of dullness lies' in each place and concludes that they are 'dull' differently. The important essay 'Prose and Verse' from April 1921 has pertinent reflections on the history of 'the long poem', arguing that Dante, Virgil and Homer were all successful in orchestrating a 'movement toward and away from intensity which is life itself.' That 'life' is clearly something which *The Waste Land* sought to achieve. Eliot's original structuring, such as the realistic passage he added at the outset about 'Tom', was geared towards such larger movements in ways that the Pound-edited, more resonantly-focused, final version was not. But 'Prose and Verse' predicates its 'enquiry' into these matters on the basis that 'the present condition of English literature is so lifeless' – a 'condition' that then seems to characterise many of the figures in *The Waste Land*.[15]

In the hinterland of Eliot's critical thinking when he was working on the sequence, therefore, is a driving impatience with the literature and environment of the post-War London in which he still felt an outsider. As he wrote in early January 1921, just as he was setting out on the major writing towards *The Waste Land*, in a letter again lambasting the 'imbecility' of contemporary London, 'I have got used to being a foreigner everywhere, and it would fatigue me to be expected to be anything else.'[16] The outsider-insider aspects of the published poem, as embodied perhaps most fully in Tiresias in Part III, 'The Fire Sermon', include, again, that dislike and scorn for the life and world Eliot found himself in, which lies behind the satiric anger of the poem's original drafts. What is notable in those drafts is the way that this anger goes along with a kind of misanthropic disgust. In one iteration of the drafts, where Tiresias sees the typist and young man together, for instance, they are described as 'crawling bugs' – a description Pound dismissed as 'Too easy'.[17]

Flittering through Eliot's contemporary critical prose is an admiration for the work of John Dryden, a kind of working-through of what makes Dryden *the* relevant poet for the early twentieth century. The admiring essay 'Andrew Marvell' measures Dryden's 'greatness' in 'wit' against Marvell's satires, and finds the latter by comparison 'random babbling'. But there is

---

[15] Ibid., 136, 160, 158.

[16] *The Letters of T.S. Eliot*, vol. 1, 532. Christopher Ricks and Jim McCue imply that the major drafting of the poem began sometime between late September 1920 and the end of January 1921 (*The Poems of T.S. Eliot*, vol. 1, 548); Lawrence Rainey writes that, although Eliot included earlier material in the papers handed over to Pound, the poem *per se* was begun in January to February 1921, and that Parts I and II were complete by April; in May 1921, Eliot saw a copy of the 'Circe' episode from James Joyce's *Ulysses* in typescript, and went back and added the 'Tom' episode, later deleted, as a different opening (*The Annotated Waste Land*, 18).

[17] *The Waste Land: a facsimile and transcript*, 45.

a typical caveat: Dryden's 'wit', Eliot suggests, is 'almost fun, and thereby loses some contact with reality ... The midwife placed her hand on his thick skull, / With this prophetic blessing: *Be thou dull*.'[18] Through Eliot's critique, we might reflect about these lines that 'thick' skull is untested; the birthing scene is absurd, but powerfully emblematic. Eliot's quotation from *Absolom and Achitophel* displays, however, those qualities of Dryden's rhetoric which elsewhere in his prose of these two years 1921–22 he views more positively. In the *TLS* piece of 9 June 1921, 'John Dryden', Eliot relishes the fact that 'Dryden always enhances: he makes his object great, in a way contrary to expectation; and the total effect is due to the transformation of the ridiculous into poetry.' For Eliot, when Pope satirizes, he 'diminishes' his subject-matter: 'The genius of Pope is not for caricature.' Eliot's 'crawling bugs' is by this definition caricature; but he was alert to other potential. For Dryden works in the opposite direction, and can orchestrate this perfectly, as even Milton cannot – he can 'rise and fall at will'.

All in all, Eliot in this period presents Dryden's satire as a discovery. He begins this essay on the poet by asserting that the nineteenth century had been almost completely unaware of Dryden's work, unlike the Romantics. To rediscover Dryden is in itself to overcome the various 'limitations' of the previous century, and so to feel 'new freedoms'. Eliot's assurance in making this discovery, and the terms in which he does so, is warranted by the book which he reviews in this *TLS* piece, Mark Van Doren's *John Dryden*. Eliot is adamant: Van Doren's book is the one 'which every practitioner of English verse should study.'[19]

Various aspects of Eliot's appreciation for John Dryden are encapsulated in Van Doren's sense of the latter's qualities, including those technical aspects which Eliot is presumably advertising to his fellow practitioners of poetry, such as 'metrical energy' in lyric moments, and the possibilities of acceleration and deceleration in longer, or narrative, work. Dryden is compared to Juvenal, not on account of his anger or roughness, but because of the 'largeness and completeness' of his satire.[20] Whatever his aspirations in this regard, as indicated, Eliot's drafts towards *The Waste Land* show in contrast a very real scorn, misogyny in the Fresca passages, and sick misanthropy else-

---

[18]   Ibid., 155.
[19]   Ibid., 173.
[20]   Mark Van Doren, *John Dryden: A Study of his Poetry* (Bloomington: Indiana University Press, [1920] 1946), 174, 209, 146. For previous discussion of the significance of Van Doren's book, particularly as helping Eliot define what he meant by 'wit' – a key term across these years – see Matthews, *T.S. Eliot and Early Modern Literature*, 97–8.

where.[21] Once Pound had helped by persuading Eliot to delete these extensive passages, the satiric remains a kind of residual atmosphere, established by
the bleak – but in its original context, risible – citation from *The Satyricon*
of Petronius. This is the epigraph as published which, on Pound's demur-
ral, Eliot used to replace his original quotation, Kurtz's dying outcry from
Conrad's *Heart of Darkness*: 'The horror! The horror!'. Arguably, Eliot's
insertion of the Latin from Petronius, however, retains something of the
tonal instability I have been discussing to this point: Eliot provides a sense
that prophecy is to be key to his sequence. Yet, and at the same time, if his
quotation 'Nam Sybillan quidem Cumis ego ipse oculis meis vidi in ampulla
vidi ...' is returned to its original context, it continues the derisory tone that
predominates in the passages excised by Pound.[22]

Most notably for our enquiry into the kinds of unsettled immediacy of
response being made to the contemporary world in *The Waste Land*, however,
Van Doren points to the way that Dryden's poetry consistently responds to
its moment, to events as they occur: 'There is a sense in which every poem
that Dryden wrote was occasional. ... Births, deaths, literary events, political
incidents tapped in him the richest commenting mind that English poetry
has known. He was the celebrant, the signalizer *par excellence*.'[23] Eliot had
shown something of his own ability in this area when obliquely referencing
the land 'corridors' established by the Versailles Peace Conference amongst
the multiple disillusionments of 'Gerontion' (the poem which, as late as
January 1922, Eliot considered printing as a kind of Preface to *The Waste
Land*, until Pound dissuaded him[24]). Significantly for the practice of *The
Waste Land*, Dryden's propensity towards enhancement includes taking (or
'plagiarizing') earlier poets' work, and creating that 'surprise so essential to
poetry from it.' Eliot, in his essay 'John Dryden,' demonstrates how Dryden

---

[21]   In his 1919 essay on 'Ben Jonson,' Eliot notably sees Jonson as more 'contemporary' to his time than even Shakespeare, because he sees a 'brutality, a lack of sentiment, a polished surface' in Jonson's satire. See *The Sacred Wood: Essays on Poetry
and Criticism* (London: Faber, 1997 edition), 102.
[22]   In their original context, the words about the Sibyl are spoken by the super-
wealthy Trimalchio, drunk at a banquet, asking about memories of myths in Homer.
His words are immediately dismissed by the work's narrator as 'blethering'. See
Petronius, *The Satyricon*, translated by P.G. Webb (Oxford: Oxford University Press,
1997), 39. Eliot had previously cited Petronius as an epigraph to his 1920 collection
of criticism, *The Sacred Wood*, there to add to his general feeling at this time that poets
were 'hated' by the wealthy, who failed to recognise merit (see *The Satyricon*, 71–2).
[23]   Van Doren, *John Dryden: A Study of his Poetry*, 107.
[24]   *The Poems of T.S. Eliot*, vol. 1, 34. The exchange between Eliot and Pound over
the possibility of including 'Gerontion' is quoted on 553–4.

transforms a 'commonplace' satirical passage from Abraham Cowley to this end.[25] Indeed, for Van Doren, and in terms that translate to Eliot's achievements in *The Waste Land*, again, this practice underpins all of Dryden's mature work. So, in Van Doren's commentary on Dryden's 'touchstone' poem, 'To the Memory of Mr Oldham', he points to the fact that 'There is not an original word in the work. It is a classical mosaic, pieces of which Dryden had had by him for a long time. It is precisely as a mosaic, as a composition, that it is a triumph.'[26]

That tension between the placing of others' words, and original 'composition', of course goes to the centre of Eliot's method with *The Waste Land*, which includes direct quotation, misremembered quotation (especially in the poem's final page), and, in the drafts as we have seen, updated parodies of eighteenth-century satire. Like Van Doren, Eliot too quotes the whole of Dryden's 'To the Memory of Mr Oldham' near the end of his *TLS* piece on him – as a 'final test' of Dryden's poetic worth. Eliot finds in the poem 'perfection' of the elegiac form, a 'satisfying completeness' of statement. However, the poem also shows Dryden's narrowness, a lack of wider metaphysical speculation, perhaps, when commemorating his friend.

Virgil-inflected commemoration around the deaths of young men in a similar vein to that undertaken by Dryden was, of course, on Eliot's mind at this very moment, since he typed up Parts I and II of *The Waste Land* at around the same time that he wrote his *TLS* review. This is especially so towards the end of Part I, 'The Burial of the Dead', with talk of corpses and of Mylae seemingly overlaying and comparing recent scenes on the Western Front with those of the First Punic War. The drafts of the first Part published in 1971, however, also show that generic instability which Pound in effect tidied up or out of the poem. These drafts bear evidence of that kind of counter-movement to the (expunged) satiric drift of the poem, as Madame Sosostris's Tarot pack fleetingly contained a 'King fishing' or 'Fisher King'.[27] For the 'literary event' (to adopt Van Doren's term for one of the instigations to poetry for Dryden) which provided the basis for Pound's salvaging of the poem as we now have it, with the recurring pattern of phrasing and imagery it contains, was the publication, in January 1920, of Jessie L. Weston's book on the Grail legend, *From Ritual to Romance*. This mythic method, as Eliot

[25]   Ibid., 174, 177, 175. Christopher Ricks has some insightful pages on Eliot's reading of Dryden's reworking of Cowley, including how Eliot himself rewrote Cowley here to further his point, in *Allusion to the Poets* (Oxford: Oxford University Press, 2002), 94–8.

[26]   Van Doren, *John Dryden*, 125.

[27]   *The Waste Land: a facsimile and transcript*, 9.

styled Joyce's modern structure in *Ulysses*, provides that baffling polarity and contrast to the satiric atmosphere which otherwise sounds through moments of the poem, including the jarring mention of Madam Sosostris's bad cold alongside the fact that she is the 'wisest woman in Europe' (lines 44–5).

Eliot variously indicated that, since childhood, versions of Arthurian tales originally by Thomas Malory remained favourites throughout his life; Weston's subject, offering a kind of anthropology of the rituals behind such stories as those, was therefore guaranteed his careful attention.[28] It is Weston's book which is given prominence by Eliot as a source, both in the headnote of his Notes to *The Waste Land*, and in his annotation to particular lines from Part V, 'What the Thunder Said'. Regarded from our present perspective, alert to allusion and intertextuality as Eliot's generation were not yet to be (but as his poetry was training readers to be), the use of 'mosaic' as a means to composition is strikingly Weston's 'method' too. At the end of Chapter I, Weston reflects that 'as to the form of these studies – they may be found disconnected', as Eliot's speaker finds himself on Margate Sands towards the end of Part III. Weston's study was written 'at intervals of time'; yet this process of her own composition might also reflect her approach to her topic, and that her ambition was to 'prove the essentially archaic character of all the elements composing the Grail story rather than to analyse the story as a connected whole.'[29] In this regard, although Weston's aim is to discover the 'origin' of the Grail legend, she frequently insists that the literary versions under discussion remain palimpsests, in which authors have consistently added to a received version of the story. As the general tone of Weston's comments around these 'additions' and interpretations indicates, Christian versions of the Grail legends are seen as limitations of original Eastern rituals. Weston's religious history in the book is not progressive, in other words.[30]

This is true of Eliot's practice in *The Waste Land* too. Layering and interplay amidst allusions and sources without hierarchy or definite progression directly determine the openness and intermixing of the poem's texture and sound-world, as several of the essays included here reveal. But what these essays inevitably also wrestle with is the fragmentary nature of the vocalisations and allusions which the poem makes, the re-voicings and dramatizations of both contemporary speech and previous texts.

[28] Robert Crawford, *Young Eliot* (London: Vintage, 2015), 53, 61.

[29] Jessie L. Weston, *From Ritual to Romance: Folklore, Magic and the Holy Grail* (Cambridge: Cambridge University Press, 1920), 24.

[30] Ibid, 19, 63, 168. Robert Crawford has important thoughts about Eliot's anti-progressive sense of history in *The Savage and the City in the work of T.S. Eliot* (Oxford: Oxford University Press, 1987), 107.

This remains, in many ways, the imperfect science in any editorial or critical response to *The Waste Land*. Christopher Ricks and Jim McCue are generous in their sense of the range or 'Scope' of what they consider 'Annotation' of Eliot's poems to amount to. Their introduction to the 876 pages of commentary in volume 1 of *The Poems of T.S. Eliot: The Annotated Text* opens straight to the point: 'From the beginning, commentators on TSE have found precedents of all kinds'. This sets the 'Annotated Edition' within an established tradition of Eliot scholarship, and also sets the method of the many pages of 'Commentary' as one solidly centred upon the discovery of 'precedents', texts which lie behind the immediate usage of words and phrases in Eliot's poems. Ricks and McCue make a decisive set of statements about a kind of factual impersonality which underpins their Editorial position and status: '2. An effort has been made not to use the Commentary for *critical* elucidation. The frontiers are uncertain, but the principle has been to provide only notes which constitute or proceed from a point of information.' Whilst acknowledging that there is a difficult line to be drawn between annotational 'Commentary' and interpretation in Eliot, Ricks and McCue return to a base line, 'information', which is itself of course 'uncertain'. That uncertainty is underlined by the fact that the word 'information' here is arguably used in a punning sense – it is what 'informs' Eliot's texts, those things which variously constitute them, which it is surely the duty of a 'Commentary' to annotate. That 'information', then, is *implicated* in the matter of 'critical elucidation': the editors, by choosing to point to certain 'points of information' rather than others, are of necessity, performing some kind of reading of Eliot. Yet, at the same time, their sense of what that 'information' might constitute is, they properly acknowledge, of 'uncertain' provenance:

> 3. Parallels with other writers will sometimes not only suggest a source but amount to an allusion. Conversely, it may not be a source but an analogue that brings back what was in the air. Notes of this kind try to put down only the parallels themselves (though in the awareness that annotation is inseparable from interpretation, selection and judgment), leaving the reader to decide what to make of what the poet may have made of this.[31]

What the reader might struggle immediately with, although the editors admit the close tie between annotation and interpretation, is the *difference*, or the scale of possibility, being drawn in the key terms here: source, allusion, analogue. This is especially so, given the rhetoric with which these terms are inscribed in their explanation. Amounting to an allusion feels something

---

[31]   *The Poems of T.S. Eliot*, vol. 1, 351–2.

more significant, for instance, than merely suggesting a source, which retains
that element of the '*may* have' about it. 'Analogue' is the term of this triad
that seems particularly vague – the suggestion of something in the atmosphere, a zeitgeist, which has somehow resonated or been paralleled in Eliot's
poetry, without being directly 'a point' of reference for which information
might be provided.

These dilemmas and uncertainties in interpretation of the poem surely
derive from Eliot's method in creating *The Waste Land* through calling upon
references that are variously proximate or remote. This leaves the annotators' and critic's tasks uniquely unresolved. It sets a limit to even the most
monumental attempt to comment upon the work, such as that in Ricks and
McCue's *Text* and their 'Editorial Composite', which integrates earlier critical opinion alongside their own hearing of echoes from literary sources in
Eliot's poem. A particular instance of this limitation might be provided by
their treatment of one element of Eliot's own editorial decision as revealed
in the 1971 *Facsimile*, the fact that Part II of the poem, now 'A Game of
Chess' alluding to a play by Thomas Middleton, initially had a different title,
'In the Cage'. This phrase is often linked to the 1913 Loeb translation of the
Petronius text which Eliot eventually chose as an epigraph for *The Waste
Land*: 'I saw with my own eyes the Sibyl at Cumae hanging in a cage. ...' But,
as critics have noted, and as Ricks and McCue indicate in their headnote and
section note, Petronius's word for where the Sibyl was 'hanging' is 'ampulla',
a vessel for carrying liquids such as wine. Both the critics, and Eliot himself,
were aware that the Loeb mistranslated the passage, which, after all Eliot
gives in Latin.[32]

Ricks and McCue leave the situation around the source for the deleted
section title unresolved. They mention the possible echo of Henry James's
1898 novella 'In the Cage', but cross-refer their reader to their note to an
earlier, unpublished poem, 'In the Department Store', with which it shares,
obviously, some locution, but also a partial setting. Yet James's novella seems
to offer more eloquent possibilities for thinking about *The Waste Land* than
this implies. The 'Cage' of the story is a 'frail structure of wood and wire'
which separates off a small telegraph office in a grocer's store in London.
The unnamed female protagonist of the story is a telegraphist who minds
an instrument called 'the sounder', the telegraph machine that both sends
and receives messages across London and beyond.[33] Through their habitual

---

[32] Ibid., 593, 621.
[33] Henry James, *The Turn of the Screw* & *In the Cage*, introduced by Hortense
Calisher (New York: Random House, 2001), 117. All subsequent page references are
given parenthetically in the text.

exchanges via the telegraph, the protagonist learns the codes deployed by
a pair of illicit society lovers, Captain Everard and Lady Bradeen; as the
story evolves, she learns that Everard is in debt, and that, on the death of
her husband, Lady Bradeen is using this financial situation to force Everard
into marrying her. Across this time, there is an unresolved flirtation and true
desire growing between the protagonist, who is herself engaged to marry,
and Captain Everard. The Captain does not truly love the Lady; he seems to
have strong feelings for the telegraphist on their own meetings outside her
working hours. Yet, in the end, she marries her fiancé, having understood
more fully what James calls the inevitable and un-crossable 'social gulf' that
prevents fulfilment in this context.

James's novella contains various features that combine and recombine
in Eliot's poem, and especially in that Part originally called 'In the Cage'.
It is a story about social class, and about the unbridge-ability between the
classes. The beautiful world of Lady Bradeen conceals adulterous relationships as a matter of course, and is, as happens in the story, aided in this by the
worker-classes such as the protagonist, who fosters that concealment at one
point. But the workers would be reconfirmed in their obscurity, were they
to desire, as she does, to break the class boundaries by sleeping with Everard:
'her sort didn't, in such cases, matter – didn't count as infidelity' (160). All
of this occurs in the world of the ugly apartment blocks of fashionable central
London – those blocks which the Eliots were moving between at the time of
his writing *The Waste Land*. Further out into the suburbs, in James's story,
pollution extends; on a November trip to Maida Vale, 'there was a thick
brown fog' which 'tasted of acrid smoke' and which has infiltrated inside
houses – Eliot's opening section has its workers proceeding over London
Bridge in a winter dawn and under a fog similarly coloured brown. Such
circumstance enforces for the protagonist the sense that her life 'in the cage',
literally or otherwise, will continue: 'Reality ... could only be ugliness and
obscurity, could never be the escape, the rise' (203).

James's novella, in short, shares something of the broad atmosphere of
The Waste Land; its examination of class (more prominent in the deleted
satiric drafts), and of desire, often illicit, seems an implicit structuring principle for Part II which was removed with Eliot's deletion of its initial title.
The society lady at her dressing table at the start is succeeded by the Cockney
pub-scene at the close, and thence by the encounter between the typist and
house agent's clerk in Part III (the Eliots presumably dealt with such clerks
during their own move to Clarence Gate Gardens in November 1920).[34] At

---

[34] *The Letters of T.S. Eliot*, vol. 1, xxix.

the heart of all of these relations, of course, is a sense of misunderstanding, miscommunication, disconnection, or of functional, 'automatic', and unfulfilling connection, in the case of the typist.

Sounds and soundings are key within the poem, as they are with James's 'sounder', the telegraph. The story's crisis between Lady Bradeen and Everard occurs around a mis-worded telegram, in a situation which the telegraphist redeems. 'In the cage' then, or 'in a cage within the cage' of the grocer's store, she is, Sibyl-like, both a centring mediator and a corrector of messages which would otherwise make little sense. (123) And yet, like the women and men in Eliot's London, she is trapped by the conditions of her world and doomed to repeat them. There is no 'escape, or rise' into love for her, or for the rich classes in the novella. The sounds she deals with each day, and which she makes sense from, continue ceaselessly to assail, as they do the figures in Eliot's sequence, and its auditors.

James's work appears consistently in ephemera across the time when Eliot was thinking about and writing *The Waste Land*, in knowledgeable letters recommending his novels to friends, and through his critical prose.[35] James's similarly 'outsider' or Tiresias-like perspective to Eliot's is literally embodied in James's caged telegraphist. The potential within his story for Eliot's concerns in the poem marks the continuing possibility for new annotation and critical commentary around *The Waste Land* for centuries to come.

*   *   *

Implicitly at the heart of many contributors' concerns in this volume is a very telling sense that the poem after one hundred years needs salvaging from the welter of social, political, and (especially) literary-critical noise to which it has been subjected across its first century. Especially refreshing, hopefully, is the way that our contributors seek to provide fresh insights into the poem almost by reading past, or in spite of, the critical industry that surrounded the work from the late 1920s at least. Whilst acknowledging, as appropriate, their debts to earlier thinking about *The Waste Land*, writers here seek to approach the text directly, and to provide narratives through its linguistic facets of all kinds – such as its use of quotation in non-English languages, of pronouns, or its sounds, voices, and musicality.

Type 'The Waste Land' into the Bodleian Library's Solo Catalogue system, and it reveals over 90 'Physical Resources' relating to the work, and over 1,500 peer-reviewed articles, together with 4,300 online resources,

[35]   See ibid., 361, and *The Complete Prose of T.S. Eliot: The Critical Edition*, Volume 2, edited by Anthony Cuda and Ronald Schuhard (Baltimore, MD: Johns Hopkins University Press, 2014), especially 23, 45, 57, 69, 397.

which contain some comment upon it. This must be a minimum calcula-
tion, neglecting passing references buried in many other works of criticism.
There is no shortage, then, of aids to reading, or of views to be echoed or
resisted about the work. And yet, aware as they are of this background, the
scholars and poets who have agreed to contribute to this special issue each
sense the need to see the poem in new lights, or to discover different things
about the poem through the responses to it of previous critics, historians,
and poets. Their successful achievement in overcoming this formidable challenge certainly reveals that the poem continues to offer potentiality and
excitement as well as new surprises, for both readers and creative writers
who continue to work in its wake. In this regard, it was important to include
writing here that considers the poem from the perspective and through the
histories of a variety of the nation-spaces which the poem itself inhabits,
including the UK, North America, and India. Since the poem stakes claim
to, or re-echoes with and through, experiences and literatures relating to
each of those spaces, it felt important to receive contemporary reflections
on the poem at this juncture from each of them. What emerges from these
various encounters is, hopefully, challenging and re-directional, in terms
of the correctives offered to assumptions within previous criticism of the
poem, and also in the way that our contributors look again at those assumptions from the perspective of the text itself, its words on the page, or in the
air when spoken aloud. There is diversity of views here; there are noticeable
cross-currents between the contributors' approaches, but also points of disa-
greement between them.

This note of corrective towards standard assumptions about *The Waste
Land* is immediately struck by Rebecca Beasley's 'A "Dangerous Model":
Resisting *The Waste Land*'. Beasley points to the difference between early
responses to the poem from Britain and North America, noting that it is
in the latter that Eliot's poem was the more easily assimilated. Through
an intense and comprehensive consideration of the presence of the poem
in British magazine and journal culture of the 1920s and into the 1930s,
Beasley discovers a notable scepticism from reviewers and critics which in
turn informed some of the thinking of creative work during this period.
Taking up the challenge of confronting 'the legend of heroic modernism'
from earlier critics, Beasley presents a deeply informed survey which, rather,
proves that *The Waste Land* was greeted with less than admiration in many
circles in the UK. Whilst Eliot's poem rapidly became a ubiquitous point
of reference across its journal culture, the perceived 'demerits' of the work
often cast it negatively within debates that presented other writers, including D.H. Lawrence, as offering more innovative ways forward within the
national poetry.

After an initial and thorough trawl of a range of journals from the early to mid-1920s, Beasley focuses upon the role that *The Waste Land* played within debates about Georgianism, romanticism, and classicism in the journal *The Adelphi*. As the discussion reveals, *The Adelphi* editor, John Middleton Murry, perceived *The Waste Land* to be a failure, but a telling failure: it forced Murry into a distinction between a 'poetry of experience', which he praised and found most fully in Lawrence's poetry, and that 'poetry of intellect' such as Eliot's, which Murry deeply disliked. As Beasley shows, this mid-20s distinction has found important afterlife in the ways that British poets from the 1950s onwards variously aligned themselves with modernity.

By the end of the 1920s, however, there was to be discerned some more positive reaction to the poem, mainly amongst what Beasley cites E.M. Forster identifying as 'the young'. Extending her discussion to cover journals including the *New Coterie*, *The Calendar of Modern Letters*, and, latterly, *Experiment*, Beasley demonstrates how the 'model' began to form a characteristic influence, at least amongst some emerging poets of the end of that decade and into the next. Whilst there was continuing circumspection and ambivalence on display in many of the discussion pieces in which the poem was included – and whilst Eliot's work continued to be pitted against more positive versions of Lawrence's potential – *The Waste Land* had become a kind of testing point for national literary development which talents such as W.H. Auden and William Empson could variously respond to and exploit.

Beasley's concern, through looking closely at the history of the poem's reception, and so to challenge assumptions about the linguistic, religious, and cultural significance of *The Waste Land*, is evident also in Rosinka Chaudhuri's contribution to the volume, 'Beyond Sanskrit Words: Eliot and the Colonial Construction of Poetic Modernism'. As Chaudhuri points out, many imperialist tropes continue to recur in critics' attitudes towards the 'Indian' elements of Eliot's poem – such as the locational pointers in Part V to 'Ganga' and 'Himavant', and the exhausted repeated 'Shantih', the Sanskrit word in translation with which the poem ends. Such imperialist response is, indeed, to an extent licensed by Eliot himself, who in his Notes gives a version of the meaning of 'Shantih' by quoting from the King James Bible. Whilst previous critics have seemingly wanted to praise the liberal education Eliot received at Harvard as a base for his interest in non-Western religion and language, Chaudhuri convincingly points out that the citation from Sanskrit, and to an extent the locations referred to, are as non-meaningful to 'Indian' readers of the poem from 1922 as they are to Europeans or North Americans. Sanskrit is on a level with the use by Eliot of Latin and Ancient Greek in his quotation from *The Satyricon* as the sequence's epigraph. The expansion upon three DA words from the *Brihadaryanaka*

Upanishad in the final Part of Eliot's sequence, often seen to represent some kind of shift towards a more settled and religious meaning when considered alongside the Gethsemane scene with which Part V opens, is equally likely to prove baffling to non-Western readers.

In suggesting that, despite this, the reception of *The Waste Land* offered further prospects for 'Indian' writers, Chaudhuri narrates how it affected the thought and poetry of four Bengali poets, Sudhindranath Datta, Amiya Chakravarty, Buddhadeva Bose, and Bishnu Dey. Rather than the imperialist tropes that often underpin earlier ideas of reception, she argues for a sense of 'simultaneity'. Between 1920s and 1930s Bengal and Eliot's London there were concurrent concerns both experiential and technical – including how to understand the confusions of the modern city through poetry, an issue as pressing in the Calcutta of that era as in Boston, London, and Paris. Most notably, the dynamism of Eliot's rendering of modern experience enabled these Bengali writers to challenge the inheritance they otherwise received from the leading Bengali poet of the previous generation, Rabindranath Tagore – an inheritance they found sentimental and cloying, and in some sense untrue to the world as it was developing around them. By citing Tagore's essay on 'Modern Poetry', Chaudhuri reveals that, like his sponsor in the West W.B. Yeats, Tagore felt that poetry's responsibility was to offer countervailing visions of beauty and meaning to the quotidian realities of modern life. In contrast, Eliot's poem provided for the emerging generation of Bengali poets a sense of the urgency with which poetry must break from such versions of the past and speak directly to that modern experience simultaneously present in all lives.[36]

That sense of the urgency and possibility encapsulated in Eliot's poem, especially with regard to its relation to contemporary culture, also forms a keynote of William Davies's '"An Icon of Occurrence": *The Waste Land's* Anniversaries'. Davies's essay takes us through significant moments down to the present to consider the resonance of the poem in political, cultural, and literary debates in Britain across its first hundred years. Beginning with its first anniversary, Davies locates the poem as a 'barometer' of discussion about the role that literature might play in society and about the inheritance that *The Waste Land* has amongst subsequent poets. Striking in terms of the

---

[36] Yeats notes the 'mere habit' of characters in Eliot's poetry, especially around their sexuality, and that 'his own art seems grey, cold, grey'. Whilst he finds 'much that is moving in symbol and imagery' in *The Waste Land*, Yeats complained about what he perceived as 'rhythmical flatness ... monotony of accent.' In sum, the poem proved that Eliot was a 'satirist', not a poet. W.B. Yeats, 'Introduction', in *The Oxford Book of Modern Verse 1892–1935* (Oxford: Oxford University Press, 1936), xxi–xxii.

poem's social and cultural legacy is the attempt by F.R. Leavis, in his influential *New Bearings in English Poetry* (1932), to cast the poem as a kind of proof that, in an otherwise unsympathetic and culturally barren age, writing could still be (that key word) 'alive'. Leavis's argument becomes typical: whilst recognising that the poem can only be read and understood properly by 'few' readers, as Davies sees it Leavis also sets the poem up as an ideal and challenging version of comprehensiveness and inclusivity in an age that otherwise lacks cohesion. In effect, Leavis sets Eliot and *The Waste Land* in particular as a touchstone for what literature might achieve both educationally and inspirationally in the twentieth century.

It is this issue which is carried onward as Davies moves us forward through *The Waste Land*'s other anniversary moments in England. Crucial in this regard is the sense that, as political readings of and around the poem became more urgent, especially in connection to a perceived rightist politics and anti-Semitism, the poem retained that sense of being a test for 'authenticity' in writing. Whilst this term had defined the so-called Movement of British poets writing in the mid-century, and was prominent in the polemics of Philip Larkin for instance, one poet associated with the Movement, Donald Davie, continued to situate the poem as a kind of testing place, both 'a challenge and an ordeal'. This testing relates more broadly to the reception of Modernism in the UK context, interestingly within the dominant shadow of Leavisite thinking in Britain. Tellingly in this regard, Davies's history moves in its final incarnation towards a figure whose response to *The Waste Land* strenuously seeks to free the poem of all such political, including literary-political, baggage. Amidst the rightly growing objections to the racial and gender attitudes in the poem which have seemed increasingly unacceptable for many writers and critics, Davies quotes the late English poet Charles Tomlinson as enjoining students and general readers to 'listen again' to the soundscape of the poem. In the final moments of the essay, Davies turns across the Atlantic to consider those African-American poets who have found inspiration within that soundscape, a fact that points, as the other essays in this special issue all do, to the continuing potential within the actual poem to speak to so many different experiences and historical contexts.

Hugh Haughton's essay here, "'O City, city": Sounding *The Waste Land*' presents us with a telling account of the sonic effects which characterise the poem, that 'lovely dissonant music' which he hears throughout the published version of 1922. This sound world, echoing Tomlinson indirectly, is for Haughton the true heart of the poem, and the reason for its continuing importance. Haughton takes a persuasively comprehensive approach to discussing the poem's sounds; he presents the sound world of the poem in all of its nuance and reference. To this end he notes the many words referring to sound and noise in the poem, both natural noises and those created by humans, and words both ancient and modern. He considers the words in the poem which are actually there to make sounds and do little more, such as 'Jug, jug'. He notes the direct references in the poem to established and more recent musical forms, from opera to jazz and modern song. Further, Haughton finds striking similarity between the sound world created by Eliot and that of contemporary composers, not only Igor Stravinsky, but surprisingly also George Gershwin.

Haughton gives a considered reflection on the tensions between voice and vocalisation and the printed text, between words that live off and on the page as they appear then recede within the poem's fabric. He thereby establishes a consistent focus within Eliot's approach to sources of influence and within the famous allusions made by *The Waste Land*: their shared consideration of sonic possibility, not only in the quotations seized within Eliot's own poetic music, but in the resonances that especially his Shakespearian – or 'Shakespeherian' – references make. Haughton gives extensive discussion to Part III, 'The Fire Sermon', to this end, revealing it as a complex and continually renewing orchestration between seemingly disparate sonic histories and soundscapes. Haughton essentially and persuasively argues that, amidst the welter of previous criticism and reading which frustratedly seeks to establish 'meaning' from the poem through its multiple cultural, historical, and religious references, it is the actual noises that the poem makes which prove the most compelling of its aspects, and which speak more immediately to us than rational 'meaning'. Adapting the thinking of Murray Schafer on soundscapes and modernity, Haughton presents *The Waste Land* as a revolutionary text with echoes that continue along the passageways of history to our present and beyond.

This issue, essentially one of how to keep reading or hearing the poem amidst its own potentially competing cultures and languages, then takes a specific and striking form in Marjorie Perloff's 'Lost and Found in Translation: Foreign Language Citations in *The Waste Land*'. Perloff asks what we can learn from Eliot's seemingly inconsistent translation practice in the poem. Some phrases in ancient or modern languages are translated, often as adaptations or variations in Eliot's English idiom. And yet the poem is punctuated by citations which are kept in their original languages – a part of that 'difficulty' in sounding and understanding which the poem presents as much today as it did in 1922. Perloff offers compelling readings of each of the passages where the issue of translation, or the refused potential for translation, occurs. What emerges is a sense of the (what is for us now racist) 'mongrelisation' of the modern world of the poem, of the shattered Europe after the First World War. But what also emerges is the spontaneousness of Eliot's creation with regard to his treatment of foreign languages in the poem, his often syncretic imagination in this and other regards. This is demonstrated by extensive discussion of the translations from Dante in 'The Fire Sermon', where, as evidenced by the *Facsimile*, Eliot works brilliantly to render immediate and pertinent, through locale and idiom, the intonations of Dante's medieval Italian.

Then again, Perloff argues, the issue of translation also serves to highlight the limitations of Eliot's imagination more generally. Eliot's deployment of Sanskrit sources in Part V – the prompt also for Rosinka Chaudhuri's essay here – is, Perloff considers, not as attentive to the context of the original source as other of his more sensitive renderings of European originals. As a result, that turn in the final section is for her 'pat', too easy, as one kind of answer to the disarray of earlier sections of the poem. Eliot is almost determinedly deaf in this reading to the complications both in the original source and in making reference to it in a poem so centred in the ruins of modern Europe. Equally, Perloff notes the failure, in a work that otherwise presents ancient languages Latin, Greek, and Sanskrit as concomitant with modern French and German, to include the Hebrew of the Bible as one of its source languages, either to be cited in the original or translated. Eliot's constant recourse to the King James Bible for reference, even when drawing upon the Hebrew Prophets as in the 'What are the roots that clutch' passage in Part I, is, Perloff suggests, a 'telling omission'. It is an omission, we might suggest in the wake of Perloff's perception, that carries darker implication in Eliot's thought, beyond the immediate moment of his choices around foreign languages and their translation.

When considering the sequence's resonance within later British and Irish poetries, Andrew Michael Roberts's 'The Poetic Afterlife of *The Waste Land*' identifies further ambivalences within Eliot's poem that establish its complex inheritance for those seeking to respond creatively. The notoriously fragmentary nature of the poetry, for instance, noted immediately by critics across the 1920s, itself becomes a kind of signature which is seen to emanate from a historical moment which in turn becomes *the* moment from which to understand later twentieth-century history. Fragmentation in the sequence is 'explained' by that post-First-World-War instant and so rendered utile to later writers, who either respond positively to Eliot's method and historical understanding, or who seek alternative unifying possibilities.

Roberts considers a scattering of poets' responses from the twenty-first century, but focuses in detail on the careers of three poets who responded variously to the ambivalence within the inheritance from *The Waste Land*: the late English poets Geoffrey Hill and Roy Fisher and the Irish poet Paul Muldoon. Hill's poetry, Roberts argues, displays both technical and thematic responses to Eliot's poem, which Hill always held in high regard against what he saw as the more compromised later work such as *Four Quartets*. Particularly in his later, book-length works, Hill deploys that fragmentariness on the surface of Eliot's text; yet across his career he accepted the 'diagnosis' that *The Waste Land* seemed to offer about fractured history and sterile contemporary culture. Fisher's poetry shows a similar interest in the formal characteristics of Eliot's poem, but uses its historical implication directly within his career-wide focus upon the cityscapes of the English Midlands. From his early collage-poem *City* (1961) through to later book-length work such as *A Furnace* (1986), Fisher digs through the layers below the modern districts and fabric of Birmingham to mount a kind of epic version of its history and the disjunctions within it. Roberts finds a similarly epic ambition in the wake of *The Waste Land* to characterise Muldoon's career, from its early 'Immram' (1980) to 'American Standard' (2019/21) – the latter a work which seems to be offering its own cautious celebration of Eliot's sequence a century on from its first publication. Through detailed consideration primarily of these two texts, Roberts relishes a performative element in Muldoon's writing which recognises further possibility within Eliot's text to decode and challenge the postures and impostures of protagonists in our contemporary moment.

Marjorie Perloff's close scrutiny of the 'La Pia' translation as it emerges from the drafts in the *Facsimile* is a practice that receives further consideration in Peter Robinson's contribution here, 'Compositional Process and Critical Product'. Robinson returns, as Davies does, to the fiftieth anniversary of the poem's first publication and to the various dissatisfactions that were revealed by critics and poets at that time with the way that the poem had been received and made to 'mean' across its first half century. These were dissatisfactions felt by Eliot himself, through his impatience that the poem was being read as a cultural or historical document when to him it was a release of personal annoyance *at* the contemporary situation. Robinson looks back to immediate critical responses to the poem as revealed by the editorial process evidenced in the *Facsimile*, in order to question particularly whether Ezra Pound's editorial work carried through on the collection of papers towards the eventual poem was universally beneficial for Eliot.

Through detailed examination of the dialogue realised between Eliot and Pound from the *Facsimile*, Robinson persuasively suggests that there are in fact losses and gains to the 'obstetric' exercise that Pound claimed to have carried out. Early critical writing around the *Facsimile* that praised Pound's work very much looked at it from the perspective of Pound's own aesthetic of clarity and condensation (Pound removed hundreds of lines and many words from the version presented to him by Eliot in Paris). This had the effect, Robinson considers, of achieving a more authoritative music in some local instances, and perhaps across the sequence as a whole. But in 'birthing' the poem, Pound's aesthetic somewhat occluded Eliot's, particularly in terms of the treatment of human relations. Especially telling was Pound's more or less consistent removal of Eliot's careful qualifications, his mature tentativeness, when figuring the relations of the couple in 'A Game of Chess' and even regarding the typist and house agent's clerk in Part III. Pound's recourse to (a version of) technique, seemingly independently of any larger meanings that the poem might have been seeking to make, leaves readers with perhaps the most sonorous poem of the twentieth century, but one in which something of its original human complexity has been silenced.

These are questions which Robinson relates to debates around Eliot about alternatively (or not) 'tone' and 'pitch', as considered in the critical work of Christopher Ricks and the critical reflections of Geoffrey Hill. Robinson uses what he sees as Hill's false division between 'tone' and 'pitch' when thinking about Eliot's career to reflect upon the insights of his close consideration of the interventions Pound made, for good or ill. Ultimately, it feels as though any 'meaning' which the poem might have resides 'uncertainly' between the two versions available to us (now three, if we include the 'Composite' in Ricks and McCue's edition). The poem's continuing power lies in its 'both and' aspects with regard to technique, in the fact that some of its originating energy escaped Pound's editorial pencil, and so, as readers, we are kept alive to continually altering sounds and voices.

Similar celebration of the technical challenge and possibility within the poem emerges from Michael Wood's 'Hypocrisy and After: Persons in *The Waste Land*'. Wood scrutinizes the whole issue of the relationship of the poem to its readers at the instigation of the citation at the end of Part I (which, after Perloff, we note is retained in its original French), from Baudelaire's address to *his* reader as 'hypocrite lecteur'. Wherein lies the hypocrisy of us as readers of *The Waste Land* across a century, Wood considers? He remarks that Baudelaire's reader is addressed as an intimate, a 'tu', but that, on the other hand, his dismissal of dishonest readerly practice seems general. Taking his prompt from the singular/plural issue in Baudelaire, then, Wood traces across Eliot's sequence the use of the second person pronoun, in each case measuring its intimacy or generality, its closeness or distance, from the 'you' seemingly addressed through the poem. This patient consideration yields an astonishing range of musics and voices or vocalisations, through *The Waste Land*'s citational and experiential accumulation.

Building on, but also resisting, earlier discussion by Michael Edwards, Paul Le Chance, and Maud Ellmann which has considered the issue of the 'many voices' in the poem, Wood argues that, through Eliot's syntax and formal design choices, the whole issue of voicing is in fact tentative. Questions of identity and identification, of how far we 'get inside' any one voice or 'character' in the poem, are forced back onto the reader continually, and often we are left in uncertain territory between the two. Sometimes, also, the very idea of a 'you' who might speak through, or be addressed by, the poem, remains implied rather than realised. At every point, therefore, the reader of the poem is embroiled in ethical uncertainties which the poem does little to help us resolve – the potential for hypocrisy in our response is everywhere. Wood's navigation of the pronominal base of the poem, then, leads us to the final question as to whether we are simply presented with a 'cacophony' which we cannot resolve into a single music, or whether there is an elaborate 'counterpoint'. Interesting in this regard is the complete lack of a 'you' for 155 lines in 'The Fire Sermon' and into Part IV – as though we are in realms of poetry which exist outside of any reader address (or 'pitch', to appropriate Hill's terms). Whilst not denying that this might in itself be a hypocritical response, Wood sees the end of the poem as revealing the incredible design that Eliot has deployed in bringing the work to this final point, one in which the technique of fragmentation is orchestrated in unrepeatable fashion.

What is noticeable in all of the essays gathered here is that, although they see the poem as everywhere locally involved in technical or citational choices that raise questions of meaning, the meaning of the poem continues to remain unresolved and uncertain. Countering the kinds of New Critical response in the poem's early years, that discovered particularly Christian resolution and trans-religious potential in its resounding 'Shantih's,[37] these new essays suggest a kind of continuing potential in the poem which equally became evident quite early on – that 'simultaneity' of recognition as Chaudhuri perceives it. Readers have consistently recognised something of themselves and of their historical situation in the poem, and it has also given subsequent writers a kind of core from which to narrate their own experience, both in literature and in the world. And yet, as Michael Wood proves, our experience by the end of the poem is largely one of what he calls 'disarray', an effect which also emerges from thinking through Eliot's way with foreign languages in the poem, as Marjorie Perloff does. Through its wonderful contradictions, as in so many other ways, *The Waste Land* presents a one-off achievement that continues, and will continue, to speak and to sound simultaneously across and between global cultures.

---

[37] On this critical history and its relation to a literary history which Eliot did so much to define, see Matthews, *T.S. Eliot and Early Modern Literature*, Chapter One.

1

A 'Dangerous Model':
Resisting The Waste Land

REBECCA BEASLEY

The Waste Land in Britain

In *Revisiting 'The Waste Land'*, Lawrence Rainey reminds us of the marked difference in the reception of *The Waste Land* between Britain and the United States:

> Because the poem was first published there (without the notes) in the *Criterion*, a new journal struggling to find an audience, and then eleven months later was issued in the Hogarth Press edition that was limited to 460 copies, it received very little media attention [in Britain]: three reviews in the wake of the *Criterion* publication, a further six after the Hogarth edition – and all but one of the nine were hostile. In the United States, in contrast, there were more than fifty reviews and notices of the poem, more or less equally divided between negative and positive evaluations.[1]

The difference is surprisingly rarely noted in studies of Eliot's poem. Surveys of the reception history tend to highlight the more positive American reviews, several of which were by names we recognise from the history of modernism – Edmund Wilson, Gilbert Seldes, Conrad Aiken, Harriet Monroe, John Crowe Ransom, and Allen Tate – and to focus discussion of the British reception on the slightly later, highly influential, positive criticism by I.A. Richards, in the Appendix to the second edition of *Principles of Literary Criticism* (1926), and F.R. Leavis, in *New Bearings in English Poetry* (1932).[2] This approach is effective in making clear the poem's relevance to

---

[1]   Lawrence Rainey, *Revisiting "The Waste Land"* (New Haven, CT: Yale University Press, 2005), 116.

[2]   Edmund Wilson, 'The Poetry of Drouth', *The Dial*, 73 (December 1922), 611–16; Gilbert Seldes, 'T.S. Eliot', *Nation*, 115 (6 December 1922), 614–16; Conrad Aiken, 'An Anatomy of Melancholy', *New Republic*, 33 (7 February 1923), 294–5; Harriet Monroe, 'A Contrast', *Poetry*, 21 (March 1923), 325–30; John Crowe Ransom, 'Waste Lands', *New York Evening Post Literary Review*, 3 (14 July

the institutionalising of modernism, and indeed the discipline of English more generally, achieved by the American New Critics and scholar-critics based at the University of Cambridge, and it underlines the continuities between the two.[3] But it can suggest that there was a kind of inevitability to *The Waste Land*'s status as the modernist poem *par excellence*. What is lost in this account is the considerable resistance to the poem demonstrated by British poets and critics. *The Waste Land* was not the only model for the modern poem.

Critics including Chris Baldick and Peter Howarth have demonstrated how 'the legend of heroic modernist insurrection' has obscured the extent to which pre-war poets, notably but not only the Georgian poets, continued to be widely published and enthusiastically read during the 1920s and 1930s. While there was certainly poetic innovation in theme, diction, and verse form during the period, what is more noticeable when one surveys post-war journals and anthologies is the continuity with the poetic conventions of the past. Baldick notes that even in Michael Roberts's *Faber Book of Modern Verse*, 'of all the period's major anthologies the most avant-gardist to the point of sectarianism in its exclusion of Hardy, Housman, and most of the "Georgian" poets', only a quarter of the poems are written in free verse, and, if one looks only at the British contributions, that proportion is less than one fifth.[4] Baldick's placing of the period's 'novelties within a larger context of continuities' and Howarth's attention to the 'non-modernists', who 'read, reviewed and wrote in the context of modernism, but who remained unconverted',[5] revisits the terrain Donald Davie and Philip Larkin sought

---

1923), 825–26; Allen Tate, 'A Reply to Ransom', *New York Evening Post Literary Review*, 3 (4 August 1923), 886; I.A. Richards, *Principles of Literary Criticism*, 2nd edition (London: Kegan Paul, Trench, Trubner, 1926), 289–95; F.R. Leavis, *New Bearings in English Poetry: A Study of the Contemporary Situation* (London: Chatto & Windus, 1932), 75–132.

[3]   See Michael Grant, 'Introduction', in Michael Grant, ed., *T.S. Eliot: The Critical Heritage*, Volume 1 (London: Routledge, 1982), 18–30; Jewel Spears Brooker, 'Introduction', in Jewel Spears Brooker, ed., *T.S. Eliot: The Contemporary Reviews* (Cambridge: Cambridge University Press, 2004), xiii–xxxix (xx–xxiv); Anthony Cuda, 'Coda: *The Waste Land*'s Afterlife: The Poem's Reception in the Twentieth Century and Beyond', in Gabrielle McIntyre, ed., *The Cambridge Companion to "The Waste Land"* (Cambridge: Cambridge University Press, 2015), 194–210 (194–96).

[4]   Chris Baldick, *The Oxford English Literary History*, Volume 10: *Britain 1910–1940: The Modern Movement* (Oxford: Oxford University Press, 2004), 75–76. See also Peter Howarth, *British Poetry in the Age of Modernism* (Cambridge: Cambridge University Press, 2005), 2–7 and *passim*.

[5]   Baldick, *The Oxford English Literary History*, 75; Howarth, *British Poetry in the Age of Modernism*, 2.

to remap fifty years ago by arguing that Hardy was the key progenitor of modern 'English poetry' and that modernism was an 'aberration' that had directed English poetry 'off on a loop-line that took it away from the general reader'.[6] In this essay, I return to this variegated landscape, to examine the role *The Waste Land* played in discussions about modern poetry in the years immediately following its publication.

The nine British reviewers of *The Waste Land* were diverse in their aesthetic allegiances. They consisted of: Eliot's Bloomsbury Group acquaintances Desmond MacCarthy and Clive Bell; the editors and poets Harold Monro and J.C. Squire, both strongly associated with Georgian poetry; Edgell Rickword, F.L. Lucas, and Humbert Wolfe, all at the beginning of their literary careers; the literary editor of the *Manchester Guardian*, Charles Powell; and a (still) anonymous reviewer for the *Times Literary Supplement*.[7] Only that anonymous review, actually a review of the first issue of *The Criterion* in the *TLS*'s survey of new periodicals, was unequivocally positive ('we have here range, depth, and beautiful expression').[8] Wolfe, in the *Weekly Westminster*, experienced 'just those thrills that I associate with what I believe to be poetry', but admitted that he did not understand the poem; Monro remarked that 'The Waste Land seems to me as near to Poetry as our generation is at present capable of reaching', yet deplored its cynical disregard of ordinary readers. The rest of the reviewers charged Eliot with unintelligibility and such excessive use of quotation and parody that it brought into question whether the poem could be considered to be by Eliot at all. 'The thing is a mad medley', wrote Powell, 'Dr Frazer and Miss J.L. Weston are freely and admittedly his creditors, and the bulk of the poem is under enormously composite and cosmopolitan mortgage: to Spenser, Shakespeare, Webster, Kyd, Middleton, Marvell, Goldsmith, Ezekiel, Buddha, Virgil, Ovid, Dante, St. Augustine, Baudelaire, Verlaine, and others'.[9] Yet almost all the reviewers had praise for Eliot's skill and his earlier poetry: *The Waste Land* was a good poet's experiment that had failed. 'To me "Prufrock" seemed a minor masterpiece which

---

[6]   Philip Larkin, 'It Could Only Happen in England: A study of John Betjeman's poems for American readers' [1971], in *Required Writing: Miscellaneous Pieces, 1955–1982* (London: Faber and Faber, 1983), 204–18 (216), and Donald Davie, *Thomas Hardy and British Poetry* (London: Routledge & Kegan Paul, 1973), 3.

[7]   See Philip Bagguley, *Harlequin in Whitehall: A Life of Humbert Wolfe, Poet & Civil Servant, 1885–1940* (London: Nyla Publishing, 1997), 173.

[8]   'Periodicals: *The Criterion*', *Times Literary Supplement*, 26 October 1922, 690.

[9]   Humbert Wolfe, 'Waste Land and Waste Paper', *Weekly Westminster*, 17 November 1923, 94; Harold Monro, 'Notes for a Study of *The Waste Land*', *Chapbook*, 34 (February 1923), 20–24 (21); C.P. [Charles Powell], 'New Books', *Manchester Guardian*, 31 October 1923, 7.

raised immense and permissible hopes: my opinion has not changed, but my hopes have dwindled slightly [...] he has not improved', wrote Bell; 'it is a pity that a man who can write as well as Mr. Eliot writes in this poem should be so bored (not passionately disgusted) with existence that he doesn't mind what comes next, or who understands it', commented Squire.[10]

Yet by the second half of the 1920s, *The Waste Land* was no longer seen as an aberration in the development of modern poetry, nor of Eliot's oeuvre, despite the quite different direction taken by his subsequent poetry. It was written about as a significant, even representative, example of modern poetry in Britain. In *Contemporary Techniques of Poetry* (1925), Robert Graves cites *The Waste Land* as an example of what he calls 'the Left Wing' of poetic experiment, and two years later he and Laura Riding included several extended discussions of the poem as representative of 'modernism' in *A Survey of Modernist Poetry* (1927).[11] Sherard Vines, in *Movements in Modern English Poetry and Prose* (1927), presented *The Waste Land* as the most important and influential poem produced by the 'intellectualist movement', in which he also placed Richard Aldington, Aldous Huxley, Herbert Read, and the Sitwells.[12] Though, unsurprisingly, it was Eliot's shorter works rather than *The Waste Land* that appeared in the decade's multiple anthologies of modern verse, prefaces and commentaries did not fail to mention it.[13] By 1930, Brian Howard could complain that 'one of the most exhausting things' about editing an anthology of verse 'by the younger English poets' was 'the numberless variations in the treble key, upon Mr. Eliot's renowned poem, *The Waste Land*'.[14]

[10]   Clive Bell, 'T.S. Eliot', *Nation and Athenaeum*, 33 (22 September 1923), 772–73 (772); J.C. Squire, 'Poetry', *London Mercury*, 8.48 (October 1923), 655–657 (656).
[11]   Robert Graves, *Contemporary Techniques of Poetry: A Political Analogy* (London: Hogarth Press, 1925), 24, 30, 42–44; Laura Riding and Robert Graves, *A Survey of Modernist Poetry* (London: William Heinemann, 1927), 50–58, 170–74, 266.
[12]   Sherard Vines, *Movements in Modern English Poetry and Prose* (London: H. Milford/Oxford University Press, 1927), 2, 74, 77–111.
[13]   See, for example, Henry Newbolt, ed., *New Paths on Helicon: A Collection of Modern Poetry*, Volume 2 (London: Thomas Nelson, 1928), 190, 217; Harold Monro, *Twentieth Century Poetry: An Anthology* (London: Chatto & Windus, 1929), 9. Eliot's response to L.A.G. Strong's request of an extract from *The Waste Land* for *The Best Poems of 1923* is relevant here: '*The Waste Land* is intended to form a whole, and I should not care to have anyone read parts of it; and furthermore I am opposed to anthologies in principle' (Eliot, letter to L.A.G. Strong, 3 July 1923, in *The Letters of T.S. Eliot*, Volume 2: 1923–1925, edited by Valerie Eliot and Hugh Haughton (London: Faber and Faber, 2009), 173.
[14]   Brian Howard, 'Mr. Eliot's Poetry', *New Statesman*, 36 (8 November 1930), 146. The anthology did not appear. See Marie-Jacqueline Lancaster, *Brian Howard:*

Recognition of *The Waste Land*'s impact and influence did not necessarily signify acceptance of its example, however. The second half of the 1920s saw the foundation of a number of literary periodicals and the publication of several anthologies which took it upon themselves to appraise their historical moment. These publications not only attempted to describe the connections between individuals and groups of the present and the recent past, they also discussed future directions. There has been little critical discussion of these debates about the state of British poetry, however, perhaps because the 20s became so strongly associated with the canonisation of the Eliot and Pound version of so-called 'high modernism', and critique of its values has tended to be telescoped into consideration of the poets of the 1930s.[15] Two of the most important studies of the period, David Ayers's *English Literature of the 1920s* and John Lucas's *The Radical Twenties*, focus primarily on prose and literature as social criticism, but these works nonetheless provide important direction. As David Ayers remarks, in the aftermath of the First World War, 'literature and the arts urgently needed to theorise their new role and define their audience', and the new 'highbrow' journals 'did not pretend to the culture-consumer readership of the pre-war journals, but were platforms from which the arts could test their purpose and very possibility'.[16] His use of 'highbrow' is taken from Q.D. Leavis, whose confidence in distinguishing between 'highbrow', 'middlebrow', and 'lowbrow' literary periodicals in *Fiction and the Reading Public* exemplifies the stratification of culture that had occurred by the end of the decade. For Leavis (and Ayers) the most significant highbrow periodicals – that is, those with 'serious standards' – were *The Criterion* (1922–39), *The Adelphi* (1923–55), and the *Calendar of Modern Letters* (1925–27).[17] *The Adelphi* was edited in the 20s by Eliot's well-established contemporary John Middleton Murry. But the *Calendar of Modern Letters* was one of several literary periodicals that appeared in the second half of the decade that sought to present the next generation. The same year that Edgell Rickword and Douglas Garman began editing the *Calendar of Modern Letters*, Russell Green and Paul Selver resurrected

---

Portrait of a Failure (London: Timewell Press, 2005), 172–73.

[15]   Chris Baldick gives a similar explanation in his *Literature of the 1920s: Writers among the Ruins* (Edinburgh: Edinburgh University Press, 2012), 1–2, noting that his book is the first to attempt a general account of literature in the twenties.

[16]   David Ayers, *English Literature of the 1920s* (Edinburgh: Edinburgh University Press, 1999), 107. See also John Lucas, *The Radical Twenties: Writing, Politics, and Culture* (Nottingham: Five Leaves Publications, 1997).

[17]   Q.D. Leavis, *Fiction and the Reading Public* (London: Chatto & Windus 1932), 20.

Coterie (1919–21) as the *New Coterie* (1925–27),[18] and three years later there appeared *Experiment*, edited by Jacob Bronowski, William Empson, William Hare, Humphrey Jennings, and Hugh Sykes Davies. To varying degrees, these periodicals engaged with and resisted *The Waste Land*, both as a model for poetry and as a repository of values.

Georgians and Romantics: *The Adelphi*

As Michael Whitworth records, John Middleton Murry had perceived his previous journal, *The Athenaeum*, as in direct opposition to the Georgian poets. In a letter to Katherine Mansfield on 29 October 1919 he describes J.C. Squire and Harold Monro as 'the anti-*Athenaeums*', and comments that 'there's no doubt it's a fight to finish between us & Them – them is the "Georgians" *en masse*. [...] in spite of the *London Mercury* and all its money and réclame, I believe we've got them on the run'.[19] *The Adelphi*, too, was framed in opposition to Georgian poetry, if in more coded terms. An advertisement for the journal reproduced in the June 1924 issue began, 'Serious but not solemn, literature but not "literary", THE ADELPHI pursues its aim of helping men and women of the present time to the discovery of a truth by which they may live'.[20] 'Serious' was a key word for Murry. He had begun his 1919 review essay, 'The Condition of English Poetry', by asking 'Shall we, or shall we not, be serious?', and went on to argue that it was 'impossible to be serious' about most of the poems in the Georgian poetry anthology he was reviewing because they lacked the truth of experience. Their 'false simplicity' was 'compounded of worship of trees and birds and contemporary poets in about equal proportions; it is sicklied over with at times quite a perceptible varnish of modernity, and at other times with what looks to be technical skill,

---

[18]   *New Coterie* does not reveal its editors' names, but evidence in the archive of Charles Lahr, the journal's publisher, internal evidence, and statements by its contributors suggest that Russell Green and Paul Selver had editorial roles. See Charles Lahr Papers, Senate House Library, University of London; and Rupert Croft-Cooke, *The Numbers Came* (London: Putnam, 1963), 128–32. My thanks to Andrew Thacker for sharing his knowledge of the journal.

[19]   Michael Whitworth, 'Enemies of Cant: *The Athenaeum* (1919–21) and *The Adelphi* (1923–48)', in Peter Brooker and Andrew Thacker, eds, *The Oxford Critical and Cultural History of Modernist Magazines*, Volume 1: *Britain and Ireland, 1880–1955* (Oxford: Oxford University Press, 2009), 364–88 (374); John Middleton Murry, letter to Katherine Mansfield, 29 October 1919, in C.A. Hankin, ed., *The Letters of John Middleton Murry to Katherine Mansfield* (London: Constable, 1983), 199, n. 2.

[20]   [John Middleton Murry], 'Our Second Year', *The Adelphi*, 2.1 (June 1924), 60.

but generally proves to be a fairly clumsy reminiscence of somebody else's technical skill'.[21] *The Adelphi*, by contrast, was presented as 'an assertion of a faith [...] that life is important, and that more life should be man's chief endeavour', and that its writers 'must be true to [their] own experience'.[22]

Nevertheless, most readers would have observed similarities between the poetry published in *The Adelphi* and the *London Mercury*, and indeed they had a number of contributors in common. *The Adelphi* published verse by five of the poets who had appeared in Edward Marsh's Georgian anthologies – Edmund Blunden, Walter de la Mare, W.W. Gibson, Robert Graves, and D.H. Lawrence – and published essays on, or recommended books by, a further four: Lascelles Abercrombie, W.H. Davies, John Drinkwater, and James Elroy Flecker. Murry had exempted de la Mare, Lawrence, and Davies from the charge of 'false simplicity' in his 'The Condition of English Poetry' review, and Abercrombie was also, he wrote, 'more or less exempt'.[23] But Drinkwater, Graves, and Gibson were all included in the charge, and indeed though Graves's *Another Future of Poetry* was included in *The Adelphi*'s 'Books to Read' section and recommended as 'within limits, apt, lively, and intelligent', it was glossed with the comment, 'Mr. Graves is not a serious writer'.[24] These poets were joined in *The Adelphi* by figures less well known today, who made up much more of the poetry provision. Poets who appeared repeatedly included Joan Arden (Melicent/Millicent Jourdain), Richard Church, Frances Cornford, H.E. (Herbert) Palmer, Margaret Radford, and, towards the end of *The Adelphi*'s run, the self-professedly romantic Harvard poet, Robert Hillyer, who also contributed poetry reviews to *The Adelphi*'s successor, the *New Adelphi*. Bar Lawrence, none of these poets contributed verse that we would now recognise as modernist: most wrote rhymed verse using regular, conventional metrical forms (notably iambic tetrameter and ballad metre), they used rural rather than urban imagery, and most deployed archaisms. Beyond Lawrence, the only exceptions to what in hindsight looks like a more consistent style of poetry than it did to contemporaries were the poems by Katherine Mansfield, whose unpublished works Murry included throughout *The Adelphi*'s (and the *New Adelphi*'s) run, two contributions from H.D., 'At Athens' and 'Antipater of Sidon', and 'The Disciple' by Iris Tree, whose work had previously appeared in Edith Sitwell's *Wheels* antholo-

[21] J.M.M., 'The Condition of English Poetry', *The Athenaeum*, 4675 (5 December 1919), 1283–85 (1283).

[22] John Middleton Murry, 'The Cause of it All', *The Adelphi*, 1.1 (June 1923), 1–11 (8).

[23] Murry, 'The Condition of English Poetry', 1283.

[24] 'Books to Read', *The Adelphi*, 4.5 (November 1926), 335.

gies.[25] Poets who had gained attention elsewhere as radical innovators, such as Eliot, Pound, and the Sitwell siblings, were not represented and were barely mentioned. In the *New Adelphi*, the relaunched version of the journal that Murry edited from September 1927 to August 1930, a slightly wider range of poetry is represented, including Theodore Morrison's 'The Singing of the Seeds', G.M. Hort's 'Afternoon at the Pension', and four poems by Michael Roberts in all of which one can hear the influence of Eliot's quatrain poems and *The Waste Land*.[26] But while the names of Eliot, John Gould Fletcher, Pound, the Sitwells, and Yeats finally appear in the journal's poetry reviews, they receive scant approbation. Eliot, Osbert Sitwell, and Sacheverell Sitwell are charged with 'eccentricity', Pound's *Selected Poems* 'are not likely to enter the living organism of our literature', Fletcher 'has not succeeded in conveying his experiences to a reader', and Yeats is 'damaged by his own theories'.[27] Hillyer is more positive about Humbert Wolfe ('too much the humanist, too keen a technician, to fall into the lovely snare in which our language delights to entrap those who think more of her than of the thoughts which alone can stimulate her full powers'), Vita Sackville-West ('here we may say farewell to the horrid contemporary trait of self-consciousness, for the poet has abandoned self-hood in the contemplation of the beloved'), Robert P. Tristram Coffin ('worth reading'), and Rupert Croft-Cooke ('pleasing but not incandescent').[28]

Though Hillyer was explicit in setting himself against his contemporaries in advocating a poetry of 'normal experience and poetic form' and a Georgian style prevailed in the earlier issues, it would be misleading to suggest that the

---

[25]   Katherine Mansfield, 'To L.H.B. (1894–1915)', *The Adelphi* 1.2 (July 1923), 136; 'Poems of Childhood', *The Adelphi*, 1.3 (August 1923), 186–89; 'Poems', *The Adelphi*, 1.6 (November 1923), 459–65; 'A Verse Fragment', *The Adelphi*, 1.9 (February 1924), 776; 'Winter Bird', *The Adelphi*, 2.2 (July 1924), 104; 'A Sunset', *New Adelphi*, 3.1 (September–November 1929), 8; 'Old Fashioned Widow's Song', *New Adelphi*, 3.2 (December 1929–February 1930), 130; H.D., 'At Athens', *The Adelphi*, 2.7 (December 1924), 618; 'Antipater of Sidon', *The Adelphi*, 3.1 (June 1925), 64; Iris Tree, 'The Disciple', *The Adelphi*, 1.3 (September 1923), 306.
[26]   Theodore Morrison, 'The Singing of the Seeds', *New Adelphi*, 2.3 (March–May 1929), 215–20; G.M. Hort, 'Afternoon at the Pension', *New Adelphi*, 2.4 (June–August 1929), 299–303; Michael Roberts, 'Four Poems', *New Adelphi*, 3.2 (December 1929–February 1930), 87–89.
[27]   Robert Hillyer, 'Verbiage, Diction, Poetry', *New Adelphi*, 1.1 (September 1927), 90–93 (90); Robert Hillyer, 'Five American Poets', *New Adelphi*, 2.3 (March–May 1929), 280–82 (281); Robert Hillyer, 'A Poet Young and Old', *New Adelphi*, 3.1 (September–November 1929), 78–80 (78).
[28]   Hillyer, 'Verbiage, Diction, Poetry', 91, 92; Robert Hillyer, 'Nine Books of Verse', *New Adelphi*, 3.3 (March–May 1930), 232–36 (235, 236).

journal actively favoured a particular style of poetry, or that it openly proposed particular models for future poetic work, because its focus was not on literary tradition nor generic distinctions, but on 'belief in life'.[29] As Murry wrote in the first issue, 'there are [...] different ways, many different ways, of believing in life', and his 'Advice for Intending Contributors' promised that 'no matter what the subject, or how apparently trivial the occasion, provided he feels strongly about it and manages to communicate the reality of his feeling in his words, his contribution will be regarded'.[30] Accordingly, over the course of its run, *The Adelphi* had less to say about contemporary literary debates than it had about philosophical, religious, and psychological issues – though Murry's personal interests in Keats and Shakespeare were well represented. The journal contained much more prose than poetry, and the 'Books to Buy', 'Books to Borrow', and 'Books to Read' columns included volumes of verse, especially recent verse, relatively rarely.

Nevertheless, the journal's philosophy could clearly be correlated to poetic values, and although these only occasionally became explicit, they are instructive in delineating a carefully considered resistance to Eliot's poetry, particularly as represented by *The Waste Land*. Murry's association of his journal with romanticism in opposition to *The Criterion*'s avowed classicism is well known, of course, and the exchange of views in essays published in the two journals has been analysed in detail by David Goldie, Jason Harding, and Dominic Rowland, among others.[31] But it is less often noted that *The Waste Land* played a fundamental role in Murry's argument. His most important essay on the subject, 'The Classical Revival', was published in *The Adelphi* in two parts in February and March 1926, and written in response to Eliot's classicist manifesto, 'The Idea of a Literary Review', which had appeared in *The Criterion* in January. In this essay Murry cites *The Waste Land* as his key piece of evidence that demonstrates Eliot is not, in fact, a classicist, and indeed that a 'serious classicism is a contradiction in terms for a modern mind'. What journalists were referring to as a classical revival, Murry preferred to term an 'Augustan' revival, characterised by a stance of scepticism and amusement, which used 'a technique of detachment for an attitude of

---

[29]   Hillyer, 'None Books of Verse', 236, Murry, 'The Cause of it All', 7.

[30]   Murry, 'The Cause of it All', 7–9.

[31]   David Goldie, *A Critical Difference: T.S. Eliot and John Middleton Murry in English Literary Criticism, 1919–1928* (Oxford: Clarendon Press, 1998), 92–127, Jason Harding, *The Criterion: Cultural Politics and Periodical Networks in Inter-War Britain* (Oxford: Oxford University Press, 2002), 25–43; Dominic Charles Edward Rowland, 'T.S. Eliot, *The Criterion*, and Literary Controversy, 1922–1939', PhD thesis, University College London, 1996.

detachment', and was unconcerned with the 'complexities and heart-search-ings of modern life'. This he saw in the work of David Garnett, Aldous Huxley, and Lytton Strachey. But *The Waste Land* was clearly profoundly concerned with modern life, and expressed 'a self-torturing and utter nihil-ism', which would be impossible to order according to classical principles, since 'there is no order in modern experience, because there is no accepted principle of order'.[32] Indeed, as Jason Harding remarks, Eliot's classicism 'really had more in common with a neo-Thomist literary revival in France and with the twentieth-century "reaction against romanticism" than with the Greek and Roman classics'.[33]

The Waste Land is thus, according to Murry, a failure, and the reasons he gives for its failure go some way towards indicating the positive values he sought in modern poetry. The poem is, he writes, over-intellectualized, it lacks spontaneity, it is 'overladen with calculated subtleties', and it fails to produce any 'unity of impression': 'the reader is compelled, in the mere effort to understand, to adopt an attitude of intellectual suspicion, which makes impossible the communication of feeling'.[34] The poetry that Murry values, in contrast, combines the ideal and the sensuous (terms he drew from George Santayana[35]) to achieve a '*direct* power': 'Poetry at its highest does not *mean* anything, it *is*; it cannot be understood, it can only be received; it is a pure conduit of mysterious and ineffable life into a man's being'. It is this communication of experience, of life, that for Murry marks out great poetry, and which he terms romantic poetry, which is indeed the only kind of poetry he believes possible for post-Reformation poets writing in the English tradition.[36] In this light, one can see that most of the poetic contributions to *The Adelphi* are valued for their emphasis on experience, especially sensuous experience, rather than intellect, and their appeals to a higher, often religious, ideal – in short, valued for their romanticism, rather than for a particular style. The fact that they nevertheless have a stylistic similarity to each other that is familiar from Georgian poetry is therefore in a sense incidental, but also, of course, the result of the fact that they are part of a twentieth-century

---

[32] John Middleton Murry, 'The "Classical" Revival [I]', *The Adelphi*, 3.9 (February 1926), 585–595 (594, 587, 591, 589, 592–93).
[33] Harding, *The Criterion*, 33.
[34] Murry, 'The "Classical" Revival [I]', 589, 591–92.
[35] See, for example, George Santayana, *The Sense of Beauty* (New York: Charles Scribner's Sons, 1896), 35.
[36] The Journeyman [John Middleton Murry], 'Poetry and Religion', *The Adelphi*, 3.10 (March 1926), 695–99 (698); John Middleton Murry, 'The "Classical" Revival: II', *The Adelphi*, 3.10 (March 1926), 648–53 (650).

neo-romanticism to which Georgian poetry also belonged, which was nourished by the models of Coleridge, Keats, Shelley, and Wordsworth.

The distinction that Murry makes between the poetry of experience and the poetry of intellect is one that other critics of 1920s poetry have also made in different, though not incompatible terms. Donald Davie read twentieth-century verse as largely divided between 'a Hardyesque style on the one hand and an Eliotic style on the other', where the former is 'confessional' and the latter 'ironical'. Two of his key examples of the Hardyesque in the 1920s were the *Adelphi* contributors, Blunden and Graves.[37] More recently, Chris Baldick has argued that one of the defining modernist techniques is 'anachronism and related disorderings of the reader's time-sense', termed by Eliot 'the mythical method' and deployed in *The Waste Land* as a 'means by which the world-anarchy may be brought under imaginative control and comprehension'.[38]

But although Hardy is praised throughout *The Adelphi* and the journal published two of his poems, Murry's major example of contemporary romanticism was not Hardy, but D.H. Lawrence.[39] Indeed, Murry later claimed that he had founded *The Adelphi* to 'prepare the place' for Lawrence when he returned to Britain.[40] Though Lawrence did not take up that place and even expressed some distaste for the journal, his work – poems, essays, and translations – appeared throughout *The Adelphi*.[41] The June-August 1930 issue of the *New Adelphi*, Murry's last as editor, was largely a Lawrence memorial. In his review of Lawrence's *Collected Poems* the year before, Murry had praised Lawrence's early work extravagantly: 'if the best work of all his contemporary poets were pooled, it could not make up a book so manifestly the work of genius as the first of these two volumes', he wrote. But he found the second volume less successful, less in tune with *The Adelphi*'s aims: 'A hard, bleak quality of dogmatic asseveration creeps in. The extraordinary richness of Mr. Lawrence's experiencing nature is curbed and straitened'. Characteristically, Murry's criticism is in part self-directed: 'We cannot feel like that; we are not like that. Perhaps we ought to be like that. Who can say?'[42]

---

[37]   Davie, *Thomas Hardy and British Poetry*, 133, 135, 132.

[38]   Baldick, *Literature of the 1920s*, 26, 87.

[39]   Thomas Hardy, 'Freed the Fret of Thinking', *The Adelphi*, 2.12 (May 1925), 959; and 'A Leader of Fashion', *The Adelphi*, 3.6 (November 1925), 395.

[40]   John Middleton Murry, *Son of Woman: The Story of D.H. Lawrence* (London: Jonathan Cape, 1931), 328.

[41]   Whitworth, 'Enemies of Cant', 387.

[42]   J.M. Murry, 'The Poems of D.H. Lawrence', *New Adelphi*, 2.2 (December–February 1929), 165–67 (165).

To what extent is *The Adelphi* evidence that Lawrence provided an alternative, non-Eliotian, model for modern poetry? *The Adelphi*'s poetry may generally have appeared consistent with Murry's definitions of romanticism, and
some contributors, such as Rupert Croft-Cooke, Edwin Muir, and Margaret
Radford were also admirers of Lawrence.[43] But others found his poetry less
compelling: Blunden and Richard Church both thought him overrated and
were much more interested in the romantic poets and Hardy.[44] But whether
they looked to Lawrence, Hardy, the romantics, or the Georgians, most of
the *Adelphi*'s contributors consciously rejected the example of Eliot's poetry.
According to Croft-Cooke, 'the poets were the Georgians, for Eliot was not
even a name to us', Blunden found Eliot's poetry 'surpassingly allusive', and
Church, though he preferred Eliot to Murry as a friend and editor, thought
Eliot's poetry was 'too dialectical and loaded with learning'.[45] Palmer would
devote a chapter of his 1938 study, *Post-Victorian Poetry*, to virulent criticism
of *The Waste Land*: 'it has little importance except as a gesture of mockery
and disillusion and contempt for the reader and critic; no value except as the
banner of present-day war weariness and spiritual barrenness – one might
almost say mental and moral degeneracy'.[46] Even Robert Graves, who shared
a warm professional correspondence with Eliot and wrote at length about
The Waste Land in *A Survey of Modernist Poetry* (1927), was somewhat
equivocal in his praise of the poem in *Contemporary Techniques of Poetry*
(1925), where he described it as 'admirably descriptive of a glorious and complete intellectual tangle, a maze thick with cul-de-sacs'.[47]

Food for the Young

In 1929, writing in *Life and Letters*, E.M. Forster remarked that one should
ask 'help of the young' to understand Eliot's oeuvre, because

---

[43]   Croft-Cooke, *The Numbers Came*, 31; Edwin Muir, 'D.H. Lawrence', in
Transition: Essays on Contemporary Literature (London: Hogarth Press, 1926),
49–63; Mark Kinkead-Weekes, *D.H. Lawrence: Triumph to Exile, 1912–1922*
(Cambridge: Cambridge University Press, 2011), 502.

[44]   Barry Webb, *Edmund Blunden: A Biography* (New Haven, CT: Yale University
Press, 1990), 133–34, 190; Edmund Blunden, *Thomas Hardy* (London: Macmillan,
1941); Richard Church, *The Golden Sovereign* (London: Heinemann, 1957), 91–92.

[45]   Croft-Cooke, *The Numbers Came*, 31; [Edmund Blunden], 'On Post-War Poets',
Times Literary Supplement, 7 March 1935, 139; Church, *The Golden Sovereign*, 233.

[46]   Herbert Palmer, *Post-Victorian Poetry* (London: Dent, 1938), 313–14.

[47]   Graves, *Contemporary Techniques of Poetry*, 43.

Mr. Eliot's work, particularly *The Waste Land*, has made a profound impression on them, and given them precisely the food they needed. And by 'the young' I mean those men and women between the ages of eighteen and thirty whose opinions one most respects, and whose reactions one most admires. He is the most important author of their day, his influence is enormous, they are inside his idiom as the young of 1900 were inside George Meredith's, they are far better qualified than their elders to expound him, and in certain directions they do expound him.[48]

Forster's contention that admiration for *The Waste Land* was generational is one frequently encountered in journalism of the period. As we saw earlier, Brian Howard made the same point in 1930, and five years earlier, Edgell Rickword had begun his review of Eliot's *Poems, 1909–1925* by imagining a Congress of Younger Poets voting on 'who has most effectively upheld the reality of the art in an age of preposterous poeticising'. Only one poet was in contention, he wrote: 'It is impossible to think of any serious rival to the name of T.S. Eliot'.[49] A review of periodicals in the second half of the twenties that focused on publishing younger poets does indeed suggest that many were inside Eliot's idiom, particularly the idiom of *The Waste Land*. Yet even among these groups, the model of *The Waste Land* was not taken up quite so unproblematically as Forster's comment might lead us to expect.

1925, the year Eliot published his *Poems, 1909–1925*, also saw the appearance of the *New Coterie* (1925–27). The *New Coterie* was the progeny of the Oxford poetry journal, *Coterie*, with which Eliot had briefly been affiliated. As Andrew Thacker has discussed, Eliot had attended the poetry reading group that gave rise to *Coterie* during his fellowship year in Oxford (1914–15), he was listed as a member of *Coterie*'s editorial board in two of its seven issues, and 'A Cooking Egg' was the concluding poem of the journal's first issue.[50] Although the *New Coterie* appeared five years after the closure of its predecessor, it shared some of the same contributors, including some of those who had belonged to the original poetry reading group: Wilfred Childe, T.W. Earp, Russell Green, and Robert Nichols. The journal provides a particularly good range of the self-consciously 'modern' poetry that was

---

[48]   E.M. Forster, 'T.S. Eliot and his Difficulties', *Life and Letters*, 2.13 (June 1929), 417–25 (420).

[49]   Edgell Rickword, 'The Modern Poet', *Calendar of Modern Letters*, 2.10 (December 1925), 278–81 (278).

[50]   Andrew Thacker, 'Aftermath of War: *Coterie* (1919–21), *New Coterie* (1925–7), Robert Graves and *The Owl* (1919–23)', in Brooker and Thacker, eds, *The Oxford Critical and Cultural History of Modernist Magazines*, vol. 1, 462–84 (463–66); T.S. Eliot, 'A Cooking Egg', *Coterie*, 1 (May 1919), 44–45.

being written during the period, partly because – despite its name – its contributors were not a clique.[51] It included humorous verse (by Clifford Bax, Earp, Green, and Aldous Huxley), intricate Georgian-influenced poetry (by Martin Armstrong, Ida Graves, Green, Evan Morgan, A.S.J. Tessimond), and imagist and futurist-influenced free verse (by Benjamin Gilbert Brooks, Robert McAlmon, Paul Selver, and Horace Shipp). Nancy Cunard's 'In Provins' engaged with the experiments Pound was undertaking in *The Cantos*; John Gould Fletcher's 'That Day' showed its imagist inheritance but prefigured a diction that would become dominant in the 1930s. A 'European Anthology' section concluded the first four issues and presented verse translations from Czech, Danish, French, German, Italian, Norwegian, Polish, Serbian, and Russian – the unusually wide range reflecting Paul Selver's interests and linguistic abilities. Unlike *The Adelphi*, the *New Coterie* did not advance any arguments about its preferred literary values: it contained no literary criticism, and though its unsigned editorials deplored the low status of literature in Britain, it blamed readers, booksellers, and newspaper magnates, not particular authors, styles or genres. Unsurprisingly, then, Eliot is not mentioned by name, but there is evidence of his influence in poems by Tessimond and – despite his protestations to the contrary – Croft-Cooke. Tessimond's 'Incident in a Drawing-Room' echoes 'Hysteria', his 'Sunday at Home' recalls the typist's teatime in 'The Fire Sermon'.[52] Croft-Cooke's 'Holy Matrimony' draws on the monologue form and locution of 'Portrait of a Lady' and syntax that alludes to 'A Game of Chess'. Croft-Cooke places his Eliotion locution within a more conventional metre and rhyme scheme, but in 'The Queen Bee' his varying of form between the six numbered sections strongly recalls *The Waste Land*.[53] Yet, for the poets of the *New Coterie*, *The Waste Land* is clearly one model amongst several.

However, the same year Green and Selver launched the *New Coterie*, Edgell Rickword and Douglas Garman edited the first issues of *The Calendar of Modern Letters*, a journal that had much more to say about Eliot's significance. Rickword had been one of the nine original reviewers of *The Waste Land*. Writing in the *Times Literary Supplement*, he had praised some passages, but ultimately criticised the poem for lacking coherence and verging on

[51]   Croft-Cooke, *The Numbers Came*, 132.
[52]   A.S.J. Tessimond, 'Incident in a Drawing-Room', *New Coterie*, 1.2 (spring 1926), 78; A.S.J. Tessimond, 'Sunday at Home', *New Coterie*, 6 (summer and autumn, 1927), 91.
[53]   Rupert Croft-Cooke, 'Holy Matrimony', *New Coterie*, 4 (autumn 1926), 17–18; Rupert Croft-Cooke, 'The Queen Bee', *New Coterie*, 4 (spring 1927), 21–23.

plagiarism.[54] Although his substantial review of Eliot's *Poems, 1909–1925* in the *Calendar of Modern Letters* begins with the warm recognition of Eliot's importance to 'younger poets' quoted above, he reiterated his reservations about *The Waste Land*. 'His success is intermittent', Rickword writes, and he concludes that 'it is the danger of the aesthetic of "The Waste Land" that it tempts the poet to think the undeveloped theme a positive triumph and obscurity more precious than commonplace'.[55] The danger of *The Waste Land*'s model is reiterated elsewhere in the journal too. In his patronizing review of Nancy Cunard's *Parallax*, Garman remarked that 'the discipline she needs must be exercised by her own personality and not by the influences to which she submits. In imitating – the word is not too strong – "The Waste Land", Miss Cunard has followed a good, but dangerous model too slavishly'.[56]

Nevertheless, the journal offered space to several poets following this dangerous model. Peter Quennell's polyvocal, free verse 'Leviathan' has multiple echoes of *The Waste Land*. The figure of Leviathan himself is attributed the androgyny that Tiresias has in Eliot's poem; Quennell's 'mitred Queen of Heaven' on 'her broad, low throne' recalls the beginning of 'A Game of Chess'; Atlantis, visited by Leviathan, is an underground world, 'all scent within the narrow throat of flowers', recalling the association of the hyacinth girl with Persephone. The end of the poem settles on a first-person speaker meditating on water, as the end of *The Waste Land* does too. Even individual word use in this context recalls Eliot, as when we are told that the Queen of Heaven 'smoothed her wrinkled snood' we recall how the typist in 'The Fire Sermon' 'smoothes her hair with automatic hand'; we see 'desires' 'carrying your torches high', as we glimpsed 'torchlight red on sweaty faces' in 'What the Thunder Said'.[57] Garman's own poem, 'Retrospect', begins by setting a scene familiar from 'The Burial of The Dead':

[54]   [Edgell Rickword], 'A Fragmentary Poem', *Times Literary Supplement*, 20 September 1923.

[55]   Rickword, 'The Modern Poet', 280–81.

[56]   D.M.G. [Douglas Garman], '*Parallax*. By Nancy Cunard', *Calendar of Modern Letters*, 1.3 (May 1925), 248.

[57]   Peter Quennell, 'Leviathan', *Calendar of Modern Letters*, 1.2 (1925), 108–110. Writing of this period, when he was an undergraduate at Oxford (1923–26), Quennell later remarked, 'we venerated *The Waste Land*', and remembered Harold Acton reciting 'the whole poem at a Conservative Oxford garden-party': see Peter Quennell, *The Marble Foot: An Autobiography, 1905–1938* (London: Collins, 1976), 126.

Spring has been dead so long –
Hyacinths fragrant in the window-pots
And the white surf of snow ebbing from the meadows –
And summer followed spring with cruel feet
Leaving a trampled corpse beneath the trees.[58]

But it is more for its criticism than its creative contributions that *The Calendar of Modern Letters* is remembered, particularly its 'scrutinies', detailed close readings of contemporary writers that provided F.R. Leavis with a name for his journal in 1932, five years after *The Calendar of Modern Letters'* demise.[59] In the criticism as well as the poetry Eliot's influence is discernible, and Malcolm Bradbury goes so far as to remark that '*The Criterion*, *The Calendar of Modern Letters* and *Scrutiny* were all classical in tone, opposed to the Romanticism of Murry's *The Adelphi* and the Dionysianism of Jack Lindsay's *London Aphrodite*'.[60] In one of the most renowned essays published by the journal, 'Thoughts on Poetic Discontent', John Crowe Ransom sets out an opposition between 'the purely romantic position' that dominated the poetry of the nineteenth century and 'irony [...] the ultimate mode of great minds', whose 'spirit transcends the Nineteenth Century mind and goes back to further places in the English tradition'. Though not identical to Eliot's classicism, Ransom's spirit of irony relies on a related critical binary and conception of literary history.

However, while *The Calendar of Modern Letters*, with Eliot, maintained that 'the characteristics of a healthy criticism are invariably "classic", tending towards an ever greater rigidity of principle, organizations more explicit, and the canalization of the wide shallow stream of taste', it distinguished itself from the *Criterion*'s 'repressive' mode of classicist criticism.[61] Particularly in

---

[58]   Douglas Garman, 'Retrospect', *Calendar of Modern Letters*, 1.4 (June 1925), 266–68 (266). 'Retrospect' was later published as the first part of Garman's long poem, 'The Jaded Hero': see Douglas Garman, *The Jaded Hero* (London: Wishart, 1927), 41–60.
[59]   F.R. Leavis, *Scrutiny: A Retrospect* (Cambridge: Cambridge University Press, 1963), 3.
[60]   Malcolm Bradbury, 'The Calendar of Modern Letters: A Review in Retrospect', *London Magazine*, new series 1.7 (October 1961), 37–46 (39).
[61]   Edgell Rickword, 'Euthanasia: Or the Future of Criticism', *Calendar of Modern Letters*, 3.2 (July 1926), 151–54 (152). Compare: T.S. Eliot, 'The Function of Criticism', *The Criterion*, 2 (October 1923), 31–42; Bertram Higgins, 'Art and Knowledge', *Calendar of Modern Letters*, 4.1 (April 1927), 56–61 (58–59); D.M.G., 'A Reply to *The Criterion*', *Calendar of Modern Letters*, 4.2 (July 1927), 154–155 (154). On this debate between the *Calendar of Modern Letters* and *The Criterion*, see Rowland, 'T.S. Eliot, *The Criterion*, and Literary Controversy, 1922–1939', 73–79.

Rickword's essays, there is sense that a certain approach to poetry he associates with Eliot has reached the limits of its use. In 'The Returning Hero', for example, Rickword argues that 'the literature of disillusionment is reaching the last stage' – his examples are Strachey, Huxley, and *The Waste Land* – and he anticipates the return of the hero and heroic action in poetry. It is significant that his diagnosis of the contemporary situation here alludes to *The Caliph's Design*, Wyndham Lewis's treatise on post-war art that was also a significant salvo in the *rappel à l'ordre* of the post-war years, but one suspicious of neo-classicism.[62] Rickword sought Lewis's, Joyce's, and Lawrence's contributions to *The Calendar of Modern Letters*: Lawrence's story, 'The Princess', opened the first issue and Lewis's writings, as Charles Hobday notes, occupy more space than any other contributor apart from Rickword himself.[63] Lewis and Lawrence, for all that they are part of the generation the journal aims to supersede, are not part of the 'literature of disillusionment', but are associated with a move to establish literature on more positive grounds. But Rickword characterises this literature not, like Murry, as a literature of expression, but rather as a literature fully connected to its world. In 'The Re-Creation of Poetry', Rickword proposes that 'relations with the life and people' around the poet need to replace the generalised emotions and fixed ideas about poetic suitability that have become hegemonic.[64] Similarly, Douglas Garman's 'Audience' is written against the current 'tendency to set poetry apart from the lively interests of existence', a tendency he associates with both the Georgian poets and the French Surrealists.[65]

A similar mixture of indebtedness and circumspection towards Eliot is displayed by *Experiment*. The first three issues were edited by a group of students who styled themselves 'the Five' – Jacob Bronowski, William Empson, William Hare, Humphrey Jennings, and Hugh Sykes Davies – and its subsequent four by Bronowski and Sykes Davies. A small group dominated contributions: as well as 'The Five', these included W.G. (William) Archer, Richard Eberhardt, Graham Noxon, Elsie Phare, Kathleen Raine, George Reavey, James Reeves, and Arthur Tillotson, all students or recent gradu-

---

[62] Wyndham Lewis, *The Caliph's Design: Architects! Where is your Vortex?* (London: Egoist, 1919), 8, 45–46.

[63] Charles Hobday, *Edgell Rickword: A Poet at War* (Manchester: Carcanet, 1989), 93. Joyce responded to Rickword's invitation by submitting 'Anna Livia Plurabelle', but the journal's printers refused to print it. See Sylvia Beach, *Shakespeare and Company* (New York: Harcourt Brace, 1959), 169.

[64] E.R. [Edgell Rickword], 'The Re-Creation of Poetry: The Use of "Negative Emotions"', *Calendar of Modern Letters*, 1.3 (May 1925), 236–41.

[65] Douglas Garman, 'Audience', *Calendar of Modern Letters*, 2.7 (summer 1925), 44–49 (45).

ates of Cambridge. Within the journal's mixture of poetry, short fiction, literary, art, film criticism, and philosophy, there was substantial attention to the state of contemporary poetry and criticism, and Eliot was the major point of reference. His influence on the poetry in the journal is striking. Although the mark of other poets' styles is evident (E.E. Cummings, H.D., Mina Loy, Pound, and Laura Riding all seem to have been read by the poets who appear in these pages), it is Eliot's voice that is by far the most audible. We hear 'A Cooking Egg' in Christopher Saltmarshe's 'Cubierto', 'Whispers of Immortality' in Arthur Tillotson's 'Movement Two-Dimensional' and 'As it is in Heaven', 'Gerontion' in Jacob Bronowski's 'Death for Odysseus', and 'Ash Wednesday' in Kathleen Raine's 'Attalus'.[66] But most of all we hear *The Waste Land*: the pages of *Experiment* are filled with rats, deserts, droughts, corpses, and flowers struggling through winter soil. Unlike *The Adelphi* and the *New Coterie*, but like *The Calendar of Modern Letters*, the poets of *Experiment* frequently used free verse and poems that, like *The Waste Land*, change form and style from section to section were not uncommon.[67] As Jason Harding, Scott McCracken, and kitt price have demonstrated, however, *Experiment*'s poetic values were by no means shared by the contributors' fellow students, and the journal drew considerable comment and criticism within Cambridge. The Georgian poems and Bloomsbury affiliations of another student journal, *The Venture*, edited by Michael Redgrave and Robin Fedden, appear to have been more representative.[68]

In fact, when we turn to *Experiment*'s critical prose, it becomes clear that the editors were more circumspect about the critical and poetic model Eliot offered than much of the journal's poetry suggests. Eliot's and Murry's debate about classicism and romanticism is invoked only to be dismissed as

---

[66]   Christopher Saltmarshe, 'Cubierto', *Experiment*, 2 (February 1929), 11; Arthur Tillotson, 'Movement Two-Dimensional', *Experiment*, 2 (February 1929), 31; Arthur Tillotson, 'As it is in Heaven', *Experiment*, 5 (February 1930), 37; Jacob Bronowski, 'Death for Odysseus', *Experiment*, 4 (November 1929), 9–10; Kathleen Raine, 'Attalus', *Experiment*, 6 (October 1930), 50.

[67]   See James Reeves, 'Cambridge Twenty Years Ago' and Kathleen Raine, 'The Poet of Our Time', in Richard March and Tambimuttu, eds, *T.S. Eliot: A Symposium* (Chicago, IL: Henry Regnery, 1949) 38–42, 78–81.

[68]   Jason Harding, 'Experiment in Cambridge: "A Manifesto of Young England"', *Cambridge Quarterly*, 27.4 (1998), 287–309 (295–97), Scott McCracken, 'Cambridge Magazines and Unfinished Business: *Experiment* (1928–30), *The Venture* (1928–30), and *Cambridge Left* (1933–4)', in Brooker and Thacker, eds, *The Oxford Critical and Cultural History of Modernist Magazines*, vol. 1, 599–622, Kate Price, '"Finite But Unbounded": *Experiment* magazine, Cambridge, England, 1928–31', *Jacket*, 20 (December 2002), http://jacketmagazine.com/20/price-expe.html.

inadequate,[69] and in the third issue 'the Five' criticise Wyndham Lewis's recent polemic in his journal *The Enemy* against the communism of the Surrealists, and include Eliot in their castigation of simplistic political oppositions:

> Mr. Lewis is not alone in creating a political (as against a literary) opposition of democratic nihilism and calling it communism: Mr. Eliot, trying in his last book to establish the continuity of a non-democratic tradition which was at the same time religious [...] invented the ingenious device of 'romantic' autocracy. Contemporary Russia was bundled into this class; and this within two pages of the reflection that 'for lazy or tired minds there is only extremity or apathy; dictatorship or communism, with enthusiasm or with indifference.' Mr Lewis is assuredly neither lazy nor tired (of Mr. Eliot it is not so easy to be certain).

The editorial ends by saying that the cause of their objection to Lewis's article is not sympathy with communism, but the belief that the abstract and inaccurate oppositions Lewis and Eliot propose mean 'there can be no clearing up of beliefs and no building up of a uniform and contemporary artistic attitude'.[70] What that attitude might be becomes clearer in later issues. In the fifth issue, Hugh Sykes Davies begins a discussion of the League of Nations by noting that among 'the people called "intelligent"' of the 'post-war generation: roughly my contemporaries' the League is regarded with apathy, in part because of problems with the League that he goes on to outline, but also because this generation has retreated from engaging with political matters into 'academicism'. The 'academic retreat is represented', he remarks, in *The Waste Land* and Pound's *Hugh Selwyn Mauberley*, and he further describes 'Mr. Eliot's Royalism' as representing 'the academic spirit applied to politics'.[71] It is not easy to judge where Sykes Davies places himself in this essay, since he aligns the 'intelligent' of his generation with the academic retreat of Eliot and Pound, yet his use of the word 'retreat' itself implies criticism. In the final editorial, published a year later, that implication is confirmed. There, Sykes Davies and Bronowski write that 'we have always avoided making protestations of policy, choosing to leave it to the reader to conclude that we really do stand for a single direction of outlook', but 'we feel it is now not arrogant to say that we are in some ways the only literary group which is positively post-war, which honestly seeks to transcend the spirit of academi-

---

[69]   E.E. Phare, 'Valéry and Gerard Hopkins', *Experiment*, 1 (November 1928), 19–23 (19); J. Bronowski, 'Symbolism', *Experiment*, 2 (February 1929), 19–22 (20, note 1).
[70]   Five, 'Wyndham Lewis's "Enemy"', *Experiment*, 3 (May 1929), 2–5 (4–5).
[71]   Hugh Sykes, 'The League of Nations', *Experiment*, 5 (February 1930), 6–10 (6).

cism and stoicism of the older generation'.[72] Yet this issue includes two signal considerations of the older generation: a section of Joyce's *Work in Progress* (with a three-page 'footnote' by Stuart Gilbert), and an essay by Bronowski on Lawrence. Although ostensibly written against 'the current estimate of Lawrence, as an advocate, a prophet and a fanatic', against, it would therefore seem, the estimate of Middleton Murry, Bronowski in fact advances an argument which has much in common with Murry's. He hastens to assure the reader that he does 'not wish in so dismissing the common misconstruction to drive the critic into any "barren aestheticism"', and that, following Matthew Arnold, he wants to postulate 'a moral interpretation of literature'. However, like Murry, Bronowski finds Lawrence unable to fulfil the promise of his aspirations. Like Murry, he values the fact that 'Lawrence's passion [...] was for the first-hand, in experience, in ethic – in living' and 'was also for the first-hand in his creation of living: for the first of all directnesses, the directness of perception. In that directness, he sought all his life to make perception and expression one thing'. But in failing to achieve this, Lawrence 'falls back' on his personal system of symbolism, so that 'as an artist, he falls short I think by lacking some central self-confidence, some completeness and stability within himself which might have made him less vulnerable', but has made him 'more valuable to this age as a man'.[73]

Lawrence, then, does not provide a model for the young artist, but he does encode values that escape the 'academicism' associated with *The Waste Land* and *Hugh Selwyn Mauberley*. This opposition relates to the journal's attention to Eliot's debate with I.A. Richards about the relation between poetry and belief that Benjamin Kohlmann has recently discussed in compelling detail. In *Science and Poetry*, Richards famously wrote that in *The Waste Land* 'by effecting a complete severance of his poetry and *all* beliefs, and this without any weakening of the poetry, he has realised what might otherwise have remained largely a speculative possibility, and has shown the way to the only solution of these difficulties'.[74] For Kohlmann, the combination of this influential characterisation of *The Waste Land* and Eliot's public profession of his politics 'made him a notoriously difficult figure in the politicized debates of the late 1920s and early 1930s', and concealed the fact that Eliot

---

[72]   [Jacob Bronowski and Hugh Sykes], Editorial, *Experiment*, 7 (spring 1931), 4.

[73]   J. Bronowski, 'D.H. Lawrence', *Experiment*, 7 (spring 1941), 5–13 (5, 8, 12, 13).

[74]   I.A. Richards, *Science and Poetry* (London: Kegan Paul, Trench, Trubner, 1926), 64–65. Empson and Jennings were supervised by Richards, and Empson, Jennings, Phare, and Raine attended Richards's lectures. See Benjamin Kohlmann, *Committed Styles: Modernism, Politics, and Left-Wing Literature in the 1930s* (Oxford: Oxford University Press, 2014), 33.

was, by the late 1920s, by no means the formalist that Marxists and New Critics alike took him to be. Kohlmann argues that *Experiment*'s engagement with the debate about poetry and belief demonstrates that it is not the high modernist journal it has been taken to be, and in fact it prefigures 'the 1930s' uneasy take on the languages of poetry and belief, as well as on the relation between literature and political involvement'.[75] Indeed, *Experiment* ends with the suggestion that it has found its model in a work which takes it firmly into the next decade's concerns. The penultimate contribution in the final issue is Empson's 'A Note on W.H. Auden's "Paid on Both Sides"', which had just been published in *The Criterion*. It concludes:

> One reason the scheme [of 'Paid on Both Sides'] is so impressive is that it puts psycho-analysis and surrealism and all that, all the irrationalist tendencies which are so essential a part of the machinery of present-day thought, into their proper place; they are made part of the normal and rational tragic form, and indeed what constitutes the tragic situation [...]. Within its scale (twenty-seven pages) there is the gamut of all the ways we have of thinking about the matter; it has the sort of completeness that makes a work seem to define the attitude of a generation.[76]

The clear affirmation of the last line is all the more striking in comparison with the equivocations about Eliot and Lawrence. Even Empson's 'Some Notes on Mr. Eliot', a close reading of 'A Game of Chess' and 'Whispers of Immortality', restricts itself to an analysis of grammar and punctuation, with no summative judgement.[77]

Both the *Calendar of Modern Letters* and *Experiment* conceive of their project as establishing the next stage for literature, a stage beyond high modernism. Unlike the *New Coterie* and *The Adelphi*, they found in *The Waste Land* idioms and arguments central to their enquiry. This is not only because of the quality of Eliot's poetry, or the attraction of his style. It is also because throughout the decade, from the first reviews onwards, *The Waste Land* was the lightning rod for the core debate about poetry, variously inflected in terms of sincerity, romanticism and classicism, and belief. In this sense, the poets of the 1930s are the direct descendants of Eliot and of *The Waste Land*, though the new decade would soon provide waste lands of its own.

---

[75]   Kohlmann, *Committed Styles*, 22, 19.
[76]   William Empson, 'A Note on W.H. Auden's "Paid on Both Sides"', *Experiment*, 7 (spring 1931), 60–61 (61).
[77]   William Empson, 'Some Notes on Mr. Eliot', *Experiment*, 4 (November 1929), 6–8.

2

Beyond the Sanskrit Words: Eliot and the Colonial Construction of Poetic Modernism

ROSINKA CHAUDHURI

Any study today of a literary work published a hundred years ago may be understood as an undertaking in archival research, but the changes in the field of literary studies have been so severe, cataclysmic almost, from the last quarter of the twentieth century onward that reading *The Waste Land* and its attendant critical exegesis again – a century after its publication – for what it used to signify (when literature still mattered) feels a lot like stepping back in time. The literary value system engendered by Eliot and his cohorts persisted in the consciousness of world literary studies well into the 1970s, ending almost abruptly after the advent of theory and neoliberalism from the next decade onward. Today, after an examination of a literary work has been proclaimed to be no different than the anthropological and ethnographic study of a Balinese cock fight, following which postcolonial studies has given way to world literature studies, the literary ethos surrounding and represented by *The Waste Land* seems strangely familiar but impossibly remotely located in a foreign country called the past.[1]

How then to approach *The Waste Land* today? Location would be key. In the time of the advent of postcolonial studies, John Mackenzie, characterising developments in the academic study of colonialism, defined the traditional point of view as a 'centrifugal' tendency: 'Imperial history and the imperial idea have been examined almost entirely in a centrifugal manner, as the radiation of influences from Britain into its wider hinterland.'[2] If we think of the manner in which *The Waste Land* was disseminated and the mode of criticism that dealt with its 'impact' and 'influence' on the colonies

---

[1] 'Ever since Clifford Geertz transformed the drama of Balinese cock-fighting into a text, and new historicism made the complementary gesture of returning culture to the centre of literary studies, students of literature, history and culture have shared a common vocabulary, key concepts and points of reference.' Stuart Blackburn and Vasudha Dalmia, 'Introduction', in *India's Literary History: Essays on the Nineteenth Century*, edited by Stuart Blackburn and Vasudha Dalmia (Delhi: Permanent Black, 2004), 1.

[2] John Mackenzie, *Propaganda and Empire* (Manchester: Manchester University Press, 1984), 2.

through the decades following its publication, we see an almost exact correspondence to the traditional study of imperialism as Mackenzie defines it. Eliot's poetry, produced in England and Europe, was seen 'radiating outward' from the centre to the periphery where, presumably, it would be studied, imbibed and imitated. Postcolonial theorists from the mid-'80s onward, straining to move away from readings that mapped such a 'centrifugal tendency', wished, rather, to offer ways of dismantling colonialism's signifying system and exposing its operation in the silencing and oppression of the colonial subject, interpreting colonialism rather as a discourse, a text without an author. Derrida and Foucault were the instruments through which the turning of the text of colonialism into an array of effects was accomplished.[3] Nowhere in this enterprise to rescue the subaltern's speech, however, was any text itself at issue (certainly no poetic text) – alongside the author, the individual text too vanished into the interstices of theory and history.

The Waste Land had an obvious and immediate connection to India in the words that it used from the Upanishads, and scholars from India or concerned with the Indian connections have not looked past the handful of Sanskrit words, Eliot's own study of the language at Harvard in 1911–13, and the interpretation of this content. Thus we have 'T.S. Eliot and the Bhagavad-Gita' in 1963, '"Shantih" in The Waste Land' in 1989, and nothing seems to have changed by the time C.D. Verma published 'The Myth of Rishyashringa: An Indian Source of the "Waste Land" ("The Waste Land" Reappraised in relation to the Mahabharata)' in 2010.[4] Damayanti Ghosh's book, *Indian Thought in T.S. Eliot*, contained a detailed investigation into the subject.[5] In each of these investigations, the concern has been what

---

[3]   For a useful overview of Jacques Derrida's impact on postcolonial thinking, see Jane Hiddleston, 'Jacques Derrida: Colonialism, Philosophy, Autobiography', in *Postcolonial Thought in the French-Speaking World*, edited by Charles Forsdick and David Murphy (Liverpool: Liverpool University Press, 2009), 53–64; for Michel Foucault and the postcolonial, see Robert Nichols, 'Postcolonial Studies and the Discourse of Foucault: Survey of a Field of Problematization', *Foucault Studies*, 9, September 2010, 111–44.

[4]   K.S. Narayana Rao, 'T.S. Eliot and the Bhagavad-Gita', *American Quarterly* 15.4, winter 1963, 572–8; K. Narayana Chandran, '"Shantih" in The Waste Land', *American Literature*, 61.4, December 1989, 681–3; and C.D. Verma, 'The Myth of Rishyashringa: An Indian Source of the "Waste Land" ("The Waste Land" Reappraised in relation to the Mahabharata)', *Indian Literature*, 54.2, March/April 2010, 151–61.

[5]   Damayanti Ghosh, *Indian Thought in T.S. Eliot* (Calcutta: Sanskrit Pustak Bhandar, 1978). The author acknowledges her father, Bengali poet and critic Buddhadeva Bose, as the person who 'suggested the particular topic, Indian Thought in T.S. Eliot, for my dissertation [at Indiana University]'.

the Sanskrit words bring to the poem – do they connote 'the mad raving of Hieronymo' as George Williamson thought, or is it that 'the Sanskrit is meant not to be readily understood' by Western readers, as A.D. Moody stated, forgetting that most Indian readers too might need the Sanskrit context explained? Chandran writes his short piece in response to Cleo M. Kearns's 'attempt to read the last line of the poem in the twin context of the Hindu tradition and the modernist poem', once again himself assuming that it is the Indian who is closest to 'Hindu tradition' although it is a fact that almost every Indian would need a gloss to understand the Upanishadic context.[6]

As every reader of *The Waste Land* knows, the last note by Eliot to the poem said: 'Shantih. Repeated as here, a formal ending to an Upanishad. "The Peace which passeth understanding" is a feeble translation of the content of this word.' 'That phrase, in turn, comes from Saint Paul's letter to the Philippians 4:7: "And the peace of God, which passeth all understanding, shall keep your hearts and minds through Christ Jesus",' explains an editor's note to Eliot's note.[7] While all of this is good to know, as indeed it is to know the meaning of the words '*dāmyata*', '*datta*' and '*dayādhvam*' as they occur in both 'What the Thunder Said' and the *Brihadaranyaka Upanishad* (which belongs to the eighth and seventh centuries before the birth of Christ), none of it is remotely relevant. ('And what is the experience referred to in the last section with all the DAs in it? Do you recognize *Le Prince d'Aquitaine de la tour abolie* or *shantih*?' wrote John Peale Bishop to Edmund Wilson two weeks after *The Waste Land* had been published.[8]) Eliot was undoubtedly Orientalist in his study and use of the Vedanta in *The Waste Land*, as Vijay Seshadri points out, but 'his study of the Vedanta had at least the advantage of giving him a developed understanding of illusion and an appreciation of the laws of action and reaction, change and permanence. (Around this time, he was actually thinking of becoming a Buddhist.)'[9] Investigating 'the Upanishadic tradition of chanting the *shantih mantra* in order to comprehend "shantih" in the later context of the Hindu tradition

---

[6] George Williamson, *A Reader's Guide to T.S. Eliot: A Poem-by-Poem Analysis* (London: Thames and Hudson, 1955), 154; A.D. Moody, *Thomas Stearns Eliot: Poet* (Cambridge: Cambridge University Press, 1979), 106; Cleo M. Kearns, *T.S. Eliot: Between Two Worlds; A Reading of T.S. Eliot's Poetry and Plays* (Cambridge: Cambridge University Press, 1987), 229, cited in Chandran, '"Shantih" in The Waste Land', 681.

[7] Lawrence Rainey, *The Annotated Waste Land with Eliot's Contemporary Prose* (New Haven, CT: Yale University Press, 2005), 126.

[8] Ibid., 33.

[9] Vijay Seshadri, 'Why T.S. Eliot Has Remained an Enigma', *Lit Hub.com*, 28 April, 2020.

and the specific context of its use in *The Waste Land* is not my intention here, not just because the work has already been done, but because it adds little to our experience of the poem itself, whether one is Indian or English or of any other nationality.[10]

This essay will return to *The Waste Land* then, still introduced to readers as 'one of the defining works of poetic modernism', as a site from which to examine the problematic relationship between the colonised subject and the avant-garde in the construction of 'poetic modernism', noting that the term is not commonly preceded by an adjective of location, such as 'Western poetic modernism', when discussed in the West (whatever that is).[11] Modernity (and its adjunct, modernism) in the rest of the world has usually been read as 'a derivative discourse', not just by 'Western' commentators but often and influentially by non-Western theorists themselves.[12] An analysis of the way in which older art historians, for instance, dealt with Indian modern art is to be found in Partha Mitter's book, *The Triumph of Modernism*, which has an example of this 'centrifugal tendency' in dealing with the East:

> The English art historian W.G. Archer wrote an influential account of Indian modernism. His analysis of the painting of Gaganendranath Tagore, one of the first Indian modernists, consisted almost entirely of tracing Picasso's putative influence on him. Unsurprisingly, Archer drew the conclusion that Gaganendranath was *un cubiste manqué*; in other words, his derivative works, based on a cultural misunderstanding, were simply bad imitations of Picasso. Behind this seemingly innocent conclusion rests the whole weight of Western art history.

Mitter goes on to comment that 'Stylistic influence, as we are all aware, has been the cornerstone of art historical discourse since the Renaissance. ... For Archer, the use of the syntax of Cubism, a product of the West, by an Indian artist, immediately locked him into a dependent relationship, the colonized mimicking the superior art of the colonizer.'[13]

---

[10]   Chandran, 'Shantih in *The Waste Land*', 681.

[11]   Jon Cook, *Poetry in Theory* (Oxford: Blackwell, 2004), 97.

[12]   The term gained currency with Partha Chatterjee's influential book, *Nationalist Thought and the Colonial World: A Derivative Discourse*. Interestingly, there was a question mark in the first few runs, but that interrogative was dropped in the course of time – the author, whom I have asked, said the Indian edition of *Nationalist Thought* has always carried the subtitle *A Derivative Discourse?* It is only the Minnesota edition that doesn't.

[13]   Partha Mitter, *The Triumph of Modernism: India's Artists and the Avant-garde 1922–1947* (Delhi: Oxford University Press, 2007), 7.

When we turn to literary studies, it is to be noted that well before the obsessive interest in content or narrative that shapes most criticism or academic research today came into its own, 'stylistic influence', or form, had almost never been mapped in the context of modern Indian poetry published from 1922 onwards by critics writing in English. Then again, one could ask what a study of form in modern Indian poetry in relation to Eliot's *The Waste Land* might, indeed, achieve even if it were undertaken. (There is, of course, no such thing as 'Indian poetry,' only Bengali, Gujarati, Tamil or Marathi poetry alongside what is called Indian poetry in English.) Looking at the manner in which modern poetic practice evolved in India in the years following Eliot's first book publication in London in 1917, it would be a pointless exercise to follow the trope of 'influence' and 'impact'. Mitter defines the notion of 'influence' as 'the key epistemic tool in studying the reception of Western art in the non-Western world'. As I have pointed out elsewhere in the context of literary studies, 'the standard terminology that characterises this particular interaction' (of literary output and its sources) 'has included words like "influence" and "impact" at one end, and "response" or "reaction" at the other; even so distinguished a commentator as Sisir Kumar Das typically titled the second volume of his *History of Indian Literature*, consisting of eight hundred and fifteen pages documenting the literary achievements of every Indian language in this age: '1800–1910: Western Impact: Indian Response'.[14] Focusing on one of the dominant Indian regional literatures of the period, Bengali Literature, we could ask: What is the point in showing how Eliot's *The Waste Land* revolutionised the form of modern Bengali poetry by tracing the manner in which Bengali poets 'imitated' Eliot?

The question is a larger one, and relates to the one famously asked by Dipesh Chakrabarty in relation to political modernity in *Provincializing Europe*. The 'modern, European idea of history' he says there, 'came to non-European peoples in the nineteenth century as somebody's idea of saying "not yet" to somebody else.' Citing John Stuart Mill, he points out that 'Mill's historicist argument' (in 'On Liberty' and 'On Representative Government') that 'Indians or Africans were *not yet* civilized enough to rule themselves' 'consigned Indians, Africans, and other "rude" nations to an imaginary waiting room of history.'[15] The literary or artistic sphere, it is

---

[14]   Sisir Kumar Das, *A History of Indian Literature 1800–1910: Western Impact: Indian Response* (New Delhi: Sahitya Akademi, 1991). Cited in Rosinka Chaudhuri, *The Literary Thing: History, Poetry, and the Making of the Modern Cultural Sphere* (Delhi: Oxford University Press, 2013; Oxford: Peter Lang, 2014).

[15]   Dipesh Chakrabarty, *Provincializing Europe: Postcolonial Thought and Historical Difference* (Delhi: Oxford University Press, 2001), 8.

worth pointing out, does not even offer that consolation of being confined to 'the waiting room of history' – Archer does not say benevolently that if Gaganendranath Tagore continued his education he would someday qualify to be let into the arena of 'Modern Art' as Mill does of the Indian citizen attempting to access democracy. An article in the *New York Times* in 2008 by art critic Holand Cotter discussed the issue in the context of reviewing a show called 'Rhythms of India: The Art of Nandalal Bose (1882–1966)' at the Philadelphia Museum of Art. Cotter wrote there of how modernity is conceived of as having happened exclusively in the West and then distributed like food aid to the rest:

> Along with detailed information about one artist's life and times, the show delivers a significant piece of news, or what is still probably news to many people: that modernism wasn't a purely Western product sent out like so many CARE packages to a hungry and waiting world. It was a phenomenon that unfolded everywhere, in different forms, at different speeds, for different reasons, under different pressures, but always under pressure. As cool and above-it-all as modern may sound it was a response to emergency. In India the emergency was a bruising colonialism that had become as intolerable to artists as to everyone else.

At the end of his retrospection on the modern art of Nandalal Bose, Cotter concluded with the thought 'that every Museum of Modern Art in the United States and Europe should be required, in the spirit of truth in advertising, to change its name to Museum of Western Modernism until it has earned the right to do otherwise.'[16]

In the political sphere, the Indian answer to the patronizing command to wait was, rather, to insist on the 'now'; to advocate, for instance, immediate universal adult franchise to all Indians at independence without waiting for the citizenry to be educated into democratic norms, implementing 'now' as the 'temporal horizon of action' rather than 'not yet.'[17] In the literary critical sphere, that demand for equal participation in the moment could be interpreted, rather, as an insistence on simultaneity. Discarding a conceptual framework which assumes 'first in the West and then elsewhere', where modernity is conceived of as having been an emanation from Europe that gradually filtered through to the rest of the world in successive stages, is pivotal to the project of mapping simultaneity in the unfolding of modern

---

[16]   Holand Cotter, 'Indian Modernism via an Eclectic and Elusive Artist', *New York Times*, 19 August, 2008.
[17]   Chakrabarty, *Provincializing Europe*, 10.

forms in poetry. Focusing on the fact that a break with the old and embracing the foreignness of the new is, of course, every modern project's foundational moment, it is possible to show simultaneous developments, under the pressures of modernity and global change, in achievements in the arts in the colonies and the metropole in a designated period. The usual complication in the context of coloniality is that the new is then interrogated for slavishness by nationalist critics – as indeed by many poets and writers too – in search of an authentic past and national tradition. On the part of critics located in the Western hemisphere, who see the borrowings of their own artists approvingly as 'affinities', perhaps the same word could apply to the resonances of the modern in the literary sphere of the metropole and the colony ('as evident in the primitivism exhibition held at the Museum of Modern Art in New York in 1985' where the 'very subtitle of the exhibition, "affinity of the tribal and the modern", characterizes Picasso's emulation of African sculpture as no more than a mere formal "affinity" with the primitive'[18]).

Once we turn to discussions on what constitutes the 'modern' in modern Bengali poetry from the 1920s onward, we see the poets and critics of the time shrug off the nineteenth-century obsession with detailing levels of borrowing. Instead, they turn, almost unconsciously, to an idea of simultaneity, of synchronicity in the development of a modern idiom in poetry. Brought about by an emergent world situation that wrought unprecedented changes globally, the poets and critics of this era in Bengal took from, discussed, and critiqued Eliot and the nature of modern poetry without any notion of lag or of mimicry, as I shall show, but rather, with a sense of 'affinity' with the commonalities in 'the predicament of culture' inaugurated by the difficult twentieth century the world over. From the 1920s onward, in any major world metropolis (which by definition would include Calcutta), ethnographic self-fashioning allowed the self to be culturally constituted as one might choose, as James Clifford shows in the case of Malinowski or Conrad, for instance, choosing to be English writers.[19] Most writers and thinkers in modern Bengal from the 1850s onward were in a similar predicament, their culture and identity inventive and mobile, their productions reflecting some of the great qualities of modernism the world over.

---

[18]   Mitter, *The Triumph of Modernism*, 8.
[19]   James Clifford, 'On Ethnographic Self-Fashioning: Conrad and Malinowski,' in *The Predicament of Culture* (Harvard: Harvard University Press, 1988), 106.

Simultaneity in the Construction of the Modern

That the content of *The Waste Land* included some significant Indian material floating in Eliot's subconscious from the time he read Sanskrit at Harvard was indisputable and factual to the modern Bengali poets of the time – almost boring. Colonial intellectuals understood instinctively that, like Edward Said, Eliot (certainly something of an Orientalist) might have said: 'There were – and are – cultures and nations whose locations are in the East, and their lives, histories, and customs have a brute reality obviously greater than anything that could be said about them in the West. About that fact this study of Orientalism has very little to contribute, except to acknowledge it tacitly.'[20] Aijaz Ahmed responded to Said by pointing out that colonial discourse analysis elided and ignored the manner in which the Western text about the Orient had been 'received, accepted, modified, challenged, overthrown or reproduced by the intelligentsias of colonised countries, not as an undifferentiated mass but as situated social agents impelled by our own conflicts, contradictions, distinct social and political locations, of class, gender, region, religious affiliation and so on'.[21]

If, then, we turn our gaze not toward Eliot or the text of *The Waste Land* yet again, but at works contemporary with it in Bengali which demonstrate the manner in which *The Waste Land* appeared on the horizon *at the same time* as a breakthrough in the understanding of what modern poetry needed to be in India, we see that, in enlisting Eliot in the fight to achieve the 'modern' in the 1920s and 30s, young poets at this time 'impelled by our own conflicts' were struggling not with Western canonicity and 'influence', but, more densely, with both the brute political reality of colonial rule as well as the ideational colonization of the literary field by the predominant celebrity poet in their vicinity, the world's first non-White Nobel Laureate, Rabindranath Tagore. Tagore's poetry both preceded their own and towered over them, throwing its vibrant shadow over every space, so that their struggle was to chart a course that would allow them to absorb him but still evade him in the effort to burst with some violence into the arena of their own modern world in that time.

For the Bengali poets and writers who grappled in the wake of Tagore in the 1920s to define the new experience of modernity, the movement began in what is now described as the *Kallol* age, i.e., the period that unfolded

---

[20]   Edward Said, *Orientalism: Western Conceptions of the Orient* (London: Penguin, 1978), 5.
[21]   Note the use of the pronoun 'our'. Aijaz Ahmed, *In Theory: Classes, Nations, Literatures* (Delhi: Oxford University Press, 1994), 172.

with the publication of the avant-garde journal *Kallol* (literally: uproar) just a year after the publication of *The Waste Land* in Britain.[22] Achintyakumar Sengupta, Buddhadeva Bose, Premendra Mitra and Nazrul Islam were all published in this journal, which arrived with the same commotion on the shores of Rabindranath Tagore's humanism as its name indicated. In a remark made by the critic Sanjay Bhattacharya while referencing *The Waste Land* in his book on the poet Jibanananda Das, we see the parallel implications of that text to the project of 'modern poetry' in Bengal:

> Bengali poetry bid farewell to Rabindranath's modernity practically from the *Kallol*-age onward. As a result, the poets of that age were labelled 'ultra-modern' [*ati-adhunik*]. The *Kallol* era was inaugurated in the same decade in which *The Waste Land* was written.[23]

The prefix 'ultra' (*ati*) was, of course, dropped in time, Sankha Ghosh writes, identifying the new 'modern' of this era with lines uttered by the aggressive nationalist Sandip in Tagore's novel *Ghare Baire* (*Home and the World*): 'Yes, I am coarse, because I am true, I am flesh, I am appetite, I am hunger, shameless, pitiless.'[24] This announcement of Sandip's seems to inaugurate a shift from an older to a newer modernity – commensurate, Ghosh reasons, with the appellation 'ultra-modern' appearing in the literary sphere.

By 'Rabindranath's modernity', on the other hand, what is being referred to here is an older modernity, marked by that period in his writing beginning from the publication of *Manasi* (1890) to that of *Balaka* (1916) – keeping these works in mind, 'to not call Rabindranath a modern poet in the context of both English and Bengali poetry in this period would be to tell an untruth.'[25] But Rabindranath's modernity was of a different character from that of the new Bengali poets of the 1920s, not least because it belonged to a different time in world history. Tracing the pattern of poetry publications simultaneously as they occurred in both England and Bengal at this time, the critic continues:

---

[22] The first issue of *Kallol*, edited by Dineshchandra Das, was brought out in April/May 1923. See Achintyakumar Sengupta, *Kallol Yug* [first ed. 1950] (Calcutta: M.C. Sarkar, 2019), 4.

[23] My translation. Bhattacharya, *Kabi Jibanananda Das* (Calcutta: Bharabi, 1969), 18. All subsequent translations from the Bengali in this essay are mine unless otherwise indicated. Bengali writers are referred to by their first name rather than their surname, which is the convention followed for all the Bengali writers mentioned here.

[24] Sankha Ghosh, *Nirmān ār Srishti* (Santiniketan: Visva-Bharati, 1982), 10.

[25] Ibid., 17.

Balaka was written at the time the First World War was starting. This was when part two of modern poetry began in English poetry. T.S. Eliot and Ezra Pound were starting the 'Imagist' revolution at this time. But Eliot didn't write *The Waste Land* until the First World War, which destroyed the meaning of European life, came to an end. It was *The Waste Land* (1922) that was in reality the victory-monument [*jayasthhamba*] of modern English poetry.[26]

In Calcutta, at the time *The Waste Land* was published, the 'Non-Cooperation Movement against the British, the waves of the Russian revolution, the inevitable bad end to the World War, the economic depression – all of this created a time when the newly arrived young poets could not be satisfied anymore with analyses of Rabindranath's poetry. That dissatisfaction was what created the *Kallol-yug* [era].'[27] Using the titles of the poetry collections published by both Tagore and Das, Bhattacharya points out that

> when Jibanananda Das published his first book of poems, *Jharā Pālak*, the wild geese buffeted in stormy flight in [Tagore's] *Balākā* [*Flight of Geese*] had given way to fallen feathers, as was evident from the title of Jibananananda's first book *Jharā Pālak* [*Fallen Feathers*] itself. In a war-weary time, a sensibility of Eliot's '*empty men*' came about, though, even then, the poet [Das] did not turn his gaze outward. When he did do that, in *Dhusar Pāndulipi*, it was not upon *The Waste Land* but on Yeats.[28]

The relationship is not a one-way street – it is not just Das who is turning his eyes upon Yeats rather than towards *The Waste Land*: the relations are reciprocal, for 'It is because Yeats or Eliot gave so much space to Indian thought in their own thinking that Indian poets have been able to receive such felt support from them without interrupting their own traditions.' Further: 'Just as Yeats and Eliot could be in a relationship with the East while at the same time being moored in their own traditions, so too, the accomplished poets of the post-Rabindranath era had no trouble at all in establishing their own relations with Yeats or Eliot.'[29]

---

[26] Ibid., 17–18.

[27] Ibid., 18. The Non-Cooperation Movement was launched by Gandhi in 1920 and rapidly gathered pace as Indians throughout the country withdrew co-operation with British rule by withholding taxes, resigning from government jobs and relinquishing their titles among other measures.

[28] Ibid. English words within a quotation used in the original Bengali essay are indicated by italicisation.

[29] Bhattacharya, *Kabi Jibanananda Das*, 19.

This notion of relationality was beautifully expressed by Jibanananda Das himself in an important essay he wrote in 1954, the year he died when he was hit by a tram in Calcutta:

> Situated as they are within the long tradition of their own country's poetry, today's foremost poets – by experiencing the world's and particularly the West's greatest poetry – have been able to establish Bengali poetry in such a place that their future will not remain confined only to the truth of the *Baishnab Padābali, Mangalkābya*, East Bengali folk songs or Madhusudan or Rabindranath – they will be found, rather, wherever man has been able to express his individual modern consciousness in great poetry.[30]

In short, what Jibanananda is doing here is establishing a relation of equivalence between the Bengali work or poet (whether in history or in his own time) and any other poet anywhere in the world – regardless of who is taking from whom, the relation between one poet and another is established on the basis of equivalence and interest. The critic writing about the poetry of Jibanananda Das concludes his argument by saying: 'A discussion of Jibanananda's poetry? Such a discussion is bound to be incomplete if it's restricted to the context of Bengali poetry alone. Jibanananda Das's poetry needs to be analysed in the context of all poetry in all ages.'[31]

The reader outside of Bengal may not know Jibanananda Das and therefore be unaware of this great poet who wrote in Bengali in the first half of the twentieth century.[32] Alongside him, the other poets of this era who 'first attempted modern poetry in Bengali in the twentieth-century sense' or in the sense of 'non-Tagorean poetry' [*arābindrik kabitā*] were Sudhindranath Datta, Amiya Chakrabarty, Buddhadeva Bose and Bishnu De (among others).[33] Each of these poets engaged with the poetry of T.S. Eliot intensively and critically. Amiya Chakravarty wrote to Rabindranath from London about a personal encounter with the poet:

---

[30]   Ibid., 19. The *Baishnab Padābali* were traditional medieval love songs/devotional songs on the love of Radha and Krishna newly recovered in the nineteenth century by Bengali critics and readers; the *Mangalkābya*, similarly, was a genre of devotional poetry to individual gods and goddesses.

[31]   Ibid., 22.

[32]   For a comprehensive treatment and a selection of his translated poetry, see Clinton Seely, *A Poet Apart: a literary biography of the Bengali poet Jibanananda Das, (1899–1954)* (Newark: University of Delaware Press, 1990) and *Naked Lonely Hand: Selected Poems*, translated by Joe Winter (London: Anvil Press, 2003).

[33]   Sutapa Bhattacharya, *Kabir Chokhe Kabi* [Poets as seen by other Poets] (Calcutta: Aruna Publishers, 1987), 4.

Argued with Eliot the other day at a meeting – he seems to want to disown all life in his search for 'pure poetry'. Poems like 'The [Waste] Land' he would value as narrative, not poetry. Keeping aside that particular method of analysis, I clearly comprehend a turn in English poetry. Eliot has not been able to keep out life's varied melody in the *choruses* of his new *drama, Murder in the Cathedral*.[34]

Sudhindranath Datta, who brought out the avant-garde Bengali journal, *Parichay, Kallol*'s successor, had published an essay in its first issue in 1931 titled '*Kābyer Mukti*' ('Poetry's Freedom') that discussed *The Waste Land* extensively in relation to image and metre and their place in modern poetry. 'Cezanne had perceived an old beauty in a fragment of a white wall when Swinburne was wandering moist-eyed through groves in search of woodland nymphs – incontrovertible proof of the inner emptiness of the latter's unworldly *art*.'[35] It was because 'the red light of insolvency was suddenly switched on above the doors of Tennyson and Swinburne's huge businesses' that:

> ... at the start of the twentieth century one could see that all wealth and passion had disappeared from poetry's body, and that all that was left was only the skeleton, a worn-out featureless skeleton left upon the echoing sands.

> What are the roots that clutch, what branches grow
> Out of this stony rubbish? Son of man,
> You cannot say, or guess, for you know only
> A heap of broken images, where the sun beats,
> And the dead tree gives no shelter, the cricket no relief
> And the dry stone no sound of water. ...
> Here is no water but only rock
> Rock and no water and the sandy road
> The road winding above among the mountains
> Which are mountains of rock without water. ...
> There is not even silence in the mountains
> But dry sterile thunder without rain (T.S. ELIOT)[36]

---

[34]   Amiya Chakravarty to Rabindranath Tagore, 20 October 1935, cited in Bhattacharya, *Kabir Chokhe Kabi*, 152. There is a misprint in the book, where the word 'Waste' is missing preceding 'Land' which is indicated by the square bracket. The italics indicate English words used in the Bengali text.

[35]   Sudhindranath Datta, '*Kābyer Mukti*' ['Poetry's Freedom'], *Parichay*, 1.1, *Srāban 1338* [1931], 26.

[36]   Ibid., 27.

This long quote, which actually continues to 'there is no water', is interspersed with ellipses of his own that show the versatility of what he himself edits out. He brings continuity to his thought through the editing – the first five lines he includes here are from lines 19–24 of 'The Burial of the Dead', and the next lines are 331–334 of 'What the Thunder Said', which continues again from line 341 in the same segment till the end of this quote. As we can see, Sudhindranath is responding to *The Waste Land* not as an Indian, but as a poet: he is not concerned at all with the reference to the 'sunken' Ganga or 'Himavant', or indeed the three DA words from the *Brihadaryanaka Upanishad*, taking, rather, to the images of drought, of dryness, hardness, and sterility. Sudhindranath then goes on to use these lines, interestingly, to denote the sterility of nineteenth-century English poetry, saying: 'that these lines are an accurate description of the nineteenth century is something not many people will be willing to agree on. They will take the name of Browning ....'[37] An involved discussion follows that then proceeds to distinguish the art of the twentieth century from that which had gone before, insisting that the art of this century is one of '*integrity*', of 'impartiality', which is why '*Eliot* called the poet a *catalytic agent*'.[38] A few pages later, he comes to 'freedom of metre' ('*chhander mukti*'), which is 'not just doing as one pleases, for free verse is itself flawlessly constructed by a self-chosen tightly bound set of rules' ('*swayamvar niyamer nibir bandhane nitol*'). 'Let me give an example', he continues:

> When lovely woman stoops to folly and
> Paces about her room again, alone,
> She smoothes her hair with automatic hand
> And puts a record on the gramophone.

T.S. Eliot has described, with the help of these civilized genteel old-fashioned four lines inserted suddenly in the middle of the self-willed, unadorned, natural metre of *The Waste Land* an insignificant love story of the contemporary world. If we think about it, we soon see why this metre is inevitable over here. The first line is taken from *Vicar of Wakefield*; *Goldsmith* had used it about his sentimental novel's loose heroine's fall from grace; further, the lines have lost all their original flavour as they have travelled from hand to hand over the last ten years – all that is left is a bitter taste. As a result, when I read these lines, at least in my mind I am overcome with the lifeless maudlin

---

[37] Ibid., 30.
[38] Ibid., 31. All italicised words within Bengali quotations are words that appear originally in English, including names of poets and books which were printed in English font within the Bengali text.

melody of love affairs today, and the next three lines oppress me with their cruel meaningless conclusion to the fussy preparation of the opening line.[39]

He goes on to describe the mechanical shout of the gramophone as a metaphor for the meaningless enticement of the insignificant drama within the story told in these lines. 'All one needs to do is to place these lines next to the lines of Homer translated by Pope or Michael's description of Meghnad to see why the modern poet does not want to pour his verse into the mould of received tradition', he says, asserting firmly: 'The poet today, if he wants to nurture the tree of poetic imagination [*kabyer kalpataru*], has to collect seeds from the entire universe, and make preparations by ploughing the mind's hard ground.'[40]

'Seeds from the entire universe' were indeed sown by each of these modern poets. Bishnu Dey, reputedly the most difficult and certainly the most aggressively intellectual Marxist among them, was also, like Jibanananda Das, a lecturer in English literature in Calcutta. Perhaps the most serious admirer of Eliot among this generation, he translated eighteen of Eliot's poems in a book he titled, simply, *Elioter Kabita* (*Eliot's Poems*, 1953).[41] Dey's involvement with Eliot was intense; looking into the aspect of prose rhythm (*gadya kabitā*), Dey reportedly sent Rabindranath Eliot's 'Journey of the Magi' without telling him who the author was; Rabindranath translated it as '*Tirthayātrī*' ('Pilgrims'), while Bishnu Dey himself later translated it again as '*Rajarshider Jātrā*'.[42] Free verse was being discussed intensively by all of these poets in these years, frequently in the context of Eliot's poetry. Thus Amiya Chakravarty's correspondence with Rabindranath towards the end of the latter's life contains an extended discussion of Eliot's *The Family Reunion* (1939), a play that shows, he feels, 'an increasing ability to capture difficult content simply in the *speech rhythm* of everyday talk – a truly new language for *poetic drama* is being constructed. You cannot call it *blank verse*, yet it's not prose either – it seems to be the ultimate apotheosis of *free verse*.'[43]

[39]   Ibid., 38.
[40]   Ibid., 39.
[41]   Bishnu Dey, *Elioter Kabita* (Calcutta: Signet Press, 1953).
[42]   First published in Sudhindranath Datta, ed., *Parichay*, 2.3, *Māgh 1339* [January 1932], 454–5. Commenting on the difficulty of successful translation, Jyotirmoy Datta has said: '*Emonki ei shedino, emanki Satyendranath ki Rabindranather anubāde, Victor Hugo ki Elioter kabitā ati śithil, ati taral, ati Gāngeya rup niyechhe*' [Even the other day, even in the translations of Satyendranath or Rabindranath, Victor Hugo or Eliot's poetry has taken on a very placid, very watery, very Ganga-esque form]. Jyotirmay Datta, '*Buddhadeva Basur Kabitā*' ['Buddhadeva Bose's Poetry'], *Kolkata*, 7–8, 2002, 140.
[43]   Amiya Chakravarty to Rabindranath Tagore, 12 April, 1939, cited in Sutapa

If, when it was published, *The Waste Land* was striking for its transitions, its techniques of collage and plurivocality and its cross-cultural, globalized field of reference, then the same could have been said of Dey's own publications, which began with a book of poems titled *Urbashi O Artemis* published by Buddhadeva Bose in 1933.[44] As his contemporary Samar Sen put it: 'Here was a poet whose Urvashi, Artemis, Ophelia and Cressida broke through with restrained lyrical beauty'; here was a poet who, alongside his friends, 'presented a different picture of the function of poets':

These were not men from whom poetry gushed forth because they were drunk with the mystery of life, nature and women. Poetry required discipline as well as inspiration. It was part of a many-faceted tradition and demanded knowledge of philosophy, music and painting, both Indian and Western – acquaintance with Abdul Karim Khan, Jamini Roy, Bach and Beethoven – and later Marx and Lenin as well as Freud. Rabindranath and Shelley were not enough. Writers in English were not enough, one had to know something about the French symbolists, Rilke and some of the Russians. One had to go deep into Sanskrit literature. ...

My conception of a poet till then was connected with the *Kallol-Kalikalam* group ... the poet ought to have a distracted look; he ought to have his punjabi (kurta) slit somewhere; it would be better if he had TB; he should also visit whorehouses to enrich his experiences. From this world to that of the *Parichay* group was indeed a very big leap.[45]

This was Sudhin Datta's magazine, *Parichay*, that signalled a generational leap for Samar Sen, the same magazine where we have seen him discuss *The Waste Land* in detail in its first number. Some, like Buddhadeva Bose, however, straddled both decades and groups. Buddhadeva wrote in *Swadesh o Sanskriti* (1957) that 'in the years following the First World War, in victorious England's un-scarred "*post-war*" landscape a different revolution arrived, a different conception of modernity, along with many other unheard-of signs of the changing times. This revolution had been preparing backstage for some time, but when it appeared on stage in the form of a "somewhat long" poem called *The Waste Land*, even then not too many people noticed, but within a few years, that waste land with its hollow men had advanced so far that it had taken over almost all of literary territory.'[46]

Bhattacharya, *Kabir Chokhe Kabi*, 156.

[44] Bishnu Dey, *Urbashi O Artemis* (Calcutta: Granthakar Mandali, 1933).

[45] Samar Sen, 'The Still Centre', in *Water My Roots: Essays By and On Bishnu Dey*, ed. Samir Dasgupta (Calcutta: Writers Workshop, 1973), 61.

[46] Buddhadeva Bose, '*Chāi - Ānander Sāhitya*' in *Swadeś O Sanskriti* (Calcutta: Bengal Publishers, 1957),116.

In his translations and criticism Buddhadeva too was another gath-
erer of seeds, famous for his accomplished translations of Baudelaire from
the French alongside extensive discussions of Rilke, Mallarme, Verlaine,
Rimbaud, Hopkins and Dostoyevsky among others.[47] In an essay written in
English titled 'Modernism in Literature' he identified the characteristics of
modernism as, first, '*the cyclic conception of time*', which was 'new and star-
tling in Europe in the 1920s, but in India, this is very, very old, lying at the
root of Vedantic philosophy.' This notion of time, he remarked, was 'at the
root of germinal works like *Ulysses*, *The Waste Land*, *The Magic Mountain*,
and Proust's *A la Recherche du Temps Perdu*.'[48] Then there was '*the position of man in the universe*', embodied in the outsider figure deployed by
Dostoyevsky, Kafka and Camus. Finally, modernism was defined by '*style*':
he places Baudelaire at the fountainhead of an aesthetic practice that contains within it Mann, Joyce, Kafka, and in Bengali letters, Jibanananda,
Sudhindranath and Bishnu Dey, who make possible his assertion about
Bengali poetry, that 'the best of it is as good as the best anywhere.'[49]

Buddhadeva Bose championed Baudelaire (quoting Rimbaud, in agreement with him that here was 'the first seer, king of poets, a true god');[50]
Jibanananda Das invoked the Surrealists; Bishnu Dey translated Eliot; but
each of these modernists also individually found in Eliot an idiom that
enabled them to speak of the city, of its trams, electric lights, libraries and
roads that made up the fabric of their modern existence:

> ... I would write a particular type of poetry which would be called *unpoetic
> poetry*,' Buddhadeva wrote to a friend. 'I would like to insert the everyday
> events of our contemporary lives into poetry. I would take situations that
> were terribly familiar. ... Our kitchens, our tea shops, our streets crowded
> with trams and buses, motor cars, trains – why would they not find a place in
> our poetry? The saris, combs, stoves and handkerchiefs of our domestic lives
> – our small joys and sorrows, arguments and quarrels, loves and hates – when
> will they shape our poetry?[51]

---

[47]   See 'Twins in Suffering: Dostoyevsky and Baudelaire' or 'In the Mouth of Fame:
Ezra Pound: A Page from Current History,' in *An Acre of Green Grass and other
English Writings of Buddhadeva Bose*, edited by Rosinka Chaudhuri (Delhi: Oxford
University Press, 2018).
[48]   See 'Modernism in Literature', in ibid., 219.
[49]   Ibid., 222. Emphases in original.
[50]   Buddhadeva Bose, 'Introduction', in *Charles Baudelaire: His Poetry: Le Fleurs
du Mal* (Calcutta: Dey's Publishing, 1961), 1.
[51]   Buddhadeva Bose, '*Bāṅglā Kabitār Bhabishyat*' ['The Future of Bengali Poetry'],
Pragati, Bhadra 1336 [August-September 1929], 126.

Buddhadeva's list is reflective of modernism the world over, a list reflected in the poetry of Pessoa and Pound, in Baudelaire's definition of the 'painter of modern life', in the 'sound images' of his own forbear Iswar Gupta (1812–59).[52] This tradition of fearless taking – not borrowing, not imitating – continued right through to the *Krittibās* writer Sarat Mukhopadhyay's wonderfully named book of poetry: *Rimbaud, Verlaine ebong nijaswa* (*Rimbaud, Verlaine and My Own*, 1963). One of the achievements of modernism and of *The Waste Land* was, of course, to make form equal to content as a bearer of significance, and, in Bengal too, the advent of *gadya kabitā* or prose poetry was only one of the elements practised in revolutionising form, which was no less wrestled with than the poetic content of contemporary urban life.

It nevertheless remained true that, though Eliot was invoked frequently, every modern Bengali poet defined his practice first and foremost against Tagore; in terms of influence, it is Tagore who needs to be addressed. Discussing the meaning of 'influence' and 'impact' in this context, Sutapa Bhattacharya gives us her gloss on the subject:

> In the context of these poets, poetic influence does not simply indicate an agglomeration of received vocabulary, imagery, or sentiment; influence may also be understood as a complete turn in opposition to the prevailing current. ... In the field of Bengali poetry, each of these poets was, in their own ways, a '*creator of ideas*'; they each evaluated Rabindranath according to their own understanding. Whether they were great poets or not may be disputable, but each of them was a powerful poet – there is no doubt about that. And their power was to be felt in the manner in which they transformed the influence of Rabindranath in their own poetic compositions.[53]

Arguably, it would be true to say this of any 'influence' upon any 'creator of ideas', and Bengali criticism has traced the transformation of Eliot in these young poets just as often and perhaps even more unselfconsciously than they have dealt with Tagore's overwhelming impression upon them.

'Modern Poetry'

In 1932, a decade after the publication of *The Waste Land*, when forced to speak (it almost seems) on 'modern poetry' for the avant-garde Bengali journal, *Parichay*, Rabindranath Tagore's only essay directly referencing

---

[52] See Rosinka Chaudhuri, 'Poet of the Present: The Material Object in the World of Iswar Gupta' in *The Literary Thing*, 59–87
[53] Sutapa Bhattacharya, *Kabir Chokhe Kabi*, 6.

T.S. Eliot was called, simply, '*Ādhunik Kābya*' ('Modern Poetry').[54] The first non-white person to have received the Nobel Prize for literature in 1913, and already a world-famous literary celebrity at this time, Rabindranath was (and continues to be) read by the public and the cognoscenti both as the very embodiment of the non-modern, even the anti-modern. A Bengali literary critic writing in English, J.C. Ghosh, described his task in writing about him in 1948 as being 'to dispose of the legend, that has grown in some quarters in recent years, of Tagore the pale-lily poet of ladies' tables.'[55] The tone had been set by Yeats's ecstatic introduction to *The Gitanjali*, in which he said the experience of reading his poetry in 1912 made him feel 'as though we had walked in Rossetti's willow wood, or heard, perhaps for the first time in literature, our voice as in a dream.'[56]

Twenty years later, Rabindranath began his Bengali essay by using the English word 'modern' twice: 'I have been asked to write something on *modern* English poetry. The task is not easy. Because, one cannot fix the limits of the *modern* by consulting an almanac. It is not a matter of periodization so much as one of emotion.'[57] He continues, in the next few lines, by pointing out that just as a river flowing straight may suddenly turn at an angle, so too, literature does not always flow in a straight line. Then he comes to the Bengali word '*ādhunik*': 'When it turns, then it is that turn that will be called *modern*. In Bengali, let us call it *ādhunik*.' 'Let us call it *ādhunik*' signals an unhappiness with acknowledging an exact equivalence between the Bengali word and the English; he had complained before of the impossibility of translating the word 'nation' into Bengali in 1902 and 1904. Trying to define contemporary 'modern' poetry a few pages into the essay, he observes, rightly, that the modern impacted painting first among the arts, and poetry only afterwards. Modern art was the first to proclaim that 'Art's job was not to captivate, but to conquer; its characteristic was not beauty but exactitude':

> Some are beautiful, some are ugly; some are useful, some are useless, but in creation we cannot use an excuse and excise anything out. That is true of literature and of art as well. ... That is why, nowadays, literature that follows

---

[54]   *Parichay*, as mentioned above on p. 58, was edited by Sudhindranath Datta.

[55]   J.C. Ghosh, *Bengali Literature* (London: Oxford University Press, 1948), 167.

[56]   W.B. Yeats, 'Introduction', in Rabindranath Tagore, *The Gitanjali* (New York: Macmillan, 1915), xvii.

[57]   All following citations from Tagore's essay are from Rabindranath Tagore, 'Adhunik Kabya' ['Modern Poetry'] in *Rabindra Rachanabali* [Collected works of Rabindranath Tagore], Volume 12 (Calcutta: Visva-Bharati Press, 2000), 463–72.

the *adhunik* dharma disdains to try and keep caste by walking carefully in the path of old manners and old lineages; it has no concept of untouchability. Eliot's poetry is this sort of contemporary poetry, but Bridges' is not.[58]

Before coming to Eliot for the first time, he approvingly quotes in some detail from Amy Lowell's poems 'A Lady' in *Sword Blades and Poppy Seeds* (1914) and 'Red Slippers' from *Men, Women and Ghosts* (1916) – these, and Ezra Pound's 'The Study in Aesthetics', he admires for imagistic qualities that make them come alive. Coming, then, to Eliot, he quotes from 'Preludes' in *Prufrock and Other Observations* (1917) in his own translation, giving us a whole page from the poem, the fourth verse almost entirely in the original English and the rest in his own Bengali version, which departs from the original in phrasing from time to time. Coming at last to the lines 'I am moved by fancies that are curled / Around these images, and cling; / The notion of some infinitely gentle / Infinitely suffering thing', he notes that 'the poet [Eliot] clearly has a distaste for this dung-gathering aged world' (referencing 'The worlds revolve like ancient women / Gathering fuel in vacant lots'), that Eliot dislikes the ugliness and the mud, but insists on walking us through it – 'not because he loves the mud, but, especially in the aftermath of the First World War, because we have to look at this muddy world and know the mud, and acknowledge it.' The second quotation from, and discussion about, Eliot occurs toward the end of the essay, from 'Aunt Helen' in the same collection, where he wonders why the poet should 'be impelled to write such a poem' – the incident described (of the second housemaid on the lap of the butler after their mistress has died and the shutters are drawn) may be 'credible and natural', but, he asks, 'is that enough?'

This is at the crux of Tagore's objection to Eliot – the forced nature of the ugliness on display involves choice and selectiveness on the part of the poet; it is an act of the will. Why choose the sick and infected leaves of a plant over the clean and natural ones? This 'modernity of the English poets' does not seem 'natural' (*sahaj*) to him, it is defiled (*ābil*), and here he seems to have *The Waste Land* in mind:

> The modernity of English poets is unnatural. It is defiled. Their mentality pokes the readers' mind with its elbow. The world that they see and show is crumbling, piled with *rubbish,* and dust-blown. Because their minds today are unwell, unhappy, unsettled. In such a state they cannot disengage completely from the world-as-object.

---

[58] '*Elioter kabya eirakam hāler kabya, Bridgeser kabya ta nay.*'

Unwell, unhappy and unsettled Eliot's mind certainly was at this time; as he said later of the time of the composition of *The Waste Land* in the context of his domestic troubles and marital difficulties: 'To me, it brought the state of mind out of which came *The Waste Land*.'[59] Rabindranath describes this state of modern poetry as 'an *influenza*' – not the natural state of the body but its diseased state. For him, this is a form of '*sentimentalism*' that cannot endure. What he valued himself, he says, in a language strongly redolent of Buddhist philosophy, is a way of seeing free from such attraction to ugliness ('*mohamukta dekha*'), to see the world without attachment and passion or desire, with a dispassionate heart (literally '*nirāsaktachitte*'). For this, he concludes, in the penultimate sentence of the essay, one needs a dispassionate mind ('*nirāsakta man*'), phrasing reminiscent of Arnold's famous emphasis on the critic's 'disinterestedness' or 'aloofness from practice'.[60] Ironically, however, they remind us most of all of those famous sentences from Eliot's 'Tradition and the Individual Talent' (1919): 'Poetry is not a turning loose of emotion, but an escape from emotion; it is not the expression of personality, but an escape from personality.'[61]

This identification of ugliness with modern poetry or the modern age was linked to the horrors of the First World War by Rabindranath himself in this essay ('In the last war in Europe, men experienced such hardness, such harshness, that the manners and dignity of many past eras was suddenly shattered by the terrible crisis of the time'). Other Bengali critics too identified its trauma as having created the crucible that birthed modern poetry:

> It was the First World War that was responsible for creating the difference between Jibanananda's mindset and Rabindranath's. The predicament of the Bengali psyche was no less [vulnerable] than that of the European psyche [after the Great War]. ... It is normal to lose one's sense of value following a war. Besides which, in the *Kallol* era, it was not enough to undertake realism in an ordinary way, it was necessary to show the ugliness of reality.[62]

In an essay titled 'Modernism and the Imagination of Ugliness', James Applewhite had stated a commonplace assumption when he began by saying that the 'expectation that art should be, or should deal with, "the beauti-

---

[59]   T.S. Eliot, *The Letters of T.S. Eliot*, Volume 1: 1898–1922, edited by Valerie Eliot and Hugh Haughton (London: Faber and Faber, 1988), xvii.
[60]   Matthew Arnold, 'The Function of Criticism at the Present Time' in *Essays in Criticism* (London and New York: Macmillan, 1895), 18.
[61]   T.S. Eliot, 'Tradition and the Individual Talent', in *Selected Essays* (London: Faber, 1972), 21.
[62]   Bhattacharya, *Kabir Chokhe Kabi*, 23–24.

ful" has long been abandoned.' In fact, he continues, '[w]e now accept an opposite aesthetic cliché: the presumption that art should be, or should deal with, the ugly. The modern ugliness involves self-limitation, an invocation of the noisome, the degrading, the inhumane, of desecration, revulsion, alienation.'[63] Rabindranath Tagore, born in 1861, preceded this era and this presumption made by a generation of modernist poets, or at least by the critics who wrote about them. The Bengali moderns themselves, however, complicated and problematised the charge of ugliness, pointing out:

> When we see the rows of smoke expelling chimneys by the sides of the Ganga, then it's true one feels like rebuking this civilization as heartless, but Calcutta's *ghāt*s [steps] by the Ganga, where so many ships from our country and abroad are moored – that too has a kind of beauty, anybody with the eyes of a poet will see that. This is a different river from the one described in *Chhinnapatra*, but this too is beautiful. It is not just ugliness [*kuśrītā*] that is engendered by the touch of the machine, a new sort of beauty too is born. ... Chimneys are unbearable, true; but sitting on the shores of the Ganga at night on the *ghats* in Calcutta who will not acknowledge that they have brought a new sort of beauty to this world? The ardour of Hopkins for the star-filled night is the same ardour the modern poet feels for the tattoo of variegated lights on the dark waters.[64]

Implicit in this appreciation of what would conventionally be termed 'ugliness' – noticeably an appreciation unattached to 'the noisome, the degrading, the inhumane' – is the charge that Rabindranath did not know how to 'see' the poetry of the city, a charge that had been gathering force since the 1920s. 'Not really like the roar of a wave, but still, the anti-Rabindranath stance of magazines such as *Kallol* or *Kalikalam* was advancing like a hum, indicating the advent of different literary tastes. In 1927, the youths behind the magazine *Pragati* declared that the age of Rabindranath was over ... and the literary sphere filled with argument and debate ...'.[65]

We therefore see that the inheritance of *The Waste Land* in relation to India, and specifically to the modern Bengali poets of the 1920s–'30s,

[63] James Applewhite, 'Modernism and the Imagination of Ugliness,' *The Sewanee Review*, 94.3 Summer 1986, 418.

[64] Buddhadeva Bose, '*E-juger Kabitā*' ['Poetry of This Age'] in *Buddhadeva Boser Prabandha Samagra*, Volume 1 (Calcutta: Paschimbanga Bangla Akademi, 2009), 330. *Chhinnapatra* refers to the collection of Rabindranath's letters to his niece written primarily from his houseboat on the river Padma in East Bengal. See Rabindranath Tagore, *Letters from a Young Poet 1887–1895* translated by Rosinka Chaudhuri (Delhi: Penguin Modern Classics, 2014).

[65] Sankha Ghosh, *Nirmān ār Srishti*, 97.

occurred not because of the Sanskrit words used in the poem, which meant little to them in relation to their cultural lineage, but as a movement against Tagore, with younger poets and Marxist materialist critics attacking him in a contest over the meaning of modern poetry. Eliot's poem became, for them, emblematic of a sensibility that Tagore was thought not to understand in debates that raged through the following decades until his death in 1941. This debate to do with Tagore's meaning and inheritance by the modern poets in Bengal at this time was predicated against what they saw as the transcendental in his writing; in the drive to represent modernity it was to Eliot, not least *The Waste Land*, that in fact a generation turned, not in mimicry, but in affinity, recognising a commonality in the perception of the crisis of the contemporary age the world over, as well as, more importantly, to be able to include the everyday of the city ('trams and buses, motor cars, trains … saris, combs, stoves and handkerchiefs') in their poetry.

Eliot's use of 'Shantih shantih shantih' as the last line in *The Waste Land* was no less ineffable than whatever element it was in Tagore's poetry that his successors in the Bengali literary sphere were so desperate to deconstruct. Eliot described his state in approaching the 'subtleties' of the Sanskrit philosophers at Harvard as one of 'enlightened mystification' – the Sanskrit words in the poem in 1922 were no doubt meant to leave the reader in a similar way. Famously, '[f]orgetting how to think and feel like an American or a European' was not something he wished to do. For the Indian poets, meanwhile, Eliot's poetry was important, but immersion in it did not mean, 'forgetting how to think and feel' like an Indian. Europe was important, and Eliot was important, for similar reasons to those outlined by the Uruguayan writer Angel Rama:

> Frantz Fanon's cry, 'Let's abandon Europe,' is nothing but a sentence. It is impossible to abandon what is already ingrained in the creative personality of the Americas, in its mental structure and hierarchy of value. This Martinican completely lacks American consciousness at the same time that he asserts a non-proved desertion because, in the last analysis, he counts on the support of a non-European cultural tradition that he assumes radically black African. He plays the role that has been imposed on him by white Europeans: Negritude. For better or worse, 'negritude' implies an autonomous cultural tradition.[66]

In their catholicity of taking from the best that was on offer in the English and European languages, the modern Indian poets in the first half of the

---

[66]   Cited in Walter D. Mignolo, *Coloniality, Subaltern Knowledges, and Border Thinking* (Princeton, NJ: Princeton University Press, 2000), 165.

twentieth century were as modern as Eliot or any other modernist in the world. That Eliot had an intuitive notion of this tie is evidenced by his original inclusion of the crucial passage from *Heart of Darkness* on the death of Kurtz as an epigraph to *The Waste Land*: 'Did he live his life again in every detail of desire, temptation, and surrender during that supreme moment of complete knowledge? He cried in a whisper at some image, at some vision – he cried out twice, a cry that was no more than breath – "The horror! the horror!"' If anything bound these two spheres of literary activity together, it was the very coloniality that was constitutive of modernity as they experienced it.[67]

[67]   Walter Mignolo, *Coloniality: The Darker Side of Modernity* (Durham, NC: Duke University Press, 2011), 1.

3

'An Icon of Recurrence':
The Waste Land's Anniversaries

WILLIAM DAVIES

The Waste Land remains a cultural and social barometer. It is a work that invites responses from each generation of readers, revealing the values of that generation through the shifting hinterlands of appreciation and critique the poem inevitably provokes. Each generation has its own Eliot, too, and this has been no more the case than when the thorny question of Eliot's politics moves into view, especially accusations of misogyny and anti-Semitism.[1] If Eliot remains a revered figure of the twentieth century, his authority has been rocked by the antiquated views which punctuated his thinking at certain stages of his life.

Concurrently, readers, above all students in the classroom, frequently now demand that the social and political content, contexts and contemporary resonances of 'great' works be taken seriously. *The Waste Land* is a prime example. Megan Quigley's 2019 edited cluster for *Modernism/modernity*, 'Reading "The Waste Land" with the #MeToo Generation', provides compelling evidence of students' perspectives in recent years.[2] Quigley's account of the difference between her own experiences as a student and that of the cohorts coming before her now is illuminating:

> The first time I heard 'The Waste Land' called an 'abortion poem' I thought I had misheard my student; now I hear it frequently (and convincingly) called a poem that stages and performs racial and gender violence and investigates trans* experience. My own teachers directed me away from Lil [and] Philomel to Nightingales and Keats – our students want Keats, but also to discuss, really discuss, the assault of the typist.

---

[1]   Useful critical overviews of these subjects can be found respectively in John Xiros Cooper's 'Anti-Semitism' and Rachel Blau Duplessis' chapter on 'Gender', both in *T.S. Eliot in Context*, edited by Jason Harding (Cambridge: Cambridge University Press, 2011), 285–294 and 295–304.

[2]   Megan Quigley, 'Reading "The Waste Land" with the #MeToo Generation', *Modernism/modernity* print plus cluster, Volume 4, cycle 1, https://doi.org/10.26597/mod.0094. All subsequent references to Quigley from this source.

What is notable is the demand to blend what we might call traditional Eliot scholarship – hunting for allusions, attempting to pin down meaning – with socially engaged readings that evaluate hitherto neglected or overshadowed topics in Eliot's work. What is equally intriguing, though, is that there *is* still this demand to read Eliot at all. As Quigley notes, Eliot's reputation has unavoidably suffered a decline:

> Eliot went from a heyday of popularity after winning the Nobel Prize in 1948 (14,000 people crammed in to hear him give a public reading in 1956) to a nadir of dislike (that one is harder to place temporally – maybe with the publication of *T.S. Eliot and Anti-Semitism* [1995], which explored Eliot's prejudice, or Carole Seymour-Jones's biography *Painted Shadow* [2001] and the film *Tom and Viv* [1994], which portrayed the breakdown of his first marriage and his wife's institutionalization.[3]

Despite such turbulence, *The Waste Land* remains one of the most cherished Anglophone cultural products of the twentieth century. Moreover, as Leslie Wheeler writes, for readers, critics and poets alike, 'Eliot endures as a rhythm, an icon of recurrence'.[4] In discussing a sequence of anniversaries and 'recurrences' in the post-publication history of *The Waste Land*, this essay examines how both the poem's and Eliot's reputations have evolved over the past century, from the ways in which they reveal the political or pedagogical priorities of a given moment to the manner in which fame and celebrity shape cultural consciousness and literary legacy.

1923 – 'Fundamental Weaknesses':
Eliot and *The Waste Land*'s First Year

For Eliot, *The Waste Land*'s publication in October 1922 represented an unburdening – it marked a moment from which he could change direction, personally and creatively. A mere fortnight after its publication, Eliot wrote to Richard Aldington that *The Waste Land* was 'a thing of the past so far as I am concerned and I am now feeling toward a new form and style.'[5] This

---

[3]   For *T.S. Eliot and Anti-Semitism*, Quigley is referring to Anthony Julius's *T.S. Eliot, Anti-Semitism and Literary Form* (London: Thames and Hudson, 1995).
[4]   Leslie Wheeler, 'Undead Eliot: How "The Waste Land" Sounds Now', *Poetry*, September 2014, accessed online: https://www.poetryfoundation.org/poetrymaga zine/articles/70143/undead-eliot-how-the-waste-land-sounds-now, last accessed 1 September 2021. All subsequent references to Wheeler from this source.
[5]   *The Letters of T.S. Eliot*, Volume 1: 1898–1922, edited by Valerie Eliot and

downbeat tone was common in Eliot's comments on the poem over the year that followed publication:

> I am very sensible of [the poem's] fundamental weaknesses, and whatever I do next will be, at least, very different; I feel that it [is] merely a kind of consummation of my past work, not the initiation of something new, and it will take me all my courage and persistence, and perhaps a long time, to do something better. But 'something' must be better. *The Waste Land* does not leave me well satisfied. (To Edmund Wilson, 11 January 1923)[6]

> I think it will take me a year or two to throw off the *Waste Land* [sic] and settle down and get at something better which is tormenting me by its elusiveness in my brain. (To Alfred Kreymborg, 6 February 1923)[7]

> There are *I* think about thirty *good* lines in *The Waste Land*, can you find them? The rest is ephemeral. (To Ford Madox Ford, 14 August 1923)[8]

And, to Otto Heller on 5 October 1923, coming up to the first-year anniversary of the poem: 'The poem is neither a success nor a failure – simply a struggle. Practically, one crucifies oneself and entertains drawing rooms and lounges. But the reception is irrelevant.'[9] The language of struggle in the aftermath of the publication is not surprising given the tumultuousness of Eliot's personal life during the composition of *The Waste Land* and the way the poem traverses Eliot's 'landscape of inward desolation', as A. David Moody puts it.[10] And though the reception was apparently 'irrelevant' to Eliot, it did not go unnoticed: 'it has been unfavourably reviewed in this country; the critics here are too timid even to admit they dislike it', he wrote to Ford Madox Ford on 4 October 1921.[11]

It is unsurprising that Eliot would zero in on negative reviews, not only due to his apparent disdain for the poem but also because they often raised questions about his inner life: 'the fact that Mr. Eliot has failed to convince

---

Hugh Haughton, revised edition (London: Faber & Faber, 2009), 596.
6   *The Letters of T.S. Eliot*, Volume 2: 1923–1925, edited by Valerie Eliot and Hugh Haughton (London: Faber & Faber, 2009), 11.
7   *The Letters of T.S. Eliot*, vol. 2, 41.
8   Ibid., 188. 'They are the twenty-nine lines of the water dripping song in the last part', he elaborated in a later letter (4 October 1923, 240).
9   Ibid., 242.
10   A. David Moody, *Tracing T.S. Eliot's Spirit* (Cambridge: Cambridge University Press, 1996), 116.
11   *The Letters of T.S. Eliot*, vol. 2, 240.

many readers that he has a soul must be laid as a black mark against him.'[12]
The mental strain of Eliot's personal life did not diminish with the publication of the poem, though: he continued working full-time at Lloyds Bank
and struggled to run *The Criterion* in the evenings, all while his wife Vivien's
health, and their marriage, deteriorated. Virginia Woolf wrote in her diary in
February 1923 that Eliot seemed a person 'about to break down'.[13]

It was not all doom and gloom, though, at least in Eliot's conversations
with Ezra Pound. He was pleased to see the poem in the public sphere and
thought it at least equal to Pound's *Cantos* in injecting modernist aesthetics
into contemporary culture: '*Waste Land* and *Cantos* do more good in this
society', Eliot wrote to Pound on 3 September 1923, 'than in the company
of cummings cowley hauptmann etc [E.E. Cummings, Malcolm Cowley and
Gerhart Hauptmann].'[14] Indeed, Eliot's ambition to see the poem doing
'good' is reflected in the positive reviews he so readily ignored. *The Waste
Land* was 'of exceptional importance' for its 'complete expression of this
poet's vision of modern life', read an anonymous review in the *Times Literary
Supplement* soon after the poem was published: 'We have here range, depth,
and beautiful expression. What more is necessary to a great poem?'[15] And,
from Edmund Wilson in December 1922 in the *Dial*: 'Mr Eliot, with all
his limitations, is one of our only authentic poets. [...] he feels intensely and
with distinction and speaks naturally in beautiful verse'; his poetry is, Wilson
concludes 'authentic crystals'.[16] Praise continued into 1923: '*The Waste Land*
is unquestionably important, unquestionably brilliant', Conrad Aiken wrote
for *New Republic*.[17] If Eliot could not reconcile such exuberance, he was at
least pleased with Wilson's review, as he confirmed in the January 1923 letter
quoted above. The affirmation of authenticity was an important one – con-
firmation that whatever interventions *The Waste Land* represented, it was
understood first and foremost as a profoundly poetic one, and Eliot as a profoundly modern poet. The significance of Eliot's efforts was felt across the
decade that followed, inspiring a generation of poets to take his endeavour
further. Critics too gathered around the poem to assert its importance for
understanding modernity – F.R. Leavis was a vital champion of the work.

---

[12]   Elinor Wylie, 'Mr Eliot's Slug-Horn', *New York Evening Post Literary Review*,
January 1923, cited in *T.S. Eliot: The Critical Heritage*, Volume 1, edited by Michael
Grant (London: Routledge, 1997), 156.
[13]   Quoted in *The Letters of T.S. Eliot*, vol. 2, xix.
[14]   *The Letters of T.S. Eliot*, vol. 2, 208.
[15]   Grant, ed., *The Critical Heritage*, vol. 1, 134.
[16]   Ibid., 139, 143.
[17]   Ibid., 157.

For these figures, *The Waste Land* was unequivocally an authentic documentation of modernity's fragmented condition and a method for poetically confronting that condition. As we shall see, this issue of Eliot and his poem as 'authentic' will recur in the anniversaries ahead, though at times in far less favourable terms than Eliot enjoyed in the twenties.

1932 – Auden, Leavis and the Tenth Anniversary

By its tenth anniversary, *The Waste Land* had become both a poetic and political object, deployed frequently in debates over the role of poetry's situation in society. The poem endeared itself to the Left interested in revolution as much as to the Right concerned with attacks on 'high-brow' culture and rise of the 'mass' in England at the time. Indicative of this reception are two texts published around *The Waste Land*'s tenth anniversary: F.R. Leavis's *New Bearings in English Poetry: A Study of the Contemporary Situation*; and W.H. Auden's *The Orators: An English Study*.

Leavis's *New Bearings* was a landmark in Eliot criticism. It provided an enormously influential critical interrogation of Eliot's poetry up to the early thirties, and remains influential in its reading of *The Waste Land*, especially on the topic of Eliot's allusive method:

> By means of such references and quotations Mr Eliot attains a compression, otherwise unattainable, that is essential to his aim; a compression approaching simultaneity – the co-presence in the mind of a number of different orientations, fundamental attitudes, orders of experience.[18]

In this 'compression', Leavis saw Eliot's poem as 'an effort to focus an inclusive human consciousness' in 'an age of psycho-analysis'.[19] The question of that 'age' underpins Leavis's approach to the poem, though; indeed, it underpins his thesis on poetry broadly. For Leavis, the majority of poetry published between 1880 and 1930, of which there was a considerable amount, demonstrated the 'very weakness' of the society which produced and received it: 'something has been wrong for forty or fifty years at least'. Crucially, he repudiated the suggestion that because more poetry was being produced than in previous centuries it must be reflective of a poetical society appreciative of verse. Instead, he viewed modern poetry as symptomatic of 'an age in which

---

[18]   F.R. Leavis, *New Bearings in English Poetry: A Study of the Contemporary Situation* (London: Chatto & Windus, 1961 [1932]), 107.
[19]   Leavis, *New Bearings*, 95.

there were no serious standards current, no live tradition of poetry, and no public capable of informed and serious interests.'[20] Modern poetry was stagnant, Leavis thought, because the twentieth century had inherited from the Victorians the Arnoldian belief (derived from Milton) that poetry 'must be the direct expression of simple emotions, and these of a limited class: tender, the exalted, the poignant, and, in general, the sympathetic. [...] Wit, play of intellect, stress of cerebral muscle had no place'.[21] Poetry arose from, and served, emotional intelligence, not rationality or, implicitly, social consciousness. Concomitantly, Leavis saw a decline in 'standards' throughout society which eroded any appreciative climate for poetry, above all represented by the rise, as he argued in *Mass Civilization and Minority Culture* (1930), in a reading public who cut their teeth not on 'Dante, Shakespeare, Donne, Baudelaire, Hardy', but on newspapers, popular fiction and the radio.[22]

The saving grace of the age, in Leavis's view, was Eliot. To Leavis, Eliot invented 'techniques' in his poetry 'adequate to the ways of feeling, or modes of experience, of adult, sensitive moderns': that is, poetry that was 'live' to *both* emotions and the intellect. Nevertheless, in Eliot and *The Waste Land* specifically, Leavis found validation of what he takes as fact: that modern society was unable to appreciate the art put before it. While in his introductory chapter, Leavis concedes that 'though there is, inevitably, a great deal of snobbism in the cult [Eliot] suffers from, mere snobbism will not account for his prestige among the young,'[23] he in the end argues that snobbism wins out. *The Waste Land* is a 'masterpiece' appropriate to a modernity in which a select few are equipped to really read such a poem (among whom Leavis of course counts himself). In turn, however, Leavis saw in the poem's evident modernity its limitations, not least due to its deep intertwinement with the modernity that fuelled its composition. He saw the deficiencies of *The Waste Land*, chiefly its inconsistent handling of external sources,[24] as recognition of the age that produced it:

> the poem in any case exists, and can exist, only for an extremely limited public equipped with special knowledge. The criticism can but be admitted. But that the public for it is limited is one of the symptoms of the state of culture that

---

[20]   Ibid., 6.

[21]   Ibid., 9.

[22]   F.R. Leavis, *Mass Civilization and Minority Culture* (Cambridge: The Minority Press, 1930), 1.

[23]   Leavis, *New Bearings*, 25.

[24]   '[R]epeated recourse to *From Ritual to Romance* will not invest it [the poem] with the virtue it assumes.' Ibid., 106.

produced the poem. Works expressing the finest consciousness of the age in which the word 'high-brow' has become current are almost inevitably such as to appeal only to a tiny minority. It is still more serious that this minority should be more and more cut off from the world around it – should, indeed, be aware of a hostile and overwhelming environment. This amounts to an admission that there must be something limited about the kind of artistic achievement possible in our time: even Shakespeare in such conditions could hardly have been the 'universal' genius. And *The Waste Land*, clearly, is not of the order of *The Divine Comedy* or of *Lear*. The important admission, then, is not that *The Waste Land* can be appreciated only by a very small minority (how large in any age has the minority been that has really compre- hended the masterpieces?), but that this limitation carries with it limitations in self-sufficiency.[25]

The Waste Land's status as a 'masterpiece' not of 'the order' of Dante or Shakespeare's best work is, in Leavis's view, indicative of the lowness of the age: it is a defective masterpiece reflective of a defective society. This is the culmination of Leavis's argument that a poet 'shall show himself to have been fully alive in our time.'[26] It was, for Leavis, the 'time' which accounted for the deficiencies in both *The Waste Land* and its reception.

A counterpoint of sorts to Leavis's diagnoses came in the form of W.H. Auden's desire to bring a social consciousness to the modernist poetics Eliot laid down; more pointedly, he wanted, as Stan Smith describes, to 'take Eliot's poetic revolution further, linking it to the social upheaval he had just lived through.'[27] The result was *The Orators: An English Study*, published in October 1932 by *The Criterion* with the accompanying note that it was 'the most valuable contribution to English poetry since "The Waste Land"'.[28] The poem was explicitly presented as coming *after* Eliot's work, and in *The Orators*' three parts we indeed find Auden attempting to marry the lessons Eliot and modernism broadly had instilled in his generation with the social commentary England at the time required.

[25]   Ibid., 103–4. The argument follows Leavis's opening remarks in *Mass Civilization and Minority Culture*: 'In any period it is upon a very small minority that the discerning appreciation of art and literature depends: it is (apart from cases of the simple and familiar) only a few who are capable of unprompted, first-hand judgment. They are still a small minority, though a larger one, who are capable of endorsing such first-hand judgment by genuine personal response' (1).

[26]   Leavis, *New Bearings*, 24.

[27]   Stan Smith, 'Remembering Bryden's Bill: Modernism from Eliot to Auden', in *Rewriting the Thirties: Modernism and After*, edited by Keith Williams and Steven Matthews (London: Routledge, 2014 [1997]), 53–70 (53).

[28]   Smith, 'Remembering Bryden's Bill', 53.

'What do you think about England, this country of ours where nobody is well?', part 1 of *The Orators* wearily begins.[29] The England in mind here is the one coming off the back of the Great Depression in which the Left were in considerable trouble: as John R. Boly writes,

> Liberals were outraged at Ramsay MacDonald's betrayal of the Labour Party, there appeared to be no real leadership in England, and the Depression had hit hard. So poets were expected, as they had not been expected since the days of Peterloo, to address contemporary social issues in a confident and authoritative fashion.[30]

Yet what was *The Waste Land*'s lesson but that modern poetry was anchored to disintegration, both external and internal? How, then, could one write socially conscious poetry that could make sense of a world so imbued with fragmentation? Auden's answer was to embrace that sense of disintegration and put into his poem minds at work in the process of ordering experience. The archetypal example here is the Airman in Book II's 'Journal of an Airman', the characterisation of whom, as Boly notes, takes its impetus from Eliot's poem by way of opposition: 'the poets of Auden's generation [...] wanted to be the Byrons and Shelleys of their age. But their modernist exemplum was Eliot's bewildered and enfeebled Tiresias. [...] [I]nstead of a despairing and enervate prophet, Auden chose as his model perceiver a self-possessed and tight-lipped technician.'[31] Importantly, Auden's Airman is also a combatant, specifically an air combatant from a form of warfare which marked the transition to the modern military methods introduced in the First World War, a conflict still looming over the nation.

The First World War was a constant preoccupation for Auden and other poets of his generation, imbuing their work with what Rachel Galvin terms 'not "survivor guilt"' but 'a structure of feeling conditioned by the conviction that combat veterans possess a non-transmittable knowledge, which endows them with special and unassailable authority concerning war'.[32] The social dimension Auden sought in modernist verse is thus directed towards the very thing that catalysed modernism in the first place (yet which few mod-

[29]   W.H. Auden, *The Orators* (London: Faber & Faber, 2015 [1932; 2nd edition 1934]), 3.
[30]   John R. Boly, 'W.H. Auden's *The Orators*: Portraits of the Artist in the Thirties', *Twentieth Century Literature* 27.3 (1981), 247–61 (248).
[31]   Ibid.
[32]   Rachel Galvin, 'The Guilt of the Noncombatant', *Essays and Studies* (2014), 205–27 (209).

ernists, including Eliot, directly experienced): the war itself, and the society that rebuilt in its wake.

Like *The Waste Land*, war as a constant condition of modern living permeates *The Orators*. Among the Airman's meditations are reports, schedules, lists and diary entries which build up to a final, imminent combat: 'The enemy are going to attack.'[33] Sometimes, war appears in a mundane treatment of death, as when 'Derek' is killed in an ambiguous flying accident which elicits unfeeling description: 'Went into a barrel roll at 8,000 ft and never came out.' Given the implication of a training mishap, 'the enemy' here are 'the mechanics' who swore 'the machine was all right when it left the hanger'.[34] Yet elsewhere 'the enemy' is a 'philosopher' who talks of 'intellect-will-sensation as real and separate entities'; elsewhere still, 'the enemy' is those whose 'victory' is 'impotence – cancer – paralysis'.[35] Sickness is a recurrent theme across *The Orators*, from that England which is 'not well' to the 'new recruits' half of whom likely 'won't get through the medical.'[36] While Eliot found comfort in old myths of the grail and the Fisher King, Auden writes of making do, of passing the medical and facing the future with as much raw data in hand. The Airman learns that 'the attack [will] take place on Aug. 28th. First penetration of the hostile position 7.10am'.[37] By the end of the Journal, when the Airman has turned to dated entries winding up to the attack, the only thing left to do before departure is take readings:

28th
3.40 a.m.
Pulses and reflexes, normal.
Barometric reading, 30.6.
Mean temperature, 34° F.,
Fair. Some cumulus cloud at 10,000 feet.
   Wind easterly and moderate.
Hands in perfect order.

Passing the medical; all hands on deck. Auden's conclusion is not some curative for the nation he deemed still as sick as Eliot portrayed it – as Leavis did too after reading Eliot – nor is his promise that poetry could improve matters ('poetry makes nothing happen', he would famously write at the

[33]   Auden, *The Orators*, 54.
[34]   Ibid., 50.
[35]   Ibid., 40.
[36]   Ibid., 50.
[37]   Ibid., 55.

end of the thirties). But, unlike Leavis, Auden's is a conclusion in which *something* happens: the Airman prepares to fight, to fly up into the blue. By taking the modernist model perfected by Eliot and injecting into it to the very themes of sickness, nation and war presumed to have been among modernism's catalysts, Auden makes Eliot's modernist verse *say* something – it becomes a social enterprise.

For Auden, then, *The Waste Land* created political potential in its poetic achievements. However, in rendering the fragmentation of modernity so acutely in poetic form, Eliot presented a problem. *The Waste Land* was undeniably a *modern* poem, but its method was poetic observation rather than engagement. Auden showed that, for socially conscious and engaged poetry to thrive in the wake of *The Waste Land*, the fragmentation Eliot laid bare had to be confronted. His solution was to put at the heart of *The Orators* a perceiving mind which thrived precisely because, against all odds, it was trying to make sense of the world around it. Ultimately, Auden's ambition, ten years on from *The Waste Land*'s arrival, was to realise what he saw in Eliot's poem, yet also to move beyond it, bringing Eliot's poetic achievements out from the depths of modernist despair which suffused its genesis (and which also coloured Leavis's ideas on the decline in modern society) and into the realm of the engaged socio-political poetry the 1930s in England called for.

1972 – *The Waste Land*'s Half-Century: Donald Davie and Authenticity

The picture was quite different at *The Waste Land*'s half-century. The poet-critic Donald Davie's appraisal of the fiftieth anniversary of the poem in 1972, marked by the publication of the drafts and transcripts facsimile the year before, demonstrates the rather low stock Eliot and modernism generally had in the 1970s:

> 1972 was recognized, dutifully but without much enthusiasm, as the fiftieth anniversary of the publication of T.S. Eliot's *The Waste Land*. Every one knew that *The Waste Land* had been the most successful twentieth-century poem in English, influential and esteemed far outside the English-speaking world. Here was a poem that had certainly reached a public. Yet how? What in this poem had 'appealed'? No obvious answer was forthcoming. Small wonder if many suspected, and a few asserted, that there had been a confidence-trick; that the élite (a new élite in which professors of English figured largely) had foisted the poem on a public long cowed and compliant, but deferential no longer. [...] [T]he anniversary of *The Waste Land* came at a very awkward time, just when more readers than ever were having rancorous

second thoughts about a poet who in his lifetime had been idolized certainly to excess. And for younger generations of readers, those who had had little or no opportunity of responding to Eliot while he was alive (he had died in 1965), a great obstacle was the social and political attitudes which the poet had espoused. How explain to a British person born since 1945 (especially if that person was not white) that in 1930 one did not have to be either crassly stupid or cynically self-interested to take seriously, as Eliot undoubtedly did, the authoritarian royalism of Charles Maurras?[38]

Davie was not alone in his assessment, particularly that it was Eliot's politics which overshadowed his literary status. His remarks followed those of Roger Kojecky, who noted in 1971 that 'the number of those who have been shocked or repelled by his [Eliot's] irreverent attitude towards ideals such as liberalism and democracy is greater than the number who have set themselves to discover what, positively, Eliot did believe.'[39] More pointedly, J.A. Morris in the *Journal of European Studies* published 'T.S. Eliot and Antisemitism' in the anniversary year, anticipating the surge in revaluations of this topic in the 1980s.

Reflecting on the facsimile publication, Davie argued that the attention to Eliot's politics in part arose from the drafts' demonstration that Ezra Pound played a central role in bringing the poem together. A great advocate of both literary figures, Davie was nevertheless forthright about their politics, chiefly Pound's 'malevolently Rightist' views and 'disastrous interventions in active politics'.[40] Pound's extreme politics conjoined with the facsimile publication to invite more serious reconsiderations of Eliot's own beliefs. Controversially, perhaps, Davie suggests that Eliot's reputation came off worse from the event precisely because Pound had been so staggeringly open about his repugnant views. 'By contrast,' Davie writes, 'Eliot's carefully qualified and camouflaged expression of similarly authoritarian and at times anti-semitic [sic] sentiments had not prevented his being accorded the Order of Merit by a grateful sovereign, nor his being commemorated in Westminster Abbey, the national mausoleum of his adopted country.' Davie qualifies this to say that it is 'unfair to Eliot', but that he states it to show the extent to which the reading public was increasingly suspicious of a poem that had previously weathered the accusations levelled against Eliot. While Eliot had been publicly and privately addressed over anti-Semitism, famously by

---

[38]   Donald Davie, '*The Waste Land* Drafts and Transcripts', in *Under Briggflatts: A History of Poetry in Great Britain 1960–1988* (Manchester: Carcanet, 1989), 98–102 (99).
[39]   Roger Kojecky, *T.S. Eliot's Social Criticism* (London: Faber & Faber, 1971), 11.
[40]   Davie, '*The Waste Land* Drafts and Transcripts', 99.

Emanuel Litvinoff in 1951,[41] and his politics had grown increasingly distant from both Left and Right as the century wore on, *The Waste Land* had by and large remained free from any taint – it retained its status as Eliot's waxed and waned. Fundamentally, Davie argued, whatever Eliot's real political positions, that status changed:

> comparisons between him and Pound were in 1972 stimulated, and exacerbated, by the publication that year of what were called the "drafts and transcripts" of *The Waste Land*; that is to say, the heterogenous packet of typescripts and manuscripts which Eliot dumped on Pound in Paris, out of which Pound had helped Eliot to extricate the poem that for fifty years had been known as *The Waste Land*.[42]

The result, when it came to the poem itself, was that it subsequently appeared 'the product not of one mind but of two' such that 'many readers were led to wonder how far the poem as they had had it all these years was in any authentic sense Eliot's at all'.[43]

The matter of authenticity – both in writing and politics – had become a central concern to English literary culture, notably among the Movement in the 1950s, that loosely associated group of English writers and poets whose work emphasised concrete ideas, familiar metrical and novel forms and a fundamentally unheroic treatment of the writer/poet as one among many undertaking a vocation. Poets were not bards or troubadours; they were civil servants, university lecturers and librarians living authentic, real lives which were visible in their work. This manifested in an anxiously 'authentic' poetry which Robert Conquest in his introduction to the anthology *New Lines* (1956) described as 'the restoration of a sound and fruitful attitude to poetry, of the principle that poetry is written by and for the whole man, intellect, emotions, senses and all'.[44] Conquest noted debts or comparisons to philosophical empiricism and claimed that, above all, this poetry 'submits to no great systems of theoretical constructs'. Importantly, too, 'on the more technical side,' he wrote, 'though of course related to all this, we see refusal to abandon a rational structure and comprehensible language, even when the verse is most highly charged with sensuous or emotional intent'. Modernism

---

[41]   See Emanuel Litvinoff, 'To T.S. Eliot', *Journey Through a Small Planet* (Harmondsworth: Penguin, 2008), 194.
[42]   Davie, '*The Waste Land* Drafts and Transcripts', 99.
[43]   Ibid.
[44]   *New Lines: An Anthology*, edited by Robert Conquest (London: Macmillan, 1956), xv.

and Romanticism alike can be seen in Conquest's sights here, and many of the Movement shared a Leavisite celebration of wit, with Davie and Thom Gunn turning to eighteenth-century Augustan poetry in particular.

While the Movement were not cohesive enough to be called a school or formal group, a shared distrust of posturing and fraudulence was a unifying force among them. The neo-Romantics of the 1940s were guilty of this, they thought, where intense emotion and recourse to images of sex and violence substituted substance and credibility in their poems. Dylan Thomas is the primary antagonist here, but he was mostly guilty, the Movement collectively agreed, of being an inconsistent, undisciplined poet.[45] Worse, though, was the inauthenticity Thomas attracted from imitators and apparent admirers. As Blake Morrison documents, the Movement shared a despair at the 'hangers-on' who surrounded Thomas, and they condemned what Davie called 'the tawd[r]y amoralism of a London Bohemia which had destroyed Dylan Thomas, the greatest talent of the generation before us.'[46] Thomas's death, John Wain wrote, comprised mostly an 'outburst of exhibitionist feeling' which involved emotionally (and at times financially) cashing in on the poet's tragic demise.[47] Unadulterated high-mindedness and intellectual indulgence were also distasteful, as such posturing eventually descended into political depravity. History was the root of this attitude, too. Pound's turn to fascism represented such a path, and Hitler its application – as Davie famously wrote of Pound, 'the development from imagism in poetry to fascism in politics is clear and unbroken'.[48] Movement novels like Kingsley Amis's *Lucky Jim* and John Wain's *Hurry on Down* are perhaps the most memorable instances of this attack on the 'phony' – a word which typified what the Movement railed against.[49] Such novels' protagonists are often working-class, provincial university graduates scraping a living while enduring encounters with stuffy or pompous characters drawn from the upper-class and Oxbridge elite.[50] The innate values of tradition and myth were put on trial, famously mocked by Larkin as 'common myth-

---

[45] Blake Morrison, *The Movement* (London: Methuen, 1980), 146–7.

[46] Donald Davie, *Purity of Diction in English Verse*, quoted in ibid., 146.

[47] Quoted in ibid., 146.

[48] Donald Davie, *Purity of Diction in English Verse* (Manchester: Carcanet, 1994), 99.

[49] Morrison identifies J.D. Salinger's *The Catcher in the Rye* (1951) and Holden Caulfield's suspicion of the 'phony' as an important influence among the Movement, particularly for Amis and Wain. Morrison, *The Movement*, 63.

[50] The irony of course is that the Movement also represented the cohort of writers and critics who were ultimately sustained by university appointments and creative writing courses.

kitty' which provided poets (chiefly Modernist and neo-Romantic poets) with tools for avoiding writing about real experiences.[51] Davie, like others among the Movement such as Thom Gunn, was less directly suspicious of the use of the 'myth-kitty' in poetry – his verse is often densely allusive – and rather more wary of 'the inauthentic', a condition he most readily attributed to confessional poetry (or writing in terms of 'sincerity') but which he also raised around Eliot's lasting impact as the poet of *The Waste Land*. For Davie, Eliot represented a problem. Eliot was a principled, authentic critic who wrote with clear convictions about the role of poetry in society. The issue, however, was that Eliot's most significant contribution to modern culture, *The Waste Land*, was all but confirmed to many at its half-century to be no more than a 'confidence-trick' pulled by Eliot and Pound.

While Davie's views on Modernism, and indeed on Eliot, changed over his five-decade career, this issue of Eliot hiding in plain sight remained a live one. Pound's involvement required confrontation, as did the extent to which his role diminished Eliot's in composing *The Waste Land* overall. Davie did not necessarily subscribe to this view, but worried over its impact on the reputation of the poem and of the Modernist legacy broadly. In an early poem, 'Twilight on the Waste Lands', in his first collection, *Brides of Reason* (1955), Davie revisits *The Waste Land* in these terms. Its middle stanzas read:

> The traveller, at dusk or dawn,
> Adverted by a trick of light,
> Starts at a meaning, hints a form
> So fugitive, the doubtful sight
> Suspects no hand of man at all,
> An artefact so natural
> It seems the work of air and light.
>
> Conceive of such a poem, planned
> With such a nicety of touch
> It quite conceals the maker's hand
> And seems a votive fragment, such
> As patient scholars make unclear
> And, hazarding their guesses, fear
> They have read into it too much.[52]

---

[51]   Quoted in Morrison, *The Movement*, 194.
[52]   Donald Davie, 'Twilight on the Waste Lands', in *Collected Poems* (Manchester: Carcanet, 2002), 14.

'Twilight on the Waste Lands' is a meditation on the dichotomy Eliot's poem presents: on the one hand, it as though it were plucked from the sights and sounds of modernity itself; on the other, it is an archly *constructed* poem, both in its appearance on the page and in its composition history and its subsequent interpretation by 'patient' but unconfident 'scholars'. The anxiety, the 'fear' that the great Modernist poem was a 'trick of light' that only 'seems' to fulfil a promise was acute for Davie. His own poem goes to great pains to retain its credentials – it is as metrically precise as any of Eliot's verse, but restrained, conscious of diverting any claims of posturing or misdirection. It is 'planned', but not interested in 'conceal[ing]' its making. These concerns, including the desire to think of poetry as manifested from nature itself, are perhaps unsurprising given that Davie's earliest appreciation of Eliot was as the poet not of *The Waste Land* but of 'Marina' from the 'Ariel' sequence.[53] That is, Davie's Eliot was the poet gearing up to write *Four Quartets*, not the one of *The Waste Land*. Davie's own poetry was profoundly influenced by the notion of 'grace dissolved in place', as Eliot puts it in 'Marina', from his early meditations on the 'small civilities' of Plymouth life ('Among Artisan's Houses', *Brides of Reason*, 1955) to his geo-poetic journeys through England in *The Shires* (1974).

Davie's appreciation of Eliot as the poet of *The Waste Land*, by contrast, came via his schooling. Indeed, in his 1972 lecture to the University of York, 'Eliot in One Poet's Life', (published a year later in *Mosaic*) Davie spelled out that *The Waste Land* had found its place in English culture in the midcentury largely as an examination piece, a poem that was in some way a test of one's own cultural acumen and, by extension, social standing:

[I]f *The Waste Land* and 'Prufrock' were already known to me by 1938, when I was 16, it was because alert and ambitious schoolmasters had pressed them upon me. And I was a very ambitious schoolboy, in those days when British education was more elitist and competitive then it is today. So I responded very readily to Eliot's early poems, in the terms in which my schoolmasters presented them to me – that is to say, as commando obstacle-course which one was not expected to complete, only to fail at more or less creditably. And I have to confess that *The Waste Land* even today lives in my mind in rather this way – as a famous challenge and ordeal, a sphinx's riddle: which is to say, not (strictly speaking) as a poem at all. Now that the publication of the drafts has made it a focus of argument once again, I see others confessing in

---

[53]   Eliot as a critic was equally important for Davie's first encounters with him, notably as the author of essays like 'The Metaphysical Poets', 'Andrew Marvell' and 'Homage to John Dryden'. See Davie, 'Eliot in One Poet's Life', in *Modernist Essays*, edited by Clive Wilmer (Manchester: Carcanet, 2004), 145–58 (146).

print that it is a sphinx's riddle to them too, and often enough they complain of Eliot or of Eliot and Pound between them, for having made a frustrating tease out of what should have been complete and satisfying. This may well be right. On the other hand, it may be that what seems unsatisfying about *The Waste Land* is not anything intrinsic to the poem but rather has to do with the reputation of the poem, with how its reputation was first made and has been sustained ever since [...].[54]

Davie's emphasis on the education sector for providing Eliot's poem with its main source of prolonged cultural life echoes his jocular aside in his essay on *The Waste Land* facsimile that it was a 'new élite in which professors of English figured largely' who oversaw matters of taste and cultural favour. Leavis looms large in this judgement, and in the influence of educators in sustaining the poem's reputation. To succeed (or fail just prior to success) with reading *The Waste Land* was a mark of prestige, a demonstration of cultural awareness and depth. It would, inevitably, also signify one's class, social background and schooling. However, fifty years on from the poem's publication, Eliot's reputation was beginning to overshadow the poem's status.

1992 – Hear It Again: R.L. Houghton and Charles Tomlinson on or around *The Waste Land*'s Seventy-Fifth.

As the 70s gave way to the 80s, it was Eliot's politics, as Davie essentially predicted, which predominated receptions of his work, chiefly the question of anti-Semitism. The issue came to a head with two studies that straddled *The Waste Land*'s seventy-fifth anniversary: Christopher Ricks' *T.S. Eliot and Prejudice* (1988), followed by Anthony Julius's *T.S. Eliot, Anti-Semitism and Literary Form* (1995). The former was careful not to accuse Eliot of an over-arching prejudicial framework to his thinking or writing; the latter concluded that Eliot's anti-Semitism underpinned his entire body of work. This debate continues, and requires careful navigation: Eliot was clearly in possession of objectionable views, notably expressed in *After Strange Gods*[55]; the degree to which they define his character and his work needs careful critical judgement. Either way, the mounting tension of the evidence against Eliot seemed to finally spill over into reappraisals of his work. *The Waste Land* subsequently received a more hostile critical gaze having long remained gilded in its status.

---

[54] Davie, 'Eliot in One Poet's Life', 145–6.
[55] T.S. Eliot, *After Strange Gods: A Primer of Modern Heresy* (London: Faber, 1934).

Echoing apprehensions over phonyism akin to the Movement and Davie's concerns at the fiftieth anniversary, the late 80s saw a more concerted effort to evaluate the authenticity of both Eliot's endeavours and the reception *The Waste Land* received. In '*The Waste Land* Revisited', for example, published in *The Cambridge Quarterly* in 1989, R.L. Houghton set out to question *The Waste Land*'s status as 'our poem *par excellence*'.[56] His trepidations over the real value of the poem stemmed in part from the ever-present force of the 'Eliot industry' propelled by scholars and publishers:

> In recent years the centre of interest in Eliot has begun to move away from the poetry, as biographical information and documents of scholarly interest have, in a limited way, become accessible. Strange academic work has begun to sprout on Eliot's Nachlass, and its efflorescence threatens the whole corpus of his poetry, but for readers generally there has been no great change. In fact little has changed for years in the commonly accepted account of *The Waste Land*.
>
> It's remarkable that the work has remained modern for so long. One cannot help suspecting that intellectual inertia set in years ago and that the poem has been fashionable, or conventionally respected, rather than of particular value to successive generations of readers. Sensibility has certainly changed since 1922, but we are still awaiting the next poet of genius who will bring the change home to us by 'altering expression' and giving us what we will recognise as a really modern poem.[57]

Houghton's account of the poem as a piece shrouded by fashion is sustained by his sense that the poem's famous Notes are a series of jokes taken too seriously by generations of readers and scholars. He argued that they reveal more about Eliot's views on potential readers, taunting an appetite to explicate rather than experience such a poem. More pointedly, though, Houghton works through the poem and argues that it is a poorly contrived sequence of linguistic quirks sustained by moments of poetic, that is lyrical, success. The final part of 'A Game of Chess', for example, is judged a series of 'set phrases' that put Eliot's snobbery on display, while the 'good night, sweet ladies' line is deemed 'odious': 'The poem consigns the women to *nox perpetua* with contempt'. Houghton laments that he once admired the 'Unreal City' sequence, taught as a young reader and critic to see its Dantean debts as a laudable form of poetic rewriting. Yet he finds verbs like 'sprout' and 'bloom' to be 'distracting oddity' on rereading, and furiously denies the 'game' Eliot sets up in the

---

[56]   R.L. Houghton, '*The Waste Land* Revisited', *Cambridge Quarterly* 18.1 (1989), 34–62 (34).
[57]   Ibid., 34.

'Stetson' dialogue as one 'we can't win'. Ultimately, it is the critical question of authenticity which returns once more:

> As I pondered this [passage], [...] my eyes moved up the page and came to rest on the phrase 'Under a brown fog'. *Under* a fog? I needed only to see the wrongness of Eliot's phrase, which out of the context of reading the poem *as* a poem was easy to do, for the whole passage to collapse.[58]

The visualisation of the city fails, in Houghton's estimations, to give the reader any experience or image of the City's unreality; instead, it is a sequence of allusions which 'send us back' without hope or purpose. 'The famous wit of this passage,' he concludes, 'is simply mystification and bluff'. Houghton's conclusion, based on the opening of 'A Game of Chess', is damning if one accepts it:

> Eliot's bad writing encouraged a style of 'reading' – and versifying – that culti-vated the arbitrarily difficult. With Eliot's authority apparently behind it this was accepted as 'modern'. The uncertainty of the syntax in the drawn-out sen-tences is due simply to Eliot's failure to write clear sense. He needed to revise the passage at all levels, from punctuation upwards. If we question the justness of words, phrases, and suggestions, time and again we find pointlessness and uncertainty.[...] Eliot, one feels, obtains a gratification from the exercise of skill in conjuring a factitious literary fancy into illusorily intense existence.[59]

'Glamour', 'mystification and bluff', 'literary fancy', all these remarks show a serious anxiety that *The Waste Land* entailed a contract between author-ity figures, be they Eliot and Pound, figures like F.R. Leavis and William Empson, or countless schoolmasters and lecturers who set the poem before wide-eyed students tasked with excavating an empty mine. The pervasive nature of extra-poetic contexts for the poem does give the impression that, like the Movement's trepidations over Dylan Thomas's fame, *The Waste Land*'s reputation has been fuelled by a desire to get away from reading the poem. Even if one does not agree with Houghton's assessment – and it is very difficult to say, out loud or to oneself, that *The Waste Land* is actually a *bad* poem – it seems that, by 1989, the gulf between Eliot and the reading public had finally come to influence readings of the poem itself. If the authority had been rested from Eliot through reappraisals of his politics, the cultural authority of *The Waste Land* itself had finally come under question too.

---

[58] Ibid., 43–44.
[59] Ibid., 45.

Some degree of rehabilitation began, however, with the seventy-fifth anniversary of the poem. A method of recuperation came from the poet, translator and painter Charles Tomlinson in 'Reading *The Waste Land*', one of his 1992 Keele University lectures. An inheritor of modernist poetics, notably from Americans such as Marianne Moore, William Carlos Williams and Wallace Stevens, as well as Pound and Eliot, Tomlinson oscillated between the margins and the centre of British poetry throughout his career. Davie was an ally, as was *Poetry Nation/PN Review*, the poetry magazine founded in 1973 by Michael Schmidt, and there was much support generated when Tomlinson was a contender for Poet Laureate, though it went to Ted Hughes. Yet he found a degree of fame in the United States during his career, in part thanks to his enthusiasms for the Black Mountain Poets, and Tomlinson's slim body of criticism is almost entirely devoted to American poets.

'Can we hear Eliot's *The Waste Land*?' was Tomlinson's question. Tomlinson was himself a profoundly sonorous poet: 'To read Tomlinson is continually to *sound*', wrote Calvin Bedient.[60] Implicit in his question was 'can we *still* hear *The Waste Land*?'. His target was the surfeit of critical and scholarly material that surrounded the poem:

> So much has been written about *The Waste Land* that we can't get at the poem's acoustics for all the commentaries. If you're just starting on Eliot, you may find that commentaries are already being thrust at you, or that, nervous, you rush for enlightenment to those famous notes at the end of the poem, only to be disappointed.[61]

Though he does not mention the tumultuous period in Eliot criticism which surrounded his lecture, Tomlinson's argument, resoundingly directed first and foremost at students, was to read the poem first, unblinkered by scholarship and commentaries, unburdened by the poem's status and reputation, or that of its poet. Indeed, read the poem first, then second, and so on was his argument: 'This is a poem that, like the rapid cutting in some films, only releases its larger meanings as you re-experience it, as you hear it again.'[62]

This sense of returning to the poem over and over, reading and listening to it carefully, of *experiencing* it, offers a rebuttal to the contentions of Davie, Houghton and others that in some way *The Waste Land* has got away with

---

[60] Calvin Bedient, 'On Charles Tomlinson', in *British Poetry Since 1960*, edited by Michael Schmidt and Grevel Lindop (Manchester: Carcanet, 1972), 172–189 (172).
[61] Charles Tomlinson, 'Reading *The Waste Land*', in *American Essays: Making It New* (Manchester: Carcanet, 2001), 22–26 (22).
[62] Ibid., 23.

something, that it is in some sense an *inauthentic* poem, or one intended
to fool the reading public. In Eliot's poem, Tomlinson argues, the soundscape 'fulfils a basic human impulse, to murmur' a poem 'aloud as we read
it, to feel out its shapes on the tongue and to inform one's browsing mind
with some sense of its overall shape when heard.' This argument provides
Tomlinson with a method of rehabilitating the allusions and quotations
which Houghton's criticism suggests readers had become impatient with:

> The cataract of quotations [...] confronts the ear with sounds in an assort-
> ment of languages. Although these are expressive of fragmentation and the
> desire to overcome it, the fragments themselves contain worlds of meaning,
> once we can listen beyond the mere noise they make. Despite the crisis at
> the centre of all this, these sounds from the Tower of Babel are strangely
> enjoyable, are thrilling both to say and hear. Art is like that. It permits us
> to confront alienation and disunity, and metamorphose them into a curious
> rejoicing. We rejoice partly in the artist's ability to so order things, or to hold
> them in such powerful *dis*order as at the climax of *The Waste Land*.[63]

Against the lamenting Leavis who saw despair at the heart of Eliot's fragmentary poem, and Houghton's sceptical denigration of Eliot's work as a kind of
con, Tomlinson's reminder is that the poem's multi-lingual tapestry is first
and foremost an experience of sound: it is a poetic experience. In wrestling
The Waste Land out of the commentaries and readings which want to see it
as the manifestation of modernity's chaos, Tomlinson lets the poem return
to a state in which it is first and foremost the interplay of language and form.

Considering again that Tomlinson's address clearly includes students (or
anyone new to *The Waste Land*), it is arguable that now, at the centenary,
when we once more demand more of such a poem, Tomlinson's argument is
simplistic and naïve. Yet in emphasising sound in the poem, he reinforces not
only the lyric qualities of the writing but also reminds us that, despite what
Eliot's own life and politics involved, *The Waste Land* entails the search for a
liberation from accepted ways of using language and culture in the formation
of experiences and beliefs: 'If we *hear The Waste Land*, putting aside for the
moment the hunting down of all literary allusions, the difficulties of speaking out and thus making things meaningful become the very heart of the
drama.'[64] It is, in these terms, a poem in search of emancipation.

Tomlinson's plea for listening to *The Waste Land* again beyond the noise
of scholarly ephemera and cultural status even chimes with Eliot's own treat-

---

[63]   Ibid., 25.
[64]   Ibid., 22.

ment of the poem in his later career. Though he lamented the poem's success, calling it mere 'rhythmical grumbling', this nevertheless emphasises sound as the poem's core. Readers, scholars and critics have remained burdened by Eliot's notes and epitaphs for the poem ever since its publication; they are a part of the poem and yet seem wholly opposed to the 'ruins' which it conjures so starkly. Eliot's recordings of the poem are instructive, on this front. When Eliot came to record readings of the poem, he left all the extra-poetical elements out. In recordings made in 1935, 1948 and 1955, the notes are set aside for the steady, precise elocutions of Eliot's uniquely Anglicised New England diction. 'It is at any rate chaste', notes Tomlinson, 'not busily interpreting every nuance by heavily underlining. It deliberately avoids the histrionic.'[65] Eliot emphasises rhythm in the poem – its shifts in metrical patterns are made all the more powerful, even with Eliot's flattened tone. As Leslie Wheeler notes, the result is one of scholarship's favourite poems freed 'from its scholarly frame' by its own composer. In turn, 'its motive and meaning root deeply, as lyric does by definition, in sound.'[66]

The recovery of Eliot as a lyric, acoustical poet is felt among contemporary poets, as detailed thoroughly by Wheeler. The American poet Major Jackson, in correspondence with Wheeler in 2012 (incidentally *The Waste Land*'s ninetieth year), is clear that Eliot's methods are what make him last:

> Eliot was an early influence. Both *The Waste Land* and 'Preludes' (and to a lesser degree such canonized poems as 'Prufrock,' 'Ash Wednesday,' etc.) lit a way for me to be highly allusive, especially with pop culture, but more importantly, his rhythmic changes and meters authorized a similar approach to composing poems.[67]

For others, there is the ambition of taking Eliot's efforts further, as in Auden's work in the 1930s. Other examples Wheeler notes include Jeremy Richards's blend of high culture and pop music in 'T.S. Eliot's Lost Hip Hop Poem', 'correlating Eliot's extremely white persona with the sound and sense of an African-American form.'

Return and reinvention – both are necessary to sustaining Eliot's work into its second century. Return involves reading the poem again for its poetical nature, for its lyric qualities, yet also asks us to read it again for the political conditions which generated it and to reflect on the politics that condition our approach to poetry and what we ask of poetry now. The pastiche and

---

[65]   Ibid., 24.
[66]   Quoted in Wheeler, 'Undead Eliot'.
[67]   Quoted in Wheeler, 'Undead Eliot'.

reimagining which contemporary poets pursue indicates that Eliot's work remains ever-present, an active resource available to nourish or react against in equal measure. If Eliot's personal life and politics are unavoidable blotches on any straightforward advocation of the poet, listening to *The Waste Land* again, as we read it to ourselves or hear it spoken aloud, is to engage in a process of delimiting Eliot's presence over the poem. It is to render *The Waste Land* a poem once more.

4

'O City, city': Sounding The Waste Land

HUGH HAUGHTON

The centenary of *The Waste Land* is a good moment to register its continuing capacity to generate a shock of recognition and to think about the relationship between shock and recognition not only in relation to the poem's interpretation and reception, but also its form.[1]

In *Shadow and Act* the African American writer Ralph Ellison gives a memorable account of the impact of Eliot's poem on him:

> *The Waste Land* seized my mind. I was intrigued by its power to move me while eluding my understanding. Somehow its rhythms were often closer to those of jazz than were those of the Negro poets, and even though I could not understand them, its range of allusion was as mixed and as varied as that of Louis Armstrong.[2]

What is striking is Ellison's re-framing of Eliot's allusive musicality in terms of Black America's greatest contribution to world music, jazz. In his *The History of the Voice*, the Caribbean poet Edward Kamau Brathwaite offers a different but complementary political angle on the poem's vocal sound. Brathwaite speaks of how in his time in the West Indies 'mainstream poets who were moving from standard English to nation English were influenced basically by T.S. Eliot and John Arlott's cricket commentary on the BBC'.[3] Since the publication of *The Drafts* of Eliot's poem, and the reconstruction of an *Ur*-version of the poem in Christopher Ricks and Jim McCue's monumental edition of *The Poems*, we are aware that the opening section of the poem was originally given the Dickensian title of 'He Do the Police in Different Voices,' and of the partly occluded American dimension of the text. It is the poem's openness to these different, non-standard voices and kinds of music that Brathwaite, like Ellison, values. It is not Eliot, the elite

---

[1]   This essay is dedicated to Mimi Ching and colleagues in the Chinese University of Hong Kong.

[2]   Ralph Ellison, *Shadow and Act* (New York: Random House, 1964), 160.

[3]   Edward Kamu Brathwaite, *The History of the Voice* (London: New Beacon Books, 1984), 30 n. 41.

cultural policeman of *After Strange Gods* or the spokesperson for tradition, but Eliot the musical outsider with an ear for rhythm and the clashing and convergence of different vocal and lyrical registers within and across cultures. In a recent essay in *Poetry* on 'How *The Waste Land* Sounds Now', exploring contemporary American poets' responses to Eliot, Lesley Wheeler observes that 'Eliot persists as a sonic obsession more vividly than as a poet who levelled important arguments or shaped literary history'. She reviews after-effects and re-mixes of Eliot in twenty-first century poets. These include Major Jackson and Kim Addonizio, whose poem 'Yes' includes the injunction, 'Now recite / The Waste Land, backwards'. John Beer's *The Waste Land and Other Poems* (2010) 'takes allusion to its limit, revisiting the modernist monument as if possessed by Eliot's ghost'. According to Wheeler, its first poem "Sound of Water Over a Rock," 'empties Eliot's poetry of meaning in favor of its tantalizing sounds.' For her, 'Sound is how Eliot expresses personal despair and social critique most forcefully, and also how he survives the apocalypse'.[4]

That word 'sound' haunts *The Waste Land* itself. In the first evocation of the desert landscape in the poem, we hear that among the 'broken images' and 'dry stone' there is 'no sound of water' (lines 22–4).[5] A little later, we are told of 'the dead sound on the final stroke of nine' of St Mary Woolnoth in the City of London (line 67), while 'The Fire Sermon' announces 'the sound of horns and motors / Which shall bring Sweeney to Mrs Porter in the spring' (line 197). The last movement, 'What the Thunder Said', which opens by evoking Christ's passion in acoustic terms as 'the shouting and the crying' and 'reverberation' of 'spring' (lines 325–7), returns us to the opening 'sound of water', repeating it with variations as 'sound of water only' and 'sound of water over a rock', and finally turns on the word again in the form of an apocalyptic question 'What is that sound high in the air / Murmur of maternal lamentation' (lines 352–66). This is the only example where the word 'sound' is related to or likened to a vocal enunciation, a communal voice of lament that is heard not as words but as a 'murmur', a non-semantic form of utterance without specific verbal meaning. Two of the other appeals are to city noises – the 'dead sound' of the traditional church clock, and the

[4]   All quotations in the preceding discussion are cited in Lesley Wheeler, 'Undead Eliot: How "The Waste Land" Sounds Now', *Poetry*. https://www.poetryfoundation. org/poetrymagazine/articles/70143/undead-eliot-how-the-waste-land-sounds-now.
[5]   All quotations from the poem are derived from *The Poems of T.S. Eliot: The Annotated Text*, edited by Christopher Ricks and Jim McCue (London: Faber, 2015), 55–77. Given the focus here upon sonic effects, references are supplied in the main text by line numbers in this edition.

industrial era 'sound of horns and motors', snappily caught in the jazz-era couplet about Sweeney and Mrs Porter. The other uses of the word refer to natural noise, the sound of water that is evoked in the fugato passage about 'if there were water' that Eliot told Ford Maddox Ford was the most successful part of the poem, culminating in the wonderful evocation of the thrush's 'water-dripping song':[6]

> If there were the sound of water only
> Not the cicada
> And dry grass singing
> But sound of water over a rock
> Where the hermit-thrush sings in the pine trees
> Drip drop drip drop drop drop drop
> But there is no water (lines 352–66)

This passage not only foregrounds sound effects in that penultimate seven-beat monosyllabically extended line, but appeals to song, another key sonic dimension of the poem. Here the cicada and grass are 'singing' just as the 'hermit-thrush sings in the pine trees.' Elsewhere the poem speaks of the nightingale's 'inviolate voice' (line 101) making its 'jug jug' song, and one of the poem's multiple speakers echoes Spenser three times in addressing London's river, 'Sweet Thames, run softly till I end my song' (lines 176–84). It is worth noting that the question 'What is that sound' near the end of the poem is an echo of the sound question asked twice earlier, 'What is that noise?' and 'What is that noise now ...?', questions answered by another voice, saying 'The wind under the door' and 'Nothing again nothing' (117–19). Sound and noise are key co-ordinates in relation to 'song', whether or not they signify nothing or just the wind. Soon after the last 'What is that sound' question, we are told of 'reminiscent bells, that kept the hours / And voices singing out of empty cisterns and exhausted wells' (lines 383–4), which remind us of the 'dead sound' of St Mary Woolnoth, but also the equally ecclesiastical Parsifalian 'voix d'enfants chantant dans la coupole' (line 202). The poem is full of such echoic effects of sounds and voices. To the words, 'sound', 'noise,' and 'singing' or 'song', we should add the violated nightingale's 'inviolable voice' and those final 'voices' out of 'empty cisterns and exhausted wells', which may or may not be 'human voices' comparable to those invoked at the end of 'The Love Song of J. Alfred Prufrock'. Like so

---

[6] *The Letters of T.S. Eliot*, Volume 2, edited by Valerie Eliot and Hugh Haughton (London: Faber, 2009), 240.

many sounds and images in the poem, these 'voices' are poised on the boundary between the human and non-human.

Sound, noise, song, and voice – Eliot's appeal to these terms in the poem tell us something fundamental about its acoustic, or, to use his own term, its 'auditory imagination' or 'feeling for syllable and rhythm'.[7] It also tells us something about its afterlife in the minds of readers like Ralph Ellison, Edward Kamau Brathwaite, and the twenty-first century poets invoked by Lesley Wheeler. Even if Ellison's 'jazz' doesn't cover the full range of effects generated by the poem, to my mind *The Waste Land* can best be understood in terms of music – of song, opera, rag-time, dance-music, vaudeville, rhythmic experiment, acoustic workshop – of noise and sound effects – as well as a piece of disintegrated vocal theatre, compounded out of Renaissance drama and music hall, and possibly cinema. (In July 1923 Eliot praised the music-hall trained Chaplin for having 'escaped in his own way the realism of the cinema and invented a *rhythm*'.)[8] It is above all a sound world. In January 1923, Eliot told Edmund Wilson, one of the first reviewers to respond to the poem's Notes, 'I think you over-understand the poem'.[9] A hundred years on, I suggest that rather than 'over-understanding' the poem on the basis of its notes (including those of those indefatigable recent annotators Christopher Ricks and Jim McCue), readers should follow Ellison, Brathwaite, and Wheeler and listen to its lovely dissonant music. We should respond to its words as 'notes' in the musical sense, treating the poem as a score as much as a text. Eliot published poems called *Preludes* and *Four Quartets* and David Fuller notes persuasively that 'although he had no technical training, music was the art that personally affected Eliot most deeply'.[10] Of no text is this more true than *The Waste Land*, which is both the first (and with *Sweeney Agonistes* most convincing) embodiment of the poet's dramatic imagination and the most complex embodiment of his responsiveness of music – and to sound more generally. To get to grips with the poem means sounding it in several senses.

The Waste Land is simultaneously a soundscape and a cityscape. It is the combination – or rather identity – of the two which gives it its unique frequency. The text represents the modern metropolis in terms of a uniquely polyvocal modernist music, which began brewing in the banker-poet Eliot's overworked brain in the City of London just over a 100 years ago. In 'The

---

[7]   T.S. Eliot, *The Use of Poetry and the Use of Criticism* (London: Faber, 1933), 118.
[8]   T.S. Eliot, 'Dramatis Personae', *The Criterion* 1 (1923), 306.
[9]   *The Letters of T.S Eliot*, vol. 2, 11.
[10] David Fuller, 'Music' in *T.S. Eliot in Context*, edited by Jason Harding (Cambridge: Cambridge University Press, 2011), 134.

Burial of the Dead', against the backdrop of Munich's Hofgarten, 'stony rubbish', and 'red rocks', we hear the sailor's song from the opening of *Tristan and Isolde*, singing to his '*Irisch Kind*'. Soon afterwards, when cutting back from the 'Hyacinth garden', we hear the watchman's desolate words from Act III of the same opera, '*Oed' und leer das Meer*'. Stravinsky thought that hearing *Tristan* was one of the formative experience of Eliot's life, and, taken beside the watery non-verbal vocables of the Rhinemaidens echoing on the Thames in 'The Fire Sermon' ('Weialala leia / Wallalla leialala'), these allusions suggest that the Wagnerian operatic sound that haunted Baudelaire, Mann and Proust is also integral to Eliot's London. But these references must be set against quite other kinds of music, harking back to the polystilism of Charles Ives and anticipating that of later composers like Alfred Schnittke. Composing his own riverine music about the Thames, Eliot repeats the onomatopoeic gobbledegook of the Rhinemaidens' song from *Götterdämmerung* twice, reprising it again after the words of his 'Thames-daughters' in trailing fragmentary form as a last 'la la' (line 306).[11] In Eliot's polystylistic verse we hear (or infer) Wagner's apocalyptic score echoing along the Thames (an English version of *The Ring* was performed in London in 1922). 'The Game of Chess' counterpoints these Wagnerian voices with allusive vocal music from across the Atlantic:

> O O that Shakespeherian Rag –
> It's so elegant
> So intelligent (lines 127–30)

Eliot is recreating the rhythms and echoing the words of a popular number from the 1912 Broadway hit, *Ziegfeld Follies* by Gene Buck and Herman Ruby, with music by David Stamper – an allusion to a rag about Shakespearian allusion ('And you'll hear old Hamlet say / "To be or not to be," / That Shakespearian Rag'). Writing to Mary Hutchinson in 1917, Eliot's wife Vivien, encouraging her to 'give a dance', said 'One day you must try Tom's Negro rag-time: I know you'd love it.'[12] Eliot clearly did too. Stravinsky composed a brilliant *Ragtime* in 1918, but as Hasse reminds us: 'To "rag" [was] to syncopate the melody of nonsyncopated work. This technique, which predates the first publication of rags by several decades, was

---

[11]   Eliot refers to his speakers as 'Thames-Daughters' in his note to line 266. *The Poems of T.S. Eliot*, vol. 1, 75.
[12]   *The Letters of T.S. Eliot*, Volume 1, edited by Valerie Eliot and Hugh Haughton (London: Faber, 2009), 239.

a common performance practice of pianists.'[13] By 1925, a writer in *Melody* magazine, was asserting that:

> Our highbrows for years have talked much of the need of declaring our independence of old world forms and inspirations. Well here we have it, in musical forms which are as intensely and significantly American as Verdi's are Italian, or Schumann and Wagner, German. It is as racy as our soil as an Irish folk song is of Ireland. It is the rush of our racing streets. It has all the bright contrasts of our racial conglomerate. It has our moods and our spirit, our impudence and irreverence, our joy in speed and force. American musical genius has in ragtime and jazz contributed something of great vitality to the art of music, in its rhythms and new colorings.[14]

Not long after publishing *The Waste Land*, Eliot wrote to Alfred Kreymborg complementing him on his *Puppet Plays*, saying he had 'got a new rhythm' which 'greatly stimulated me' and could be called 'jazz drama'.[15] We can feel it surfacing in the 'Shakespeherian' lines from his own 1922 sequence, with its insertion of the sound of 'hear' into 'Shakespeherian', and mix of 'high-brown' and 'low-brow', Germanic Wagner, and what *Melody* calls 'American musical genius'.[16]

Alex Ross's account of European and American music is entitled *The Rest is Noise: Listening to the Twentieth Century* and *The Waste Land* could be sub-titled 'Listening to the Twentieth-Century, London, 1922'.[17] For it, too, the relationship between music and noise is primary. As both its notes and its early reception foreground, *The Waste Land* is famously haunted by traditional cadences as well as allusions to earlier literary culture. But it is also simultaneously alert to the syncopated, fragmented, dissonant idioms of Wagner and of modernist composers like Stravinsky and Satie as well as popular jazz.[18] Eliot and his first wife Vivien were both popular dance affi-cionados, as well as being devotees of the Ballets Russes ('the finest ballet

[13]   J.E. Hasse, *Ragtime: Its History, Composers, and Music* (New York: Schirmer Books, 1985), 4.

[14]   Cited in Ted Tjaden, 'The Interplay between Classical Music, Ragtime and Jazz'. http://www.ragtimepiano.ca/rags/classical.htm.

[15]   *The Letters of T.S. Eliot*, vol. 2, 192.

[16]   For a fuller discussion of Eliot and Rag-time, see David Chinitz, *T.S Eliot and the Cultural Divide* (Chicago, IL: University of Chicago Press, 2003), 8–52.

[17]   Alex Ross, *The Rest is Noise: Listening to the Twentieth Century* (London: Fourth Estate, 2012).

[18]   Writing from Margate in October 1921, Eliot asked Richard Aldington whether he liked *Fanfare: A Musical Causerie*, which had carried statements of support not only from Eliot himself, but de Falla and Satie. *The Letters of T.S. Eliot*, vol. 1, 591.

in Europe', according to his 'Commentary' in *The Criterion* in 1924), and of Massine in particular. Eliot lived in the early jazz age and the resonant aftermath of *The Rite of Spring* and, like the jaded post-coital typist in his poem, liked stooping to put a record on the gramophone. The 'King of Ragtime' Scott Joplin wrote a popular and haunting piano piece from 1902 called 'Elite Syncopations' and if *The Waste Land* has a reputation for being the epitome of modernist elitism and/or elite modernism, it is also a poem of syncopations, inflected by rag-time and stylish musical pastiche, as well as by verse music from the past in warped echoic forms. In this, it is not unlike Stravinsky's turn to 'neo-classicism' in the early 1920s, described by Taruskin not as 'pastiche but an ironic mixture of styles in which everything is used with equal self-consciousness and nothing can be taken stylistically for granted.'[19] It is also, however, a response to the echoic soundscape of the modern metropolis.

*   *   *

Eliot's poem inevitably takes on a different site-specific resonance in rela-tion to its two original places of publication, London and New York, where it appeared in Eliot's own *The Criterion* as well as *The Dial* in 1922. Set in post-war London in the wake of the First World War, it generates a music of syncopated metropolitan crisis as well as more obliquely of the poet's per-sonal and poetic crisis. In a letter of 7 April 1921 to Richard Aldington, Eliot throws some light on his traumatic sense of the political situation. He talks of 'having only contempt for existing political parties, and profound hatred of democracy' as well as feeling 'the blackest gloom':

> Whatever happens will be another step towards the destruction of Europe. The whole of contemporary politics etc. oppresses me with a continuous physical horror like the feeling of growing madness in one's brain. It is rather a horror to be sane in the midst of this: it is too dreadful, too huge, for one to have the comforting feeling of superiority. It goes too far for rage.[20]

That 'hatred of democracy' sounds a disturbingly dissonant note, reminding us that Eliot was a self-consciously reactionary poet even before *For Lancelot Andrewes* and *After Strange Gods*. It also suggests the breakdown of any clear demarcation between the personal and political; a sense of horror, madness, and destruction that encompasses his 'brain'. In a later lecture at Harvard,

---

19   Richard Taruskin, *Music in the Early Twentieth Century* (Oxford: Oxford University Press, 2010), 482.
20   *The Letters of T.S. Eliot*, vol. 1, 550.

Eliot gave a rather different gloss on his state of mind when writing *The Waste Land*, saying that 'various critics have done me the honour to interpret [it] in terms of a criticism of the contemporary world' but 'to me it was only the relief of a personal and wholly insignificant grouse against life; it is just a piece of rhythmical grumbling.'[21] His terms 'grouse' and 'grumbling' strategically displace attention from his 'criticism of the contemporary world' but also downplay the intensity of the 'rhythmical' force of the poem and its psychological origins.

We are bound to be sceptical about Eliot's display of discomfort, given the scale of his patently ambitious, poly-allusive, palimpsest of a poem, by far the longest and most comprehensively-composed text of his to that point. Nonetheless, the relationship between 'physical horror' towards the contemporary world on the one hand, and the 'personal' and the 'rhythmical' on the other, goes to the heart of this uniquely sonic text. In his great study on *A Transnational Poetics*, Jahan Ramazani argues that in modernism 'poetic compression demands that discrepant idioms and soundscapes, tropes and subgenres, be forced together with intensity' and few texts do this with as much intensity as *The Waste Land*.[22]

Ramazani's term 'soundscape' returns us to music as well as the pioneering work of Murray Schafer, particularly *The Soundscape: Our Sonic Environment and the Tuning of the World* (1977, reprinted 1994). Schafer offers an account of the seismic transformation of the entire sound world during the late nineteenth and early twentieth centuries as a result of urbanisation, industrialisation, and mechanisation, charting its effect on both music and the human environment. In his chapter on 'The Meeting of Music and Environment', Schafer argues that 'From our point of view the real revolutionary of the new era was the Futurist experimenter Luigi Russolo', who not only invented numerous mechanical noise-makers, but in 1913 published a manifesto entitled *L'Arte dei Rumori* (*The Art of Noises*). In it, Russolo argues that 'Noise was not really born before the 19th century, before the advent of machinery'. Schafer quotes the following passage:

> Let's walk together through a great modern capital, with the ear more attentive than the eye, and we will vary the pleasures of our sensibilities by distinguishing among the gurglings of water, air and gas inside metallic pipes, the rum-

[21] A quotation from Theodore Spencer during a lecture at Harvard University, recorded by Eliot's brother Henry, cited in *The Waste Land: A Facsimile and Transcript*, edited by Valerie Eliot (London: Faber, 1971), 1.
[22] Jahan Ramazani, *A Transnational Poetics* (Chicago, IL: University of Chicago Press, 2009), 4.

bling and rattlings of engines breathing with obvious animal spirits, the rising and falling of pistons, the stridency of mechanical saws, the loud jumping of trolleys on their rails, the snapping of whips, the whippings of flags. We will have fun imagining our orchestration of department stores' sliding doors, the hubbub of the crowds, the different roars of railway stations, iron foundries, textile mills, printing houses, power plants and subways.[23]

We might also say that Russolo, and Eliot after him, was writing under the spell of Marinetti's *Futurist Manfesto* of 1901, where the charismatic and dogmatic Italian spokesman of the Future reported that: 'Under our windows we suddenly heard the famished roar of automobiles. "Let's go!" I said.'[24] We have already noted Eliot's repeated question 'What is that noise?'; and comparable 'noise' becomes a crucial dimension of Eliot's poem, including (briefly) the noise of automobiles in 'The Fire Sermon', the central section of the poem where we are aware of the poet walking through the kind of 'great modern capital' Rossolo mentions.

I have already noted Eliot's admiration for Stravinsky, and while finishing the drafting of *The Waste Land*, Eliot addressed his work directly in one of his 'London Letters' for *The Dial*. Here he raises precisely the relationship between noise and music, modernity and rhythm:

Whether Strawinsky's [*sic*] music be permanent or ephemeral I do not know; but it did seem to transform the rhythm of the steppes into the scream of the motor horn, the rattle of machinery, the grinding of wheels, the beating of iron and steel, the roar of the underground railway, and the other barbaric cries of modern life; and to transform these despairing noises into music.[25]

These words are reminiscent of Eliot's remarks on the relationship between art and modern life in '*Ulysses*, Order and Myth' (1923), a response to another hyper-musical modernist text, but they also represent a revealing take on the Russian composer's new sound world. Charles Rosen has written that '[i]n both *Le sacre du printemps* and *Les noces* the disruption of the bodily expectations of rhythm and accent are essential parts of the tradition of the sentiment of the twentieth-century', a century where 'the density of the attacks on

[23]   Quoted in Schafer, *The Soundscape*, 110–11.
[24]   Cited in Gary Leonard, 'The famished roar of automobiles': Modernity, the Internal Combustion Engine, and Modernism' in *Disciplining Modernism*, edited by Pamela L. Caughie (London: Palgrave Macmillan, 2009), 221.
[25]   'London Letter', *Dial*, September 1921, cited in *The Annotated Waste Land with Eliot's Contemporary Prose*, edited by Lawrence Rainey (New Haven, CT: Yale University Press, 2005), 189.

our bodily reliance on regular rhythm and harmonic resolution was greater ... than at any time before.'[26] Like Eliot's poem, *The Rite of Spring* continually shifts its rhythmic pulse, abruptly and unpredictably changing its time signature from bar to bar. Of its 'Sacrificial Dance', Taruskin says its 'metric processes' are 'mosaic', 'concretized in specific, discrete and (above all) minuscule "tesserae", with the variations in the ostensible "metric" patterns actually reflecting permutations of the order in which these tiny fixed elements are juxtaposed.'[27] Much the same could be said of the constantly shifting, line-by-line metrics of *The Waste Land*, which also combines violent rhythmic disruption with recreations of archaic myth. *The Rite of Spring* was based on the research into Russian myth, ritual and music by the Slavic painter and archaeologist Nikolai Roerich, and its archaism anticipates *The Waste Land*, with its comparable re-mashed allusions to J.G. Frazer's *The Golden Bough*. The poem, after all, opens with another rite of spring ('April is the cruellest month'), built around the 'despairing' or 'barbaric cries of modern life.'[28] Though initially composed for Diaghilev's Ballets Russes in Paris and premiered there in 1912, Stravinsky's ballet does not itself reflect on the modern metropolis as Eliot's poem does. Eliot's account of Stravinsky's musical modernity in the London letter, with its translation of 'noise' to 'music', is more suggestive of the whole acoustic environment of his own poem – and its literary method.

Other composers were more attuned to acoustic modernity. Eliot is unlikely to have been aware of Arseny Avraamov's contemporary 1922 composition *Symphony of Factory Sirens*, performed in Baku in the year of *The Waste Land*, which involved 'ship sirens, bus and car horns, foghorns, machine guns, and a steam-whistle machine.'[29] Nonetheless, *The Waste Land* is part of the same musical *Zeitgeist*. Eliot must, however, as Nancy Hargraves has argued, have been aware of the premier of Satie's *Parade* in Paris in 1917, or at least its London debut in 1919. The Satie/Cocteau/Picasso/Diaghilev ballet made hay with such extra-musical materials as a dynamo, Morse code machine, steam engine, airplane motor, sirens and typewriters. Eliot's remarks on Stravinsky situate Stravinsky's music squarely in the modern city, and his reference to 'horns and motors, which shall bring / Sweeney to Mrs Porter in the spring' (lines 197–8) typify the new ambient soundscape we

---

[26]   Charles Rosen, *Music and Sentiment* (New Haven, CT and London: Yale University Press, 2010), 128–9.
[27]   Taruskin, *Music in the Early Twentieth Century*, 184.
[28]   On Stravinsky and Roerich, see Taruskin, *Music in the Early Twentieth Century*, 170–90.
[29]   See the Wikipedia entry on Arseny Avraamov: http://en.wikipedia.org/wiki/Arseny_Avraamov.

see in *The Waste Land*. Early in 'The Fire Sermon', we are told 'the human engine waits / Like a taxi throbbing waiting' (lines 216–17), before the poem unnervingly segues to 'I, Tiresias' speaking of 'throbbing between two lives' (line 218), thereby collapsing the boundary between human and machine in 'the human engine.' The projection of the trans-historical, trans-sexual Tiresias out of Oedipus and Ovid onto the London taxi changes both. It is as much part of the acoustic world of 'The Fire Sermon' as 'the gramophone' (line 256), conjuring two new machines that enter intimately into human consciousness in the contemporary London of the poem: the motor car and the record player.[30] This is not really a poem of ideas, but a reflex of what the Russian poet Osip Mandelstam called 'The Noise of Time', as it was heard in Eliot's own time in post-war London.[31]

In a letter of 1922, in which he discusses sending the now published manuscripts of the poem to John Quinn, Eliot said that: 'Perhaps the greatest curse of my life is noise and the associations which imagination immediately suggests with various noises.'[32] The association with the composition of the poem published that year is telling, as is the connection between noises themselves and associations. Noises and associations – and even the noise of associativeness itself – are primary materials Eliot is working with. We can see this in the theatrically entitled 'The Game of Chess', which we have already quoted ('"What is that noise?" / The wind under the door', lines 117–18). The voice asking about noise is in quotation marks, whereas the answers given by the implicit second speaker have none, complicating the relationship between noises and voices while foregrounding the importance of that question, 'What is that noise?', to the relationship between noise and meaning.

It arises again with another question at the end, where an unknown voice asks in 'What the Thunder Said': 'What is that sound high in the air / Murmur of maternal lamentation' (lines 367–8). 'A murmur' is a vocal noise where you cannot quite catch what is being said (by the Thunder or the lamenting mothers). The words 'noise' and 'murmur' both speak of acoustic realities that are not reducible to semantic analysis, phenomena the poem is

---

[30] Cf. Hart Crane in *The Bridge* (1930): 'The phonographs of hades in the brain / Are tunnels that re-wind themselves, and love / A burnt match skating in a urinal.' Hart Crane, *Complete Poems and Selected Letters*, edited by Langdon Hammer (New York: Library of America, 2006), 68.

[31] 'My desire is not to speak about myself but to track down the age, the noise and the germination of time.' Osip Mandelstam, *The Noise of Time and Other Prose Pieces*, translated by Clarence Brown (London: Quartet Books, 1988), 109.

[32] *The Letters of T.S. Eliot*, vol. 1, 750.

acutely sensitive to, like the 'sighs short and infrequent' (line 64) heard on London Bridge in Part I, or the 'chatter' (line 262) in the bar in Part III, the bones picked 'in whispers' (line 316) in Part IV or the woman's 'whisper music' (line 379) in Part V. The drafts, assembled into Ricks and McCue's 'Editorial Composite' offer two more uses of 'noise', as when we hear of 'faint perceptions of the noise / Of the movement, and the lights!' (lines 346–7) and its absence when we are told of someone 'Who only knows that there is no noise now' (line 357).

While revising the text for publication and boiling down these drafts into the final version, Eliot had a serious nervous breakdown, spending time on leave from the bank in Margate and in a clinic in Lausanne in Switzerland. There he told his brother Henry that 'at least there are people of many nationalities, which I always like.'[33] He told another friend that the 'chief recommendation' of Switzerland was that it was 'full of foreigners – American countesses, Russian princesses Rumanians, Greeks and Scandinavians, Czecho counts, Belgian punks etc.'[34] This is true of the sound world of the poem he was completing too, where at the outset we hear someone saying 'Bin gar keine Russin, stamm' aus Litauen, echt deutsch' ('I'm not Russian, I'm from Lithuania, genuinely German', line 12), while later someone called 'Mr Eugenides the Smyrna merchant' speaks 'in demotic French' (lines 209–12) and we hear of the death of the patently anachronistic corpse of 'Phlebas the Phoenician' (line 312). If we add the manifestly Greek Tiresias, it is quite an international cast list and lends a particular polyglot resonance to the poem, comparable to the international ambience Eliot enjoyed in Lausanne. Much of the musical and cultural force of the poem depends on its vision of London as full of foreigners and foreignness, and overlaid with other places, as when its 'Falling towers' are listed tersely in broken, unpunctuated lines in 'What the Thunder Said' alongside other capitals: 'Jerusalem Athens Alexandria / Vienna London / Unreal' (lines 375–7).

The text is notoriously peppered with non-English words – German ('Frisch weht der wind', line 31), French ('hypocrite lecteur, mon semblable', line 76), Italian ('Poi s'ascose', line 428), and Sanskrit ('Damyata', line 433). This offers an international frame of literary reference, of course, but it also creates an international sonic effect. It situates English in a polyglot auditory world. The poem is alive to the music of speech, and rather than being mediated through the poet's diegetic voice, is created out of a cacophony of voices. The poem is full of different, mainly unnamed speakers – whose speech is

---

33 Ibid., 200.
34 Ibid., 614, 617.

sometimes framed with quotation marks or with speech-marked indenta-
tions, but mainly spliced together without obvious joins or separations or
indications of who exactly is speaking. It is also notoriously, full of the voices
out of earlier texts – in the form of quotations from Dante, Shakespeare,
Marvell, Wagner, Kyd, and a host of others (another case of 'So many, / I
had not thought death had undone so many'). This is particularly vivid in
the final moments of the poem, following the play on the perfectly in-place
nursery rhyme echoing in 'London Bridge is falling down falling down falling
down' (line 426). The effect is to make us hear numerous languages and styles
of language, voices from different historical and geographical cultures, speaking by turns across each other and to each other and over each other, generating an acute sense of overwhelming cultural crisis as well as a spell-binding
polyglot polyphonic fugato music:

> Poi s'ascose nel foco che gli affina
> Quando fiam uti chelidon – O swallow swallow
> Le Prince d'Aquitaine à la tour abolie
> These fragments I have shored against my ruins
> Why then Ile fit you. Hieronymo's mad againe.
> Datta. Dayadhvam. Damyata.
> > Shantih   shantih   shantih (lines 427–33)

A nursery rhyme, associated with the bridge near Eliot's place of work, triggers a whirlwind of fragments. We hear the Italian of his beloved Dante in
Purgatory ('Then he hid him in the fire that refines them') where Dante
quotes the Provençal of his fellow-poet Arnaut Daniel praying 'Sovegna vos
del temps de mon dolor' ('be mindful in due time of my pain'), followed by
the Latin of the Spring poem *Pervigilium Veneris* ('when I shall be as the
swallow', a salient part of the sentence 'when I shall be as the swallow, that
I may cease to be voiceless'), a fragment that in turn triggers, as by Freudian
association, Tennyson's 'O Swallow, Swallow, flying South' from *The Princess*
and Swinburne's 'Swallow, my sister, O sister swallow'). The poem then
jumps to the opening line of De Nerval's 'El Desdichado', an Orphic poem
about surviving a trip to Hell, and on to fragments from a mad scene from a
Revenger's Tragedy ('Why then I'll fit you. Hieronymo's mad againe'), and
then broken words from a Sanskrit *Upanishad*, that returns us to Eastern
Religion (as in the Buddha's 'Fire Sermon'). The shattered jigsaw of splin-
tered allusions offer condensed references to high points of literary history
which mattered deeply to Eliot, turning on moments of pain, ruin, crisis, and
madness. Crisis finds utterance in a broken, allusive music – a score created
out of quotations and allusions, that 'range of allusion' that Ellison describes
as being 'as mixed and as varied as that of Louis Armstrong'.

Readers and critics of the poem have been made hyper-aware of the poem's allusiveness – this is a poem where it is impossible to know what is and is not a quotation or who is being quoted or doing the quoting. Quotation generates its own complex, indeterminate musical texture. It is the *sound* of the different languages, the music of words originating in different languages and texts from the literary past, harmonising, or dis-harmonising together, that we hear.

*   *   *

In order to foreground the poem's signature music – or musical signature – I want to turn to Eliot's most concerted conjuring of the music of the modern city in a paragraph in its central section, 'The Fire Sermon'. This is the passage which follows on the Sex and the City scene where the resurrected prophet Tiresias watches a male twentieth-century office worker and a female typist act out an erotic encounter in her cramped inner-city apartment, where her sofa bed is covered with underwear ('Stockings, slippers, camisoles, and stays', line 227). It is an almost cinematic scene of everyday metropolitan domesticity, ending with the typist putting on a record. It is followed and framed by one of Eliot's most haunting musical evocations of London:

> 'This music crept by me upon the waters'
> And along the Strand, up Queen Victoria Street.
> O City city, I can sometimes hear
> Beside a public bar in Lower Thames Street,
> The pleasant whining of a mandoline
> And a clatter and a chatter from within
> Where fishmen lounge at noon: (lines 257–63)

The first thing to note is that the lines themselves are *about* being haunted by music, and they follow the poem's most direct allusion to modern musical technology, when we are told the post-coital typist 'smoothes her hair with automatic hand / And puts a record on the gramophone' (lines 255–6). This reminds us that the unspecified music she is playing represents music in Walter Benjamin's 'age of mechanical reproduction', a sign of the quantum leap that occurred in the first quarter of the twentieth century and enabled people to 'play' (and hear) music in a completely new sense due to its technological reproduction in 'record' form. The poem puts on record a scene of putting a record on the gramophone. Eliot's suavely prosaic pentameter ends the seduction scene and its final equivocal cadence ends on the sound (and sense) of the word marking the new sound technology: 'And puts a record on the gramophone'. Like Tiresias earlier, and the Ionian church later, the word 'gramophone' derives from Greek, being a compound of the word 'gramma' (meaning 'something written') and 'phono' (meaning 'of or related to sound, acoustic'). In other words, it captures the gist of Eliot's enterprise here, the registering of ambient sound in graphic form.

The gramophone here is more than an incidental contemporary detail like the 'silk hat' or 'camisoles'. It draws attention to the way the poem records new ways of hearing and reproducing music, responding to a new automated technology of reproduction as well as source of unprecedented musical sounds. Reproduction of music and the ambient sounds of the city are crucial in the poetic technology of Eliot's poem. Thanks to sound recordings, we are able to hear Eliot's own reading of the passage in question at different times for gramophone records, and on a record-sleeve he wrote that 'Good poetry ought to be read aloud', it offers a 'guide to the rhythms'. This presumably includes what he calls this poem's 'rhythmical grumbling.'[35] One of the first people to have heard him read it was Virginia Woolf, who records the event in her diary for Sunday 11 June 1922. She was particularly struck by how he 'rhythmed it':

> Eliot dined last Sunday & read his poem. He sang it & chanted it rhythmed it. It has great beauty & force of phrase; symmetry; & tensity. What connects it together I'm not so sure. But he read till he had to rush ... and discussion thus was curtailed. One was left, however, with some strong emotion. The Waste Land it is called; & Mary Hutch, who has heard it more quietly, interprets it to be Tom's autobiography – a melancholy one.[36]

Nothing gives stronger evidence of the essentially musical and auditory reality of the poem as Eliot conceived and performed it in the year of its publication.

The passage itself is actually about words, rhythms and music emanating from another place and time (as well as another text), as they are heard sounding or re-sounding in the streets of 1920s London (or wherever we are reading today, in Hong Kong, London, New York, Beirut, or Tokyo). Though this is not quite the same as the way the typist's record reproduces music from elsewhere, it is analogous to it (as in her work as a typist she reproduces spoken words in written form, and she reproduces recorded sounds recorded elsewhere in her London flat). These intensely musical lines begin with the experience of music, music heard in the streets in the heart of the City (with a capital C) as well as in the city of London more generally. Both cities – or both senses of the city – are captured visually (if not audibly)

35 Author's note, HMV recording of *Four Quartets*.
36 *The Diary of Virginia Woolf*, Volume 2: 1920–24, edited by Anne Olivier Bell and Andrew McNeillie (Harmondsworth: Penguin, 1981), 178.

in the printed line 'O City city' (upper case, lower case). The repeated noun phrase ('O City city') is one of countless repetitions in the poem and has a particular acoustic electricity. The poetic opening – 'This music crept by me on the water' – is of course a quotation from *The Tempest*, bringing not only Shakespeare's Jacobean play into post-war London, but Ariel's haunting music, recalled by Ferdinand on the desert island, which Caliban had also earlier evoked in terms of noise and music:

... the isle is full of noises,
Sounds and sweet airs, that give delight, and hurt not.
Sometimes a thousand twangling instruments
Will hum about mine ears; and sometime voices ... (Act 3, scene 2)

Ferdinand's recall of Ariel's 'Full Fathom Five', sponsors a journey through a twentieth-century London geography, marked by street names. Eliot's London streets are local toponymic allusions, drawing on streets named for a monarch, the river, and the river bank. The rather archaic apostrophe 'O city', as well as quotation from the great French city poet Baudelaire, echoes earlier comparably archaic-Shakespearian apostrophes in the poem: 'O keep the dog far hence', 'O O O O that Shakespeherian Rag', and 'O the moon shone bright on Mrs Porter', all of which insist on the sonic instant of utterance and inject an off-key lyricism into the modern urban stream.

Music in the city – *sounded in the city* – is Eliot's focus here.[37] This provides the keynote to this allusive, polyphonic topographical and toponymical paragraph, built around London place names. Beginning with that uncanny creeping music, or a voice talking about creeping music, the syntax records the music moving acoustically with the speaker 'along the Strand, up Queen Victoria Street' to a place where he says 'I can sometimes hear / Beside a public bar in Lower Thames Street, / The pleasant whining of a mandolin / And a clatter and a chatter from within.' In this musical epiphany in the London streets, Eliot foregrounds the verb 'hear', which hangs suspended at the end of the line, drawing attention to the acoustic dimension of the text as well as that of the London streetscape. The 'pleasant whining of a mandoline' is crossed with the 'clatter and chatter' of pub-noises: simultaneously registering the thrum of a fashionable instrument, the noise of glasses, and the murmur of conversation in the pub (like that recorded in the final section

---

[37]   For an account of this in Eliot's earlier poetry, see John Xiros Cooper, 'Thinking with your ears: Rhapsody, Prelude, Song in Eliot's Early Lyrics', *T.S. Eliot's Orchestra: Critical Essays on Poetry and Music*, edited by John Xiros Cooper (New York: Garland Publishing, Inc, 2000), 103.

of 'The Game of Chess'). In a letter of 4 November 1921 from the sea-side resort of Margate, written while composing 'The Fire Sermon', Eliot said he had done a rough draft while 'sitting in a shelter at the front', where he would also 'sketch people, after a fashion, and practise scales on the mandoline'.[38] Mandolins were all the rage but Eliot's mandolin sets up a personal connection. In a letter of January 1920 to Mary Hutchinson, Eliot imagined bringing another instrument, saying 'it is a jazz-banjoline I should bring, not a lute'.[39] 'Banjoline' is the French name for a hybrid instrument with a banjo body, and neck of a violin or mandolin, so related to the mandolin Eliot was given by his wife Vivien. In the poem, Eliot's mandolin gets transposed back to the City and the Strand from 'Margate Sands', making ambient noise essential to the poem's sense of music and carrying the poet's instrument into the London streetscape.

Despite the comment from Margate Sands about failure to connect, the poem is full of auditory connections, echoes, repetitions. Crossing voices, crossing sound-effects, and crossing rhythms, are crucial to the suspended, synthetic and echoic acoustic of these lightly-punctuated lines, which also 'sketch people, after a fashion.' They sometimes involve something like practising scales. Odd one-off patterns of sound emerge and disappear, like the two symmetrical 'Str' consonantal compounds in 'And along the *Str*and, up Queen Victoria *Str*eet', and then the assonantal carry-over falling 'r' sounds in 'hear', 'bar' and 'lower' as well as the onomatopoeic 'whining of a mandoline', which is followed by the comparably onomatopoeic internal rhyme of 'a clatter and a chatter'. 'Chatter' reminds us of the founding relation between the poem and speech, which Eliot dwells upon in 'The Music of Poetry', but also suggests that much that is audible is not intelligible – like a 'murmur', it has meaning but not one that is graspable. In the final lines of the paragraph, these subtle, wavering, syncopated sound-patternings are consummated in fully resonating rhymes, firstly between 'mandoline' and 'within', and then by the plangent tonic-like resolution of the final rhyme of 'hold' and 'gold' associated with Wren's St Magnus Martyr.

If Eliot foregrounds the verb 'hear' at the close of the line here, the same verb occupies the same position twice earlier in 'The Game of Chess', each time with a full rhyme (first with 'ear' and then 'year'). The first time is with reference to an uncanny 'rattle of bones' and a 'chuckle' (line 186) – two non-verbal sounds. The second is in response to the internal combustion engine, 'But at my back from time to time I hear / The sound of horns and motors,

---

38   *The Letters of T.S. Eliot*, vol. 1, 600–1.
39   Ibid., 432.

which shall bring / Sweeney to Mrs Porter in the spring' (lines 196–8), a sequence of two-rhymed couplets. At the end of the poem too, a voice reports 'I have heard the key / Turn in the door once', again foregrounding the act of hearing, before going on to speak of the different soundscape of 'aethereal rumours'. Ethereal they may be, but the word 'rumour' comes from the Latin from 'noise' as well as meaning 'hearsay', insisting on the acoustic rather than semantic. In his recent collection *Eavesdropping*, the visually impaired contemporary US poet Stephen Kusisto reports on walking in New York, saying 'I was looking for noises that stirred the imagination,' saying he responded to the 'neural, icy soundscape of a large city', 'waking up to the quick transformations in a soundscape, especially the ugly ones.' The same is true of the poet of *The Waste Land*, moving through his metropolitan echo-chamber in London, and responding to 'noises that stirred' his imagination.[40]

These little sound effects in the paragraph do not advertise themselves, but when read in the context of the opening reference to creeping 'music', we register their irregular, constantly modulating, and syncopated city music. In 1928, Eliot's musical fellow countryman George Gershwin composed his jazz-influenced *An American in Paris*, and we could think of *The Waste Land* as *An American in London*, especially if we read it in terms of the drafts and Composite Ur-Text produced by Christopher Ricks and Jim McCue (Eliot was still technically an American, and did not become a British citizen until 1928). If the Gershwin comparison might seem far-fetched, we should remember that when Eliot was working on the poem, he was writing regular 'London Letters' for the American periodical *The Dial*. In 1919, Eliot told his English friend Mary Hutchinson to 'remember that I am a *metic* – a foreigner', and the original typescript has a much stronger American provenance, as we have seen, including multiple allusions to popular song. Indeed, the poem is full of signs of being written by a *metic*, a foreigner, if not necessarily an American. In 'The Burial of the Dead', walking over London bridge amid the crowd, the speaker addresses an acquaintance who was with him at the battle of Mylae as 'Stetson!' (lines 69–70). This gives him the same name as the world's most popular hat, mass-manufactured in Philadelphia, and more associated with 'the Boss of the Plains Hat' and Westerns rather than a classical Greek sea battle.

With that 'Stetson!' in Part I, and the jazzy 'Shakespeherian Rag' in Part II, Eliot injects a different slant on the London represented by the Cockney pub-scene in 'A Game of Chess'. Eliot's Joycean coinage 'Shakespeherian' (not in the original) incorporates the verb 'hear' into Shakespeare's name.

<hr>

[40]   Stephen Kuusisto, *Eavesdropping* (New York: W.W. Norton, 2006), 123, 75.

The Stetson and the 'Rag' certainly give an American accent to the poem's first part, and, as David Chinitz points out, 'the Manuscript of *The Waste Land* shows Eliot drawing on popular song to a greater extent than the Grail myth in the final version.'[41] This is particularly true of the first section, 'He do the Police in Different Voices', where Eliot drew on Boston memories of vaudeville and popular culture, with lines from 'Harrigan' and references to 'By the Watermelon Vine', a 1904 'coon song', and 'My Evaline', a vaude-ville-minstrel number, as well as a marginal allusion to 'The Cubanola Glide' noted by Valerie Eliot in her edition of the drafts.[42] If this opening Boston scene had been retained, along with the later sailing scene, *The Waste Land* would be more obviously transatlantic, and more aligned to Gershwin in Paris. As it happens, Gershwin incorporated Jazz into his one-act 'vaudeville' opera *Monday Morning Blues* in 1922, as well as the later *Rhapsody in Blue* and *An American in Paris*, while in Paris Stravinsky had already incorporated jazz into *Piano Rag Music* (1919) and *The Soldier's Tale* (1919, which he later described as 'a Russian émigré's dream of Jazz'[43]). The transatlantic 'jazz' dimension of *The Waste Land* is an another émigré's dream.

The 'Inexplicable splendour of Ionian white and gold' (line 265) of Wren's church might seem an instance of the visual rather than auditory imagina-tion, but even here, the 'splendour' is primarily conjured by the ear; indeed, in the drafts Eliot tried out different terms for the church, with 'inviolable music' offered as a discarded earlier version of 'inexplicable splendour'[44]. 'Magnus Martyr' follows in the wake of the earlier 'Saint Mary Woolnoth', a church acoustically recalled via 'the dead sound of the final stroke of nine' (line 68), a short-hand presumably for the moment the commuter arrived at the office. Of this sound, one of the weirdest of Eliot's notorious Notes to the poem records: 'A phenomenon I have often noticed' (note to line 68) In 1923, Eliot told his fellow poet Richard Aldington that his office was '75, Lombard Street, First floor ... opposite clock of St Mary Woolnoth', and the phrase 'Dead sound' shows how alive to sound (and place) the poem is.[45] Going back to St Magnus, the falling cadences of 'inexplicable' and 'splen-dour' (with their clotted '*spl*' sounds) opens out into the expansive tribute to the 'Ionian white and gold' of Wren's church. The topographical, musical, and linguistic adjective 'Ionian' reenforces the association of its names with Christian martyrdom, Latinity ('Magnus') and Classical Greece ('Ionian'),

41 Chinitz, *T.S Eliot and the Cultural Divide*, 43.
42 These lines are listed as variants in *The Poems of T.S. Eliot*, vol. 1, 598.
43 Quoted in Alex Ross, *The Rest is Noise*, 98.
44 Eliot, *The Waste Land: a facsimile and transcript*, 37.
45 Letter of 4 January 1923, *The Letters of T.S. Eliot*, vol. 2, 5.

naming a London church but also opening a vista onto European classical and ecclesiastical tradition. It also, however, evokes the Ionian mode, the name for the diatonic scale in Western Music.

The repeated 'O City, city' echoes his earlier 'Unreal City', which Eliot's note identifies with Baudelaire's 'Fourmillante Cité, cité pleine de rêves', confirming the centrality of Baudelaire for Eliot's poetics of modernity, and subliminally making Paris, though unnamed, one of the poem's palimpsest of capital cities (like Vienna, Jerusalem, Carthage).[46] Jean Starobinski speaks suggestively of Baudelaire's Parisian soundscape in 'Paysage', which speaks of 'the spires, the bell-towers, these masts of the city' evoking 'eternity', noting the coexistence in his cityscape of two worlds where industrial chimneys soar up amid the spires. For Starobinski, this is the characteristic subject (or stance) of modernity: 'Loss of the subject among the crowd – or, inversely, absolute power, claimed by the individual consciousness.'[47] Baudelaire's studio 'qui chante et bavarde' ('sings and chats'), is the precursor of Eliot's pub where 'fishmen lounge at noon', as Baudelaire's 'clochers' or 'bell-towers' anticipate Eliot's evocation of 'the peal of bells / white towers' in the river lyrics (lines 288–9). The church music of St Magnus Martyr's 'inexplicable splendour of Ionian white and gold' has something of this redemptive Baudelairian music, returning us in some measure to something like the self-transcending spell of 'This music crept by me upon the waters' (Act 1, scene 2), and recalling the benumbed, traumatised Ferdinand's coming to consciousness on hearing Ariel's song in *The Tempest*.

*   *   *

That opening line here, 'This music crept by me upon the waters' (line 257), has a stealthy inevitability to it. We recognize it as familiar, though we are unsure about its bearing on contemporary London, or the bearing of Shakespeare's *The Tempest* on the modern city. Eliot's echo of Ariel gives a sense of a double time, with modernity and Renaissance theatricality happening simultaneously, or London and some exotic island colonial other (such as Singapore or Hong Kong). Regardless of its meaning in Shakespeare's play, its reference in Eliot's text is ambiguous – moving in different directions (back to the typist's recorded music and then out into the street, back to Shakespeare and other *Tempest* allusions in the poem recast in a world of gas works and city directors). It comes complete with inverted commas which, unlike many other references, announces its allusive status, but reading it or

---

[46]   Eliot, 'The Lesson of Baudelaire', *Tyro* 1 (March 1921).
[47]   Jean Starobinski, 'Les cheminées et les clochers', *Magazine Littéraire* 280 (September 1990).

hearing it, we do not know what the phrase 'This music' refers to within the poem. If we do not automatically detect the specific creeping allusion in the line itself, the Notes refer us to 'V. *The Tempest*. See above.' There the lines are spoken by Ferdinand, under the spell of Ariel's song:

> Where should this music be? I' th' air or th' earth?
> It sounds no more, and sure, it waits upon
> Some god o' th' island. Sitting on a bank,
> Weeping again the king my father's wrack,
> This music crept by me upon the waters,
> Allaying both their fury and my passion
> With its sweet air. (Act 1, scene 2)

Ariel's words play a structural part in the polyphonic texture of Eliot's city, uncannily crossing Shakespeare's exilic magical island with the modern metropolis, injecting the place with a sense of mourning, exile, bereavement, and magic. As early as in 'The Burial of the Dead', where it is quoted by Mme Sosostris, we hear a fragmentary memory of Ariel's song 'Full fathoms five' ('Those are pearls that were his eyes'), but it is in the second paragraph of 'The Fire Sermon' where the mourning figure of Ferdinand comes into focus, framed in a modern urban landscape, but still 'sitting on a bank' as in Shakespeare. Though city acoustics are not initially the focus of the passage, we need to hear the whole verse paragraph to get the force of Eliot's transposition of 'this music' from Prospero's island to contemporary 1920s London:

> A rat crept softly through the vegetation
> Dragging its slimy belly on the bank
> While I was fishing in the dull canal
> On a winter's evening round behind the gashouse ... (lines 187–90)

We note immediately that, where in *The Tempest*, 'this music crept by me upon the waters', here it is initially the *rat* which 'crept' by, dragging itself on 'the bank.' 'Rattled by the rat's foot', with the play on the 'rat' in 'rattled', generating an eerie punning acoustic. The 'bank' refers to the canal or river bank, as in Shakespeare, but in the wake of 'the loitering heirs of City directors', and our knowledge of Eliot's job in Lloyd's Bank in the city, the reader might pick up on the close affinity here between 'on the bank' and 'in the bank'. Perhaps that word 'bank' helped trigger the echoing of Shakespeare's words at the heart of London in the wake of the poet's own father's death. At any rate, we are given a figure of mourning, caught up in memories of Shakespearian music, heard while the speaker is fishing by a modern canal.

This setting thereafter provides the springboard for an extraordinary acoustic cacophony – a flood of voices, idioms, noises, allusions, and sound effects, at the centre of Eliot's city poem. The couplet rhymes of 'year' and 'hear' and 'bring' and 'spring' generate a series of assonantal sound-patterns, with 'Porter', followed by another 'Porter', 'daughter' and 'soda water' – the effect is like Cole Porter – and then the French poet Verlaine's extraordinarily assonantal line echoing with its four simultaneous '*an*' sounds ('en*fants*, *chantant dans* le coupole'). In his 'L'art poétique' Verlaine proclaimed 'La musique avant toute chose', and the quotation of his intensely musical line from his poem 'Parsifal' about Wagner's opera, with its children singing music in the dome of a church, triggers the series of broken formulaic bird-song noises, a three-beat line followed by a six-beat line of pure onomatopoeia ('Twit twit twit / Jug jug jug jug jug jug'). The result is a kind of exuberant lyric haemorrhage, not far away from the contemporary sound poems of the Dadaist Tristan Tzara in Zurich or the *Zaum* poetry of the Russian transsense poet Khlebnikhov.[48]

In 'The Frontiers of Criticism', Eliot suggests that 'poetic originality is largely an original way of assembling the most disparate and unlikely material to make a new whole.'[49] Later, in his great essay on 'The Music of Poetry', discussing the relation between verse and conversation, he says:

> Of course we do not want the poet merely to reproduce exactly the conversational idiom of himself, his family, his friends and particular district: but what he finds there is the material out of which he must make his poetry. He must, like the sculptor, be faithful to the material in which he works; it is out of sounds that he has heard that he must make his melody and harmony.

The same could certainly be said of the sonic collage assembled in *The Waste Land*. In the same essay, he speaks of the mistaken assumption that 'all poetry ought to be melodious, or that melody is more than one of the components of the music of words'. 'Some poetry is meant to be sung', he says, but 'most poetry in modern times is meant to be spoken'. He also notes that 'Dissonance, even cacophony has its place', and a long poem needs 'a rhythm of fluctuating emotion essential to the musical structure of the whole'.[50] The Shakespearian music that creeps by him on the waters, that is, has to be

---

[48]   Despite Eliot, in 'The Lesson of Baudelaire' (1921), describing Dadaism as 'a disease of the French mind' not 'applicable to London'. Cited in Rainey, *The Annotated Waste Land*, 144.

[49]   T.S. Eliot, *On Poetry and Poets* (London: Faber, 1957), 108.

[50]   Ibid., 32.

taken up into a larger structure where 'Dissonance, even cacophony' plays a part, so that we get his own 'apeneck Sweeney' mixed in with 'Mrs Porter', and a fragment of Verlaine about children's voices singing in Wagner's Grail opera *Parsifal*, mixed in with what Chinitz has identified as a bawdy popular parody of the 'Red Wing'.

David Chinitz has made much of Eliot's interest in American popular music and dance music, while David Fuller notes that Eliot and Stravinsky both incorporated 'popular materials, especially jazz – the most obviously American element in the poetry of Eliot the adopted European, and a mark of Stravinsky's adopted American identity'.[51] Stravinsky actually first made most use of jazz during the post-war Paris years, and *The Waste Land* gathers its affinity with Gershwin's *An American in Paris* because of its incorporation of 'O that Shakespeherian rag' in 'The Game of Chess'. The reference suggests an analogy between the poem's elite syncopations and its Shakespearian allusions, but also gives us a cue (or clue) how to read its jazz-like rhythmic playfulness and understand its tendency to riff on popular tunes. If the music of *The Tempest* creeps by the speaker on the water, it is crossed with other kinds of creeping music, some inescapably modern, all of which embody an unstable, multi-vocal, multi-stylistic modality of the audible.

Murray Schafer's sense of *Our Sonic Environment and the Soundscape* speaks of the sound world of the modern secular city – that of 'horns and motors' – in contrast to 'Sacred Noise' symbolised by 'church bells' and the spectacular 'acoustic events' that once took place in churches. In 'The Music of Poetry', Eliot said 'it is out of sounds that he has heard that [the poet] must make his melody and harmony.'[52] In the case of 'The Fire Sermon' and *The Waste Land* as a whole, the 'sounds he has heard' create a uniquely complex weave of 'melody and harmony' with 'dissonance', incorporating noises, rumours, cacophonies, and many different kinds of songs from Ariel's to 'The Shakespeherian Rag'. Eliot said that from Laforgue:

> I learned that the sort of material that I had, the sort of experience that an adolescent had had, in an industrial city in America, could be the material for poetry; and that the source of new poetry might be found in what had been regarded hitherto as the impossible, the sterile, the intractably unpoetic.[53]

W.H. Auden wrote that T.S. Eliot had 'made it possible for English poetry to deal with all the properties of modern city life, and to write poems in

51   Fuller, 'Music', 135–6.
52   Eliot, *On Poetry and Poets*, 108.
53   T.S. Eliot, *To Criticize the Critic* (London: Faber, 1965), 126.

which the structure is musical rather than logical.'[54] That is true, and it is so in part because the 'experience' his poetry embodies is both 'musical' and acoustic ('the sounds that he has heard'). It puts acousticity into the city, and the modern city into acousticity. Having done this in *The Waste Land*, with the exception of the unfinished *Sweeney Agonistes*, Eliot turned away from such poetic music as he did from the modern metropolis. Though the poem did not resolve the cultural and personal crisis Eliot felt in post-War London in 1922, it managed to turn crisis into art, intolerable noise into memorable music. An unmistakably modern music that sounds as uncannily haunted and haunting a hundred years after first publication.

---

[54]   W.H. Auden, 'The Example of Yeats', in *Prose*, Volume 2: 1939–1948, edited by Edward Mendelson (London: Faber, 2002), 388.

5

Lost and Found in Translation: Foreign Language Citations in The Waste Land

MARJORIE PERLOFF

The Waste Land, as everyone knows, is a collage of allusions to texts in other languages, ranging from Greek and Latin to German, French, Italian, and even Sanskrit in the poem's dramatic conclusion. But although the main allusions have long been identified and their thematic import endlessly explicated and discussed,[1] there is one question that has been oddly overlooked: when and why does Eliot cite a line or passage in the original and when does he translate it? Line 307, for example – 'To Carthage then I came' – is footnoted by Eliot himself as referring to St. Augustine's *Confessions*: 'to Carthage then I came, where a cauldron of unholy loves sang all about mine ears.'[2] In Latin, this sentence from Book 3, Chapter 1, reads, '*Veni Karthaginem, et circumstrepebat me undique sartago flagitiosorum amorum.*' Why did Eliot render Augustine's famous opening words in English when, in line 431, he reproduced the reference to Arnaut Daniel in Dante's *Purgatorio, 'Poi s'ascose nel foco che gli affina'* ('Then he dived into the refining fire'), in the original?

What determines the decision to translate? If we include the epigraph and dedication, there are, by my count, thirteen instances in which Eliot retains the original line or passage – a rather small amount in a poem of 433 lines in which every other line contains an English-language allusion to one literary text or another? I propose here to look at Eliot's foreign-language citations – the distribution is Greek-1, Latin-2, Italian-2, French-4, German-2, Sanskrit-2 – more closely so as to try to understand when and why the original is retained and how successfully these foreign phrases function in the poem.[3]

---

[1]   The monumental Christopher Ricks and Jim McCue edition of *The Poems of T.S. Eliot*, Volume 1 (London: Faber, 2015), contains extraordinarily detailed commentary on and source study of each and every possible allusion in *The Waste Land*.

[2]   See *The Poems of T.S. Eliot*, vol. 1, 75.

[3]   In the case of the citations from Wagner's *Tristan and* Isolde (lines 32–5, line 42), I count the two references as one. In the case of the Sanskrit, I count the repetition of the three words *Datta, Dayadhvam, Damyata*, first used separately and then together in line 432 as one example – one which also includes the name *Ganga* for

The facsimile edition of the *The Waste Land*, with Pound's annotations, provides us with what are probably the most important clues. When Pound, himself the master of citational poetry, was going through Eliot's manuscript, he did not delete a single one of Eliot's foreign-language passages; indeed, the ending of Part V ('What the Thunder Said'), whose last seven lines contain a bewildering sequence of colliding fragments – beginning with the '*Poi s'ascose*' cited above, followed by lines from the *Pervigilium Veneris*, Gerard de Nerval's sonnet, 'El Desdichado,' Thomas Kyd's *Spanish Tragedy*, and the *Brihadaranyaka Upanishad* – was left entirely intact. Moreover, the La Pia passage in 'The Fire Sermon' (lines 291–4), based on a striking passage in Dante's *Purgatorio* V, lines 133–6

> ricorditi di me, che son la Pia:
> Siena mi fe', disfecemi Maremma:
> salsi colui che innanellata, pria
> disponando, m'aveva con la sua gemma[4]

won Pound's highest praise, with a big *echt* (the real thing!) written in the margin.

The interesting thing about the Dante passage above is that Eliot's rendering is in English, whereas what is probably its immediate source, Pound's 'Hugh Selwyn Mauberley' (1920), which Eliot surely knew, used the *Inferno's* line, 'Siena mi fe': Disfecemi Maremma,' as the title of a brilliantly satiric poem about a littérateur 'out of step with his decade' named Mr Verog, who is recalling the drunken antics of Ernest Dowson and friends and consequent decline of poetry in the Yellow Nineties.[5] Pound characteristically emptied the Italian line of its original reference to sexual assault and uses the words of La Pia for ironic purposes. Eliot, in contrast, takes the story quite seriously when he composes the section on the three 'Daughters of the Thames,' with its pathetic tales of acquiescence to unwanted sex.

Here is Eliot's first draft, which wholly lacked the concision of either Dante or Pound:

---

the river Ganges, and *Himavant* for Mt. Everest, since these words all come from the same source.

4   'Remember me, who am La Pia: Siena made me, Maremma unmade me: 'tis known to him who, first plighting troth, had wedded me with his gem.' For the Dante passages, I use the Temple Classics three-volume bilingual edition by Israel Gollancz (London: J.M. Dent, 1954), with its straightforward prose translations. The real Pia was evidently murdered by her husband in her Maremma castle.

5   See Ezra Pound, *Personae: The Shorter Poems*, revised edition, edited by Lea Baechler and A. Walton Litz (New York: New Directions, 1990), 190.

Highbury bore me. Highbury's children
Played under green trees and in the dusty Park.
~~We~~ Mine were humble people and conservative
As neither the rich nor the working class know.
My father had a small business, somewhere in the city
A small business, an anxious business, ~~whi~~ provided/ing only
The house in Highbury, and three weeks at Shankin, Bognor

This is crossed out and a second draft is made:

Highbury bore me, Richmond and Kew
Undid me. At Kew we had tea.
~~At~~/Near Richmond on the river at last I l raised
                                                    my knees
~~Stretched o~~/On the floor of a perilous canoe.

To this, Pound responds 'O.K.' But Eliot tries once more:

Trams and dusty trees.
Highbury bore me. Richmond and Kew
Undid me. ~~Beyond~~ By Richmond I raised my knees
Stretched on the floor of a perilous canoe.

And it this third version, except that 'perilous' is replaced by 'narrow', that
is marked by Pound as *echt*.[6]

Why does Eliot render Dante's passage in English and change the place
names? Siena and Maremma were both towns in Tuscany; Highbury is,
according to Ricks and McCue's notes, 'a dreary lower middle class suburb of
London'; whereas Richmond and Kew, in southwest London, were attractive
districts, the site of outdoor weekend pleasures including canoeing on the
lake at Kew Gardens.[7] For Eliot, the allusions had to support the poem's
larger meaning, the poet's vision. This Pia had to be similar to the other two
anonymous 'daughters of the Thames': all three had to represent the larger
degradation of society in the 'wasteland' of modern non-believers. Pound
might use 'Siena mi fe'; disfecemi Maremma' as a witty title for the undoing
of the late pre-Raphaelite poets; Eliot, by contrast, adapted and transformed
Dante's material for his own thematic purposes.

---

6   T.S. Eliot, *The Waste Land: A Facsimile and Transcript*, edited by Valerie Eliot
(London: Faber, 1972), 51.
7   *The Poems of T.S. Eliot*, vol. 1, 678.

An even more elaborate verbal transformation occurs in the 'Unreal City' passage of Part I. Eliot's own notes refer the famous opening words, 'Unreal City,' to Baudelaire's 'Fourmillante cité, cité pleine de rêves' in 'Les Sept Vieillards,' but the French poet's 'fourmillante' – swarming, bustling – city is anything but 'unreal.' Eliot's phantasmagoria continues with another Dantean allusion: his note acknowledges the debt to two tercets from the depiction of Limbo in *Inferno* III, 55–7 and *IV*, 25–27, or, more accurately, though Eliot does not say so, 25–30:

> e dietro le venia si lunga tratta
> di gente, ch'io non avrei mai creduto,
> che more tanta n'avesse disfatta

> [and behind it came so long a train of people,
> that I should never have believed death had
> undone so many]

> quivi, secondo che per ascoltare,
> non avea pianto, ma' che di sospiri,
> che l'aura eterna facevan tremare

> e ciò avvenia di duol senza martiri
> ch'avean le turbe, ch'eran molte e grandi
> d'infanti e di femmine e di viri.

> [here there was no plaint, that could be heard,
> except of sighs, which caused the eternal air
> to tremble

> and this arose from the sadness, without torment,
> of the crowds that were many and great,
> both of children and of women and men.]

In Eliot's poem, the 'crowds that were many and great' are transferred to the beginning of the passage and are amalgamated with the first two lines from Canto III above:

> Under the brown fog of a winter dawn
> A crowd flowed over London Bridge, so many
> I had not thought death had undone so many. (lines 61–3)

Eliot's terse rendition 'I had not thought death had undone so many' is rendered more powerful by the repetition of 'so many.' And Dante's 'sighs, which caused the eternal air to tremble,' become 'Sighs, short and infrequent, were exhaled, / And each man fixed his eyes before his feet, / Flowed up the hill and down King William Street' (lines 64–6).

The Dante scenario is, in other words, kept intact except that Eliot localizes and specifies, giving us London Bridge and London weather, as well as King William Street, and he eliminates Dante's women and children in order to focus on the mechanized movement of the men, fixing their eyes 'before their feet' as they move along to the City to work.

Such syncretic adaptation was Eliot's characteristic mode: his mind almost intuitively created the necessary variations on his chosen topos, be it Baudelaire's city or Dante's Limbo or Augustine's unholy lusts. All the more reasons foreign citations had to be selected with special care, as was the case with the *Waste Land's* wide-ranging epigraph – ironically, a second choice. Eliot's original choice came from Joseph Conrad's *Heart of Darkness*, where the narrator Marlow relays the dying words of the ill-fated Colonial trader 'Mr. Kurtz,' who is understood, by Marlow, to have lost his soul:

> Did he live his life again in every detail of desire, temptation, and surrender during that supreme moment of complete knowledge?
>   He cried in a whisper at some image, at some vision – he cried out twice, a cry that was no more than a breath –
>   'The horror!   the horror!'[8]

Pound, editing Eliot's first draft, and always more conscious of the *who* than the *what* in poetry, objected to this epigraph on the grounds that 'I doubt if Conrad is weighty enough to stand the citation.'[9] Today, the objection may strike us as ironically off-base, given the great fame of *Heart of Darkness*, not to mention the very real link between its 'horror' and that of *The Waste Land*. But Eliot did not contest Pound's view and chose instead the passage in Chapter 48 of Petronius's late first-century Menippean satire *The Satyricon*, in which the vulgar and ostentatiously rich Trimalchio, boasting of his adventures, declares:

> 'Nam Sibyllam quidem Cumis ego ipse oculis meis vidi in ampulla pendere, et cum illi pueri dicerent: Σίβυλλα τί θέλεις; respondebat illa: ἀποθανεῖν θέλω.'

---

8   *The Waste Land: A Facsimile and Transcript*, 3.
9   *The Poems of T.S. Eliot*, vol. 1, 591.

(I saw with my own eyes the Sibyl at Cumae hanging in a cage, and when the boys said to her, 'Sibyl, what do you want? She answered: 'I want to die.')

The Cumaean Sibyl was the famous prophetess (painted by both Raphael and Michelangelo) who asked Apollo for immortal life but, according to Ovid, forgot to ask for eternal youth and hence withered away, her body growing smaller and smaller with age and finally kept in a jar. Her story is very appropriate for *The Waste Land*, whose inhabitants are the living dead. Eliot, moreover, clearly admired the contrast between Trimalchio's colloquial Latin and the Sibyl's more formal Greek. The contrast between the two foreshadows the mongrelized language of *The Waste Land*, where one speech register quickly morphs into another, emphasizing the complex history and geography incorporated into Eliot's collage poem. Then, too, in Virgil's *Aeneid* (VI 86–87), the Cumaean Sybil prophesied the destruction of Rome – a note of doom that fittingly introduces the poem.

In English translation, the effect of the Latin-Greek contrast is, of course, lost, and so it makes sense for Eliot to cite the passage in the original, with the Greek citation inside the Latin narrative so as to enhance the strangeness of the Sibyl's response. The epigraph thus nicely sets the stage for the image of the 'dead land,' where 'memory and desire' motivate the action. And here the first foreign-language citation, which occurs in the 'Marie' sequence in lines 8–12 is relevant:

> Summer surprised us, coming over the Starnbergersee
> With a shower of rain, we stopped in the colonnade, and went on
> In sunlight, into the Hofgarten,
> And drank coffee, and talked for an hour.
> Bin gar keine Russin, stamm' aus Litauen, echt deutsch.

This, Eliot's first compound portrait in 'The Burial of the Dead,' is a brilliant amalgam of overheard conversation and allusions to Marie Larisch's memoir *My Past* of 1913. Larisch was a cousin of Ludwig II of Bavaria and evidently the confidante of the Austrian Crown Prince Rudolf (*Mayerling*), who committed the double suicide with his mistress Marie Vetsera. The Hofgarten chit chat between upper-class socialites who have come in out of the rain – the life-giving rain of *The Waste Land* – to drink coffee, foregrounds the words of the anonymous society woman, who says, 'Bin gar keine Russin, stamm' aus Litauen, echt deutsch.' The lady protests that she is *not* Russian – a country whose population was considered wild and barbaric by Western Europeans of the World War I years especially after the 1917 Revolution. Her admission that she is Lithuanian gives her away: Lithuania had a large Jewish population at the time and she is, in any case, déclassé since, however much she protests that she is 'echt deutch,' she is obviously not a 'real' (*echt*) German.

The German line encapsulates the anomie and deracinated quality of international café society as Eliot saw it: the mood could not be evoked as effectively in English. The mongrelization of Europe was, we know, one of Eliot's obsessions (and today we would say a deeply racist one!), and even Marie, the genuine aristocrat, is characterized by a free-floating fear that neither a resort in the mountains nor a spa in Italy or Southern France can alleviate.

The German citation from Richard Wagner fits perfectly into this context. The 'fear in a handful of dust' (line 30) that has been running through the poem from the beginning, gives way, for a moment, to a sudden note of hope:

> *Frisch weht der Wind*
> *Der Heimat zu.*
> *Mein Irisch Kind,*
> *Wo weilest du?*

> [Fresh blows the wind
> Toward home.
> My Irish child,
> Where are you lingering?]

This is the song of the young sailor that opens Wagner's *Tristan and Isolde*, an opera Eliot evidently first came to know through his beloved Jean Verdenal in 1911 Paris. The opera opens with Tristan bringing the Irish princess Isolde to Cornwall to be married to Tristan's uncle, King Mark, a journey that will culminate in Tristan and Isolde's drinking of the love potion that induces their oath of undying love. The *Tristan* lines nicely introduce the Hyacinth girl passage, the one moment in *The Waste Land* when love seems possible: 'Looking into the heart of light, the silence' (line 41). But after those words, there is a sharp break, followed by the single German line, '*Oed' und leer das Meer*' ('Desolate and empty the sea', line 42), spoken by the Watchman in Act III of *Tristan*, warning the dying lover, who is back at his ancestral castle in Brittany, that the ship bringing Isolde, for whom he is anxiously waiting, is nowhere in sight. So, in *The Waste Land*, the hyacinth moment, 'the awful daring of a moment's surrender / which an age of prudence can never retract' (lines 404–5), ends in desolation and emptiness.

Is the retention of the German original more than an exoticism? Yes, I think so because in English, 'Desolate and empty the sea' or 'Fresh blows the wind. …' would not be nearly as dramatic or evocative as this passage.

And the minimalism of the lines looks ahead to Verlaine's related treatment of *Parsifal* in 'The Fire Sermon,' where the hellish scene of the second verse paragraph, culminating in the bawdy ballad, 'Oh the moon shone bright on Mrs. Porter / And on her daughter / They wash their feet in soda water' (lines 199–201) gives way to the momentary vision of spiritual beauty in: '*Et O ces voix d'enfants chantant dans la coupole!*' ('And Oh, those voices of children, singing in the church dome!', line 202).[10] Sound, of course, also plays a role in all these instances: *Oéd und leér das Meér*, with its internal rhyme and three stresses on long open vowels deftly conveys the loss of love, contrasting with the jaunty dance rhythms of 'Frísch wéht der Wínd,' just eight lines above it.

There are two more French citations in *The Waste Land*. The last line of 'The Burial of the Dead' cites the final line of Baudelaire's opening poem in *Les Fleurs du Mal:*

> *Tu le connais, lecteur, ce monstre délicat,*
> *– Hypocrite lecteur, – mon semblable, – mon frère!*

In its context – the Stetson passage that so artfully collages the vegetation myth that animates the entire poem with Dante's calling on the shadows in the *Inferno* and John Webster's *White Devil*, with its cruel reference to the Wolf that digs up corpses – Baudelaire's ironic twist, turning his bitterly cruel account of *ennui* right back on his reader, seems at first rather out of place, an intimate lyric address with a very different register from the epic sweep of *The Waste Land*. But on further thought, it can be argued that Baudelaire's '*monstre délicat*' perfectly sets the stage for the profound ennui of the Wastelanders in Part II – the rich lady in 'A Game of Chess', whose mantra is 'What shall we do tomorrow? / What shall we ever do?' (lines 133–4) and the mean-spirited woman in the pub who has nothing to do but gossip about her friends and relatives. Eliot here and then in the portraits of typist and clerk in Part III, sees Baudelaire's *ennui* as the very condition of modern life and the 'hypocrite' reader as equally involved. The inability to *feel*, to have any sexual energy or passion for anything is central throughout the poem, although, unlike the Catholic Baudelaire, the American Protestant T.S. Eliot always looks for a way out:

> O City, city, I can sometimes hear
> Beside a public bar in Lower Thames Street,
> The pleasant whining of a mandoline
> And a clatter and a chatter from within (lines 259–62)

---

[10]   *The Poems of T.S. Eliot*, vol., 656.

Those are not lines Baudelaire could have written. And Eliot himself quickly turns to the image of 'The river sweat[ing]/ Oil and tar' (lines 266–7) and the narrative of the three degenerate Daughters of the Thames. The poet's mood – the next French citation – reverts, in *The Waste Land's* final montage, to Gérard de Nerval's 'Prince d'Aquitaine à la tour abolie' (line 430), the disinherited prince at the broken tower, recapitulating those 'Falling towers' of lines 372–5, those emblems of 'Jerusalem Athens Alexandria / Vienna London / Unreal.'

This brings me to the Sanskrit citations in 'What the Thunder Said.' In the Appendix to *Notes toward a Definition of Culture*, Eliot remarked, 'Long ago I studied the ancient Indian languages, and while I was chiefly interested at that time in Philosophy, I read a little poetry too; and I know that my own poetry shows the influence of Indian thought and sensibility.'[11] Since that time, much has been written on Eliot's use of Indian religious ideas in *The Waste Land*, and specifically his insertion into the text of the Sanskrit words *Ganga* (the Ganges), *Himavant* (Mt. Everest in the Himalayas), the capitalized *DA*, which evidently encompasses the next three – *Datta* (give), *Dayadhvam* (sympathize), *Damyata* (control) – and finally *Sānti*, which Eliot transliterates as *Shantih* and translates in his notes as 'the Peace which passeth understanding.'[12]

'Why ... Dadda, Dayadhvam, Damyata? Or Shantih?,' Eliot's close Harvard friend, the poet Conrad Aiken asked him. 'Do they not say a great deal less for us than "Give: sympathise: control" or "Peace?"' It is a good question. Eliot responded that he was interested, not just in the meaning of these enigmatic words but in how they mean.[13] The distinctions he uses come directly from his reading of C.R. Lanman's 'The Great Forest Upanishad.' The passage in question, cited by the editors of the *Poems of T.S. Eliot*, is worth quoting in full:

Three kinds of children of Praj-pati, Lord of Children, lived as Brahman-students with Praja-pati their father: the gods, the human beings, the demons. ... Living with him as Brahman students, the gods spake, 'teach us, Exalted One.' – Unto them he spake this one syllable Da. 'Have ye under-

[11] T.S. Eliot, *Notes towards the Definition of Culture* (London: Faber & Faber, 1948), 113.
[12] See *Poems of T.S. Eliot*, vol. 1, 77. On pages 698–709 of the commentary, the editors provide the key sources for Eliot's allusions.
[13] See Conrad Aiken, 'An Anatomy of Melancholy,' *Sewanee Review*, 74, no. 1 (Winter 1966), 193. Cited in G. Nageswara Rao's 'Why Sanskrit Words in *The Waste Land*,' *East and West*, 26, no. 3/4 (December 1976), 531–7. I am indebted to this excellent essay in my discussion.

stood?' – We have understood,' thus they spake, 'it was dámyata, control yourself, that thou saidest unto us.' 'Yes,' spake me, 'ye have understood.'

Then spake to him human beings, 'Teach us, Exalted One.' Unto Them he spake that selfsame syllable Da. 'Have ye understood?' – 'We have understood,' thus they spake. 'It was dattá, give, that thou saidest unto us.' – 'Yes, spake he, 'ye have understood.'

Then spake to him the demons. 'Teach us, Exalted One.' – Unto them he spake that selfsame syllable Da. 'Have ye understood?' – 'We have understood,' thus they spake. 'it was dáyadhvam, be compassionate, that thou saidest unto us.' 'Yes,' spake he, 'ye have understood.'

This it is which that voice of god repeats, the thunder, when it rolls 'Da Da Da, that is dámyata, dattá, dáyahdvam. Therefore these three must be learned, self-control, giving, compassion.[14]

'Had Eliot translated [the original Sanksrit words],' G. Nageswara Rao suggests, 'he would have forfeited their whole wealth of evocative power and emotive value so appropriate to the texture of the verse and so indispensable to the intention of the poem'. And he explains: 'What is significant is that the same syllable *da* here conveys different messages to different beings.' The gods, who have so much power, must learn to control themselves, men who are selfish by nature must learn to give, and the demons, 'possessed as they are with diabolic strength,' must learn to be compassionate. 'From the message of the thunder', Rao observes, 'the protagonist realizes the true ideals that make life meaningful. Each ideal sets him to an uncompromising introspective self-scrutiny'.[15] Once the poet has, so to speak, confessed his sins, he is ready to make peace with himself: 'Shall I at least set my lands in order?' Following the tightly woven mosaic of 'fragments' that has been 'shored' against his 'ruins,' the poet is ready to move toward *Shantih*.

Rhetorically and sonically, it all makes good sense. 'Ganga,' with its two hard *g*'s, dramatically points to the holy river, still 'sunken' but, given the breaking of the 'black clouds' over 'Himavant' with their life-giving rain, about to replenish its sacred waters. And the variations on DA – *Datta, Dayadhvam, Damyata* – produce a striking set of chords, representing what the thunder 'said' and carrying the reader to new heights.

Nevertheless, I find the Sanskrit citations somewhat problematic. Who, to begin with, are the gods, demons, and men of Eliot's own world that match the Upanishad's tripartite cast of characters and why, for that matter, this particular triad of imperatives, give, sympathize, control? Then, too, Eliot knew very well that his readers, those who might know a little French and

---

14   *The Poems of T.S. Eliot*, vol. 1, 699.
15   Ibid., 533, 535.

German and might well have studied Latin at school, would not know his Indian sources and would read the Sanskrit primarily as an exotic heightening of the command to *Datta, Dayadhvam, Damyata.* The *control,* ironically enough, is that of the poet himself, demanding assent from his audience to what is a legendary Indian tale.

And there's the rub. The narrative about demons, men, and gods, each group responding to the word DA in their own way, is a little too easy – too pat a response to the chaos and suffering depicted so brilliantly earlier in the poem. Give, sympathize, control: can those admonitions, coming from the Buddha, really transform the world of those crossing London Bridge (now 'falling down falling down falling down'), or strolling in the Hofgarten, or occupying a humble bed-sitting room like the typist who 'lays out food in tins' (line 223)? Or do the Thunder's words speak only to the poet himself, prompting him to recall, vis-à-vis '*Datta*' ('Give'), 'the awful daring of a moment's surrender / Which an age of prudence can never retract,' to repudiate (*Dayadhdvam*) his status as 'each in his own prison,' and finally to be willing, at least hypothetically ('would have'), to respond 'Gaily', when 'invited' by the 'controlling hands,' presumably of God (*Damyata*)? It is a very personal response to what began as a much more public poem. Indeed, the Sanskrit curiously masks the turn to lyric in the last section of *The Waste Land.*

And this raises a further question, this time about the important passage early in the poem that is intentionally *not* translated. The second verse paragraph of 'The Burial of the Dead' draws heavily upon the Hebrew Prophets in the King James Bible. I have italicized the words and phrases that allude to the Bible here:

> What are the roots that clutch, what branches grow
> Out of this stony *rubbish? Son of man,*
> *You cannot say, or guess,* for you know only
> *A heap of broken images,* where the sun beats,
> *And the dead tree gives no shelter, the cricket no relief,*
> *And the dry stone no sound of water.* Only
> *There is shadow under this red rock,*
> *(Come in under the shadow of this red rock),*
> And I will show you something different from either
> Your shadow at morning striding behind you
> Or your shadow at evening rising to meet you;
> I will show my fear in a handful of *dust.* (lines 18–30)

In his notes, Eliot himself here refers us to Ezekiel 2:1–2:5 and 6:4 and Ecclesiastes 12:5, while the reference 'Come in under the shadow of this red

rock' and 'handful of dust' come from Isaiah 32:3 and 2:10 – all from the
King James Bible:

Ezekiel 2:1–2:5
And he said unto me, Son of man, stand upon thy feet, and I will speak
unto thee.
And the spirit entered into me when he spake unto me, and set me upon
my feet, that I heard him that spake unto me.
And he said unto me, Son of man, I send thee to the children of Israel, to
a rebellious nation that hath rebelled against me: they and their fathers have
transgressed against me, even unto this very day.
For they are impudent children and stiffhearted. I do send thee unto them;
and thou shalt say unto them, Thus saith the Lord GOD.
And they, whether they will hear, or whether they will forbear, (for they
are a rebellious house,) yet shall know that there hath been a prophet among
them.

Ezekiel 6:4
And your altars shall be desolate and your images shall be broken:
And I will cast down your slain men before your idols.

Ecclesiastes 12:5
Also when they shall be afraid of that which is high, and fears shall be in
the way, and the almond tree shall flourish, and the grasshopper shall be a
burden, and desire shall fail: because man goeth to his long home, and the
mourners go about the streets.

Isaiah 2:10
Enter into the rock, and hide in the dust, from the terror of the Lord and
the glory of His majesty.

Isaiah 32:3
And a man shall be as an hiding place from the wind, and a covert from
the tempest; as rivers of water in a dry place, as the shadow of a great rock in
a weary land.

The 'Son of man,' in this scheme of things, is badly needed to bring about
renewal from the Waste Land landscape with its 'roots that clutch,' 'stony
rubbish,' and 'heap of broken images.' Ecclesiastes' flowering 'almond tree' is
replaced by 'the dead tree [that] gives no shelter,' the green grasshopper, once
capable of quick, agile movement, replaced by the black 'cricket' that brings
'no relief,' and with 'the dry stone no sound of water.' But not all is gloom:
the poet is attentive to Isaiah's call to 'Enter into the rock, and hide in the

dust, / From the terror of the Lord.' Isaiah suggests that 'man shall be as an hiding place from the wind' and 'as the shadow of a great rock in a weary land.' Eliot's rock is 'red,' suggesting the strength of fire or the sun, but man cannot confront the 'red' directly; he must 'come in under the shadow of this red rock,' and his own shadow becomes a source of 'fear in a handful of dust.'

Biblical imagery runs through *The Waste Land*, but what is important to note, in the context of the Latin epigraph and Sanskrit ending, is the total absence of that other ancient language – Hebrew. The Prophets and Ecclesiastes could, after all, be quoted from the Hebrew Bible where they originate rather than from the King James. But for Eliot such an idea would have seemed preposterous. Certainly Hebrew was taught at Harvard and Oxford during Eliot's tenure at these universities, but it was a subject for Biblical scholars, not Liberal Arts students – much less, gentlemen. Sanskrit was exotic and romantic: one was pleased to dabble in Indian thought – as long as the India in question was ancient, not modern. But the Old Testament was somehow regarded by educated Anglophone speakers of Eliot's day as the domain of the King James Bible. Of course one cited one's Isaiah or Ezekiel from the KJB: it was as if the prophets had spoken in English.

Robert Alter, who has over the last decade produced a monumental and highly praised translation of the entire Hebrew Bible, argues, in a little book called *The Art of Biblical Poetry*,[16] that Old Testament Hebrew was rich in puns, double entendres, complex metaphors, and sonic play, especially in the *Song of Solomon* and the *Book of Prophets*. And yet the Eliot who does cite the Upanishads would not have dreamt of trying to track down the original language or wording of his Biblical citations. To put it another way, '*Poi s'ascose nel fuoco che gli affina*' may be cited in the original Italian, but the words of the prophets remain the property of Renaissance England.

A century later, now that Hebrew is widely studied, this telling omission will surely raise eyebrows. And the mention of Dante's Italian brings me back to the poem's dedication, which I have not yet considered: 'For Ezra Pound: *il miglior fabbro*' ('the better craftsman'). Arnaut Daniel, the Provençal troubadour poet, seen in *Purgatorio XXVI* as submitting to the refining fires of Purgatory so as to purge himself of sexual lust, was one of Dante's favourite poets: he praises Arnaut for being 'il miglior fabbro del parlar materno ('of the mother tongue') – in this case, the vernacular rather than the Latin which was still the 'literary' language of his day. But in this

---

[16] Robert Alter, *The Art of Biblical Poetry* (New York: Basic Books, 2011). Cf. Robert Alter, *The Art of Bible Translation* (Princeton, NJ: Princeton University Press, 2019); and Robert Alter, *The Hebrew Bible: Translation with Commentary*, 3 volumes (New York: W.W. Norton, 2018).

context, Eliot's comparison of Pound to Arnaut is not entirely complimentary, Dante, everyone would agree, being a much greater poet than Arnaut. For Eliot to use Dante's phrase in praising Pound is, in fact, to compare himself to Dante. Pound-Arnaut may well be 'the better craftsman' but the reader is to understand that Eliot-Dante is surely the greater poet. And many of Eliot's readers would agree.

We know that Eliot was deeply grateful to Pound for his revisions of *The Waste Land*. Pound in essence made the published poem what it is. But we also know that Eliot always had his doubts about Pound's poetry. He praises the metrics as well as translations, but on the subject of *The Cantos*, Eliot says as little as possible. Indeed, his correspondence and critical prose make clear that he never quite approved of Pound's poetics. And so the dedication is produced in a foreign language, in which it sounds as complimentary as it is terse. A moment's thought, however, reveals that *Il Miglior Fabbro* is something of a backhanded compliment.

Eliot's foreign-language insertions thus serve as an important index to a set of convictions and contradictions that might otherwise remain hidden. Hebrew, the language of the Jews, was as unfashionable as Sanskrit was considered, in Eliot's circle, as charming and 'different.' French, German, and Dante's Italian were, even after World War I, the languages of European culture, and of course Latin and Greek the admired and necessary classics. The Cumaean Sybil may address us in Greek, but you will not find the woman in the Hofgarten speaking Lithuanian, nor will Phlebas the Phoenician utter a word of that other Semitic language. As for the Words of the Prophet, in the multilingual, multicultural landscape of *The Waste Land*, those words are inscribed in the Biblical English everyone could recognize.

But then English itself has a curious status in *The Waste Land*: Eliot's poem may be said to dramatize the moment when the poet's own language seems to break down, as other languages and hence their cultures impinge upon it, breaking all norms of consistency or uniformity. In this sense, *The Waste Land* is indeed a war poem. But change was imminent. After 1922, Eliot turned away from the language of citation, foreign or otherwise. *Ash Wednesday*, the *Ariel* Poems, and *The Four Quartets* avoid the heterogeneity of multiple languages, opting for a remarkably purified English. Except for Dante's *sovegna vos* ('be mindful'), used in Part IV of *Ash Wednesday*, recalling the need for purgatorial transformation, there is not a single foreign phrase in these late poems. Having experimented with *le côté Ezra Pound* in his earlier years, Eliot firmly – almost ruthlessly – put the Poundian collage mode behind him and became, for better or worse, the more conceptual 'Anglo-Catholic, Classicist, Royalist' poet of the *Four Quartets*.

6

The Poetic Afterlife of The Waste Land

ANDREW MICHAEL ROBERTS

This chapter explores some of the ways in which Eliot's most famous poem remains a significant and sometimes a ghostly presence, in poetry of the later twentieth and early twenty-first centuries.[1] A number of critics have considered its influence on, or parallels with, later poets or poems, some of which will be discussed here.[2] What follows is not by any means a complete survey of its widely-diffused poetic afterlife, but a consideration of both some generally influential elements of *The Waste Land* and examples of how specific poets writing in the last seventy years have engaged with its legacies.

There are many ways of conceiving of a relation between a poem and its potential precursors. The venerable concepts of 'imitation' (with classical and religious origins) and 'influence' are always ready to hand. There are various genre-based categories: 'imitation' again but also parody, pastiche, tribute, version, adaptation. Then there are conceptions which carry a psychological, social or evaluative view of such relation: Harold Bloom's well-known anxiety of influence, which conceives of it in Oedipal (masculinized) and competitive terms is a psychological theory; in contrast, Christopher Ricks's metaphor of friendship uses primarily social terms (such as 'a nod to', 'generosity', 'livingly grateful'). What Ricks proposes is less a theory than a mode of discussion.[3] With grander cultural claims, there is of course Eliot's

---

[1] The poem's critical afterlife is assessed in Anthony Cuda, 'Coda: *The Waste Land*'s Afterlife: The Poem's Reception in the Twentieth Century and Beyond', in *The Cambridge Companion to The Waste Land*, edited by Gabrielle McIntire (New York: Cambridge University Press, 2015), 194–210.

[2] *The Waste Land* is, unsurprisingly, most often evoked in the context of 'late modernist' poetry; for example, Jeremy Noel-Tod compares J.H. Prynne's 'As Mouth Blindness' to the end of Eliot's poem, in terms of a sense that the reader is 'impatiently' dismissed. Jeremy Noel-Tod, 'In Different Voices: Modernism since the 1960s', in *Oxford Handbook of Contemporary British and Irish Poetry*, edited by Peter Robinson (Oxford: Oxford University Press, 2013), 111–19 (114).

[3] Harold Bloom, *The Anxiety of Influence: A Theory of Poetry*, 2nd edition (New York and Oxford: Oxford University Press, 1997); Christopher Ricks, *True Friendship: Geoffrey Hill, Anthony Hecht, and Robert Lowell Under the Sign of Eliot and Pound* (New Haven, CT: Yale University Press, 2010), 15, 17, 39.

own concept of the 'tradition'. While his idea of 'the literature of Europe' as a 'simultaneous order' may now seem monolithic and overly Platonic, the claim that this order is modified by the introduction of new works, that 'the past should be altered by the present', remains resonant and of particular relevance to *The Waste Land*.[4] In contrast to human forms of relation such as rivalry or friendship, 'intertextuality' displaces the relation from author to text, while approaching an encompassing view of all literary texts, in a way which may tend to dissipate specificity of relation.[5] The metaphor of the 'afterlife' of texts, which has become popular in academic circles over the last twenty years or so, brings in connotations of ghostly presence, responding perhaps to the persistent fascination of the gothic, and has a certain appropriateness to a discussion of *The Waste Land*, given the poem's staging of ghostly encounters.

The canonical status of *The Waste Land*, both in academic and critical accounts of modernism and in the popular idea of 'modern' poetry (the latter reflected in parodies and cross-media versions of the poem) is perhaps the most obvious factor in the scope of its influence.[6] There are lines, images, passages and ideas which almost every English-speaking poet and reader will know, whether at first or second hand: the opening inversion of Spring as a time of renewal, the image of the crowd flowing over London Bridge, the pub scene, the idea of fragments, the symbolism of sterility, deserts and water. Echoes of these can readily find their way into later poetry, by design or sometimes even half-conscious memory.[7] The poem's deployment of multiple 'voices' has proved prescient of a persistent fascination with multiplicity and polyvocalism in later twentieth and twenty-first-century writing, while its putative unity (and arguable lack of unity) make it exemplary and a test case for preoccupations and debates around postmodernism.[8] Both these

---

[4]   T.S. Eliot, 'Tradition and the Individual Talent', in *Selected Essays* (1932; 3rd edition, London: Faber, 1951), 13–22 (14).

[5]   See Graham Allen, *Intertextuality* (London: Routledge, 2011), 9–15.

[6]   For example: Wendy Cope's 'Waste Land Limericks', in *Making Cocoa for Kingsley Amis* (London: Faber, 1986), 20–23; Martin Rowson's graphic novel version, *The Waste Land* (London: Penguin, 1990).

[7]   It is beyond the scope of this chapter to chart the influence of *The Waste Land* on other media forms, but it is worth noting an instance such as Michael Tippett's *The Midsummer Marriage*, which has a version of the Fisher King in the form of King Fisher, and a clairvoyant called Madame Sosostris.

[8]   Michael Levenson attempts to 'negotiate between the two assessments, the poem as a submerged unity and the poem as a chaos of fragments'. *A Genealogy of Modernism: A Study of English Literary Doctrine 1908–1922* (Cambridge: Cambridge University Press, 1984), 176.

aspects of the poem are susceptible of conflicting forms of appropriation and reworking. Seen as a dramatic, performative work in which 'voice' is dominant, *The Waste Land* may hold a place within forms of poetry which value the idea of speech, individuality and the evocation of consciousness. Conversely, if the collaging of multiple, conflicting voices is understood (as implied by 'Tradition and the Individual Talent') as an 'escape' from personality towards impersonality, *The Waste Land* can stand as a point of departure for the forms of 'innovative', experimental or alternative poetry which are suspicious of the centrality of subjectivity or voice, often associating this with consumerist ideology or excessive individualism.[9] The hermeneutic instability of *The Waste Land*, its susceptibility to alternative interpretations and modes of reading, enable these different appropriations of its legacy. An account of the poem which takes seriously Tiresias' organizing role and thus sees the poem as in some sense a continuous stream of consciousness offers a different sort of legacy to one which sees the poem as an experimental collage of conflicting forms of discourse, responsive to inter-art modernist techniques and media such as the gramophone. Thus, in keeping with the often paradoxical imbrication of modernist and postmodernist modes, *The Waste Land* could be seen to follow two opposing trajectories over the last one hundred years.

Somewhat in accord with Lyotard's proposal that 'a work can become modern only if it is first postmodern', what appeared to early readers as the poem's radical abandonment of rationality and order (making it prescient of postmodernist dissemination and relativism and indicative of what Lyotard terms the attempt to present the unpresentable) has been progressively tamed, both by academic canonisation and exegesis and by the increased media-driven familiarity of multiple and fragmented forms of expression (it has become, in various senses, highly 'presentable').[10] Conversely, *The Waste Land*'s early reception, framed by the assumptions of readers, reviewers and the author himself, that 'unity' was a key feature of a successful work of art, meant that it was in some quarters in effect read initially as a work of modernist 'disjunctive irony', in which (in Alan Wilde's terms) an 'aestheticizing

---

[9]   Robert Sheppard comments that 'Eliot's theories of impersonality were bypassed by American writers who have used Eliot's "lesson" to write technically proficient verse on highly personal themes: the so-called "confessional" writers'. Robert Sheppard, *The Poetry of Saying: British Poetry and Its Discontents 1950–2000* (Liverpool: Liverpool University Press, 2005), 29.

[10]   Jean-François Lyotard, 'What is Postmodernism?', appendix to *The Postmodern Condition: A Report on Knowledge*, translated by Geoff Bennington and Brian Massumi (Minneapolis: University of Minnesota Press, 1984), 79–80.

consciousness' rescues a world from indeterminacy through 'the sublimity of form' or which (in Lyotard's terms) 'allows the unpresentable to be put forward as the missing contents' within a beautiful form.[11]

Even a somewhat sceptical early review, such as that in the *TLS* of September 1923, suggested that there may be a key to unlocking the poem: 'in the concluding confession, "These fragments I have shored against my ruins", we receive a direct communication which throws light on much which had preceded it'.[12] This inaugurates a long tradition of reflexive recuperation, in which the poem's seeming fragmentation becomes itself a form of unity because it represents a unifying intention of historical mourning and repair. Similarly, Eliot himself proffered Tiresias as a unifying consciousness and F.R. Leavis, whose book *New Bearings in English Poetry* played a major role in the canonisation of the poem, asserts a strongly unified view of the poem by recuperating its fragmentariness through consciousness and myth. Quoting Eliot's note asserting that Tiresias unites all the personages in the poem, Leavis says that this 'provides the clue' and 'indicates plainly enough what the poem is: an effort to focus an inclusive human consciousness'. Acknowledging that 'the mode of consciousness' lacks 'organizing principle' or 'inherent direction', he turns to myth, and to *From Ritual to Romance* to provide 'something in the nature of a musical organization'.[13] From this starting point, there is a trajectory in the inverse direction to that proposed above: as both critical ideas and cultural practices become more open to and familiar with the fragmented or collaged, *The Waste Land* opens itself to reinterpretation as proto-postmodernist, in accord with Maud Ellmann's reading of the poem as a 'sphinx without a secret': 'Most commentators have been so busy tracking its allusions down and patching up its tattered memories that they have overlooked its broken images in search of the totality it might have been'.[14] The poem, one might say, finds itself belatedly inhabiting a culture of suspensive irony, with 'a willingness to live with uncertainty, to tolerate, and, in some cases, to welcome a world seen as random and multiple, even,

---

[11]   Alan Wilde, *Horizons of Assent: Modernism, Postmodernism, and the Ironic Imagination* (Baltimore, MD: Johns Hopkins University Press, 1981), 40; Lyotard, 'What is Postmodernism?', 81.

[12]   Review of *The Waste Land*, *Times Literary Supplement*, 20 September 1923, printed in *T.S. Eliot, 'The Waste Land': A Casebook*, edited by C.B. Cox and Arnold P. Hinchcliffe (London and Basingstoke: Macmillan, 1968), 31.

[13]   F.R. Leavis, *New Bearings in English Poetry: A Study of the Contemporary Situation* (London: Chatto & Windus, 1932), 73–4. See Eliot's note to line 218 of *The Waste Land*.

[14]   Maud Ellmann, *The Poetics of Impersonality: T.S. Eliot and Ezra Pound* (Cambridge, MA: Harvard University Press, 1987), 91–2.

at times, absurd'.[15] In this context, the poem will seem both more contemporary and less radical.

All of this means that the legacy of *The Waste Land* for later poets is an ambivalent one, and their response can readily take many forms, including imitation, parody, tribute, selective influence, negative reaction, avoidance, explicit or implicit dismissal and creative transformation. Such responses can be triangulated using categories such as 'mainstream' and 'alternative' (key to many late twentieth-century debates); also 'late modernist', 'modernist' and 'postmodernist'. While for most poets the well-known published version of *The Waste Land* will be the first-encountered and perhaps definitive experience, for others the availability (since 1971) of the facsimile of drafts and Pound's annotations, offers further possibilities – explicitly referenced, for example, by Paul Muldoon in 'American Standard' (as discussed below).[16] For a number of poets and critics, the two versions of the poem represent a key dividing line. For Geoffrey Hill, as we shall see, Pound in effect rescues the poem from a drift, which Hill finds over Eliot's writing career, away from a certain openness of 'becoming' towards a certain 'apathy' or 'tone' associated with closure.[17] Paul Muldoon's comments are found in poetry, and are characteristically oblique and ironic: he refers to Pound as a 'great believer in less / being more' and always ready with his (editor's) 'blue pencil'.[18] That Muldoon makes this observation in a long and rather repetitive poem involves a certain irony. For Marjorie Perloff, the difference between Eliot's draft and the final result after Pound's intervention approaches a distinction between modernist and postmodernist poetics. Commenting that *The Waste Land* is 'by no means a "dialogic" poem' and that its conclusion appeals to 'an outside source of authority', she argues that this 'makes for more authorial control ... than the fragmentation, parataxis, and collage structure ... would suggest – a structure that ... is largely the product of Pound's severe cuts'.[19] The judgements of Hill, Muldoon and Perloff are made in different modes

[15]   Wilde, *Horizons of Assent*, 45. Is Wilde, consciously or unconsciously, echoing 'The Love Song of J. Alfred Prufrock'? ('At times, indeed, almost ridiculous – / Almost, at times, the Fool')?

[16]   T.S. Eliot, *The Waste Land: A Facsimile and Transcript of the Original Drafts*, edited by Valerie Eliot (New York: Harcourt, 1971).

[17]   Geoffrey Hill, *Collected Critical Writings*, edited by Kenneth Haynes (Oxford: Oxford University Press, 2008). Despite this, Ricks finds many echoes and convergences of concerns between Hill's poetry and *Four Quartets*.

[18]   Paul Muldoon, 'American Standard', in *Howdie-Skelp* (London: Faber, 2021), 12. The sequence first appeared in *Times Literary Supplement*, 1 February 2019.

[19]   Marjorie Perloff, *21st-Century Modernism: The 'New' Poetics* (Malden, MA and Oxford: Blackwell, 2002), 37–8.

and registers, and hardly neatly aligned, but nevertheless have significant parallels. They indicate some of the ways in which *The Waste Land* may offer a model of *either* closure and aesthetic ordering via myth and consciousness, *or* dislocation and chaotic collage.

Traces of *The Waste Land* in later poetry range from isolated allusions to sustained engagement. The most powerful general influence of Eliot's poem is to be found, not in specific allusions or echoes, but in the underlying formal conception which emerged from Eliot's writing and Pound's editing. In broad terms, this consists of using 'traditional', classical, or earlier myths and canonical works to provide a structuring conception within which late modernist or postmodernist style and techniques can be given free play. In this respect Joyce's *Ulysses* is a shared source of influence, but of course provides a model in fiction rather than poetry. The model has proved amenable to adaptation to postmodernist techniques (aided by the arguably proto-postmodernist elements of *The Waste Land* which I have mentioned). Elements of such a model can be found in poems which are very different in mood, values and implication from Eliot's poem, such as Paul Muldoon's *Immram*. It carries with it both a tendency to ironic relation between elements of form (between a sense of overall form and a local impression of formlessness) and a poetic, in itself crucial to modernism across the arts, which stresses the role of the reader, viewer or audience in negotiating the indeterminacies of meaning and value which that irony generates. Throughout *The Waste Land* and poems which show its formal influence, the reader is confronted with the question of how far to 'read into' the poem's lines and passages a determining or quasi-determining set of mythic meanings. In the case of the original, how far does the reader attempt to 'hear' every line as emanating from the cross-gender consciousness of Tiresias (something which is far from evident in the text), and to construct or detect associated forms of unity? And how far does the reader interpret every allusion to water or dust in terms of biblical and mythical echoes and values?

Geoffrey Hill

Amongst poets writing in English since 1950, Geoffrey Hill is perhaps the most engaged with Eliot's legacy – an engagement which is reflected in complex ways in Hill's own critical writing, and which has been widely noticed, both by those who admire Hill and by those who don't.[20] Christopher Ricks has

---

[20] When Tom Paulin described Hill as 'a parasite upon Eliot's imagination', the basis for his observation is not so different to Ricks's statement that 'The heart of

explored this relation in detail. His concept of 'friendship' includes elements of the adversarial: 'Hill's poems as well as his criticism wrestle angelically with Eliot, with Pound, and with Lowell'.[21] Ricks also deploys the somewhat ritualistic phrase 'under the sign of' (derived from Eliot's comment on Laforgue), and the more familiar idea of influence, quoting again from Eliot himself: 'People are only influenced in the direction in which they want to go'; 'A poet cannot help being influenced, therefore he should subject himself to as many influences as possible'.[22] Ricks's overall view of the relation centres on a distinction between Hill as poet and Hill as critic: 'the prose Hill ... was to become estranged from Eliot, but there remain some massive concurrences of principle and of practice'.[23] He nevertheless distinguishes the trajectories of their poetic developments: '[t]he trajectory in Hill has taken him towards tragic farce ... in Eliot, away from it ... In Hill, toward popular culture; in Eliot, away from it'.[24] Ricks's examples of echoes are mostly from *Four Quartets*; this may be in part because he wishes to demonstrate that, against the drift of Hill's prose critique of late Eliot, and in particular of the plays and *Four Quartets*, his own poetry is indebted to the latter. Ricks does detect a few echoes of *The Waste Land*: in 'Pindarics' 21 (from *Without Title*) the imagery of key and lock applied to choice and free will, and an epigraph from Pavese, whose 'lamentations' are refracted through the 'maternal lamentation' of *The Waste Land*: 'one of the things I hear in the severe beauty of Hill's "Pindarics" 21 is "What the Thunder Said," and, rumbling behind that, What T.S. Eliot said'. But Ricks also observes that 'Eliot's words may have prompted or precipitated or fertilized, without this being in the shaping spirit of allusion'.[25] In an earlier book, Ricks traced the influence of Eliot's use of parentheses in *The Waste Land* on Hill's creative use of brackets.[26]

Hill's matter, the heart of his fertile darkness, is undoubtedly Eliot, Hill's doubts about Eliot.' Ricks, *True Friendship*, 38. Paulin was hostile to Hill's work because of what he took to be Hill's politics. See Tom Paulin, 'The Case for Geoffrey Hill', review of *Geoffrey Hill, Essays on His Work*, *London Review of Books*, 4 April 1985, 13–14 (13). As Ricks notes, a number of 'charges' have been 'uniformly levelled at Eliot and Hill: charges of inaccessibility, obscurity, elitism, inspissation and foreign paraphernalia; charges of prejudice, nostalgia, and the idealizing of the past; charges of scabrousness and obscenity, and even of mystification and outrage'. Ricks, *True Friendship*, 19.

21   Ricks, *True Friendship*, 1, ix–x.
22   Ibid., ix, 21.
23   Ibid., 24–5.
24   Ibid., 27.
25   Ibid., 48, 39.
26   Christopher Ricks, *The Force of Poetry* (Oxford: Clarendon Press, 1995), 307–9.

Ricks's finely nuanced and detailed discussion of Hill's indebtedness to Eliot focuses on the one hand on verbal echoes and nuances of style, and on the other on large questions of theme and idea:

> all the cruces that Eliot and Hill agree to be inescapable, even if they disagree about just what it would be fully to comprehend them: the recalcitrance of the self in relation to art, the distinguishable but not distinct claims of religion and literature, the centrality of blasphemy, the intertwining of humility with humiliation, and what it might mean to 'redeem the time.'[27]

Ricks doesn't discuss to any great extent questions of overall structure, nor techniques such as the evocation of myth as a form of cultural critique. Hill's most obvious affinity with Eliot, and *The Waste Land* in particular, lies in the allusiveness of his work; the ways in which quotation, allusion, imitation and parody are not merely intermittent elements but integral to the construction and meaning of most of his poems. Hill's essays 'Word Value in F.H. Bradley' and 'Eros in F.H. Bradley and T.S. Eliot', as well as 'Dividing Legacies', show the depth and intensity of his engagement with Eliot's poetry, prose and wider influence, involving as they do a meticulous analysis of strands of ideas and evaluation of Eliot's development.[28] His critical evaluation of Eliot's oeuvre, favouring those works which show 'the way of apprehension' (*Sweeney Agonistes*, *Ash Wednesday*, *Mariana*, *Coriolan*) over those which display 'discursive intelligence' (*Four Quartets* and the plays), has been assessed, along with some of its significance for Hill's own poetry, by Steven Matthews.[29] Hill's distinction of terms is characteristically subtle, but in essence 'the way of apprehension' (a phrase from F.H. Bradley[30]) is here is associated with ideas of 'becoming', 'belonging' and 'recognition', whereas 'discursive intelligence' is stigmatised as seeking 'closure at a rational level' and writing 'infected by ... public apathy'.[31] As already noted, *The Waste Land* occupies a somewhat uncertain place within this divided evaluation of Eliot's work: it belongs to the 'discursive intelligence' of which Hill disapproves 'in the form in which Eliot originally presented it to Pound's scru-

---

[27]   Ricks, *True Friendship*, 25.
[28]   Hill, *Collected Critical Writings*, 532–47, 548–64, 366–79.
[29]   Steven Matthews, '"Felt Unities": Geoffrey Hill, T.S. Eliot and David Jones', in *Strangeness and Power: Essays on the Poetry of Geoffrey Hill*, edited by Andrew Michael Roberts (Bristol: Shearsman Books, 2020), 31ff.
[30]   F.H. Bradley, *Appearance and Reality: A Metaphysical Essay* (London: Oxford University Press, 1959), 76.
[31]   Hill, *Collected Critical Writings*, 534; Matthews, '"Felt Unities"', 33; Hill, *Collected Critical Writings*, 547.

tiny'; the implication seems to be that Pound rescued it from that fate.[32] However, the pub scene is still cited by Hill as presaging Eliot's later, inadequate understanding of 'the People'. It is not quite clear whether the somewhat stereotyped characterisation of the working classes in the pub scene is taken by Hill to be the other side of the coin to Eliot's alleged infection by 'public apathy' as his career progressed.[33] Matthews finds in 'De Jure Belli ac Pacis' from *Canaan* 'a middle Europe reminiscent of *The Waste Land*', but on the whole, like Ricks, he sees the post-1922 Eliot as the more important influence on Hill's work.[34]

The broader significance of *The Waste Land* for Hill's poetry arguably lies less in specific echoes or features of style than in two broad aspects: one technical, the other thematic. The technical aspect is located in Eliot's use of voices: dramatic, multiple, dispersed, sometimes at the edge of coherence; at times evoking but then undermining a sense of autobiographical 'speaker'. Hill's *Speech! Speech!*, for example, is marked by interruptions, shifting registers and a pervasive ironization of subject positions and 'authenticity' of voice:

> Erudition. Pain. Light. Imagine it great
> unavoidable work; although: heroic
> verse a non-starter, says PEOPLE.
>
> On self-advisement I erased
> WE, though I is a shade too painful,[35]

It is possible to read the whole poem as the 'voice' of an author-persona, anticipating and responding to critics, media and the wider culture; it is also possible to read it as a hearing of multiple voices within a culture and a time: 'do / you, as I do, sit late by the Aga / with clues received from sputtering / agents of Marconi'.[36] This indeterminacy is akin to that of *The Waste Land*. However, here, as elsewhere, the crucial legacy of Eliot's technique in later poetry lies in all those forms of poetry which 'hear voices' rather than seeking to 'find' a voice. Hill's intense concern with history, especially English history, has more connections with the later Eliot of *Four Quartets*. Hill's own poetry

---

[32] Hill, *Collected Critical Writings*, 534.

[33] Ibid., 547.

[34] Matthews, '"Felt Unities"', 31, 23.

[35] Geoffrey Hill, *Broken Hierarchies: Poems, 1952–2012* (Oxford: Oxford University Press, 2013), 289, 291.

[36] Ibid., 289.

combined this interest in history and historical forms of understanding with the technique of 'hearing' and ventriloquising multiple voices, a combination which enables a conception of the long poem or poetic sequence as formally diagnostic of social, political and cultural configurations. This sense is apparent in some of Hill's own comments about his poetry as when, responding to accusations of indulging in cultural nostalgia, he put forward a diagnostic conception of the role of poetry: 'To be accused of exhibiting a symptom when, to the best of my ability, I'm offering a diagnosis appears to be one of the numerous injustices which one must suffer with as much equanimity as possible.'[37]

The conception of *The Waste Land* as offering a diagnosis of a supposedly fragmented and 'sterile' culture, which became a staple of critical reading, can be seen echoed in sequences such as Hill's 'An Apology for the Revival of Christian Architecture in England' and *Speech! Speech!* where shifting voices, viewpoints, contexts and registers enact a critical and satirical conception of a culture and its history. Although Hill writes comparatively little about *The Waste Land* in his critical writing, his positive assertion of its value, found in a footnote, rests on the quality that some have found unsympathetic in the poem: '*The Waste Land*, at its first appearance, could only be understood exegetically; that is its remaining strength.'[38] Jeremy Noel-Tod applies to the modernist multiplication of voices in *The Waste Land* and 'The Love Song of J. Alfred Prufrock' Adorno's concept of a 'dialectical philosophical proposition' and an 'identification with language' on the part of the poem.[39] (Noel-Tod applies this specifically to J.H. Prynne, whom he sees as a key inheritor of this strand of modernism.) The idea of the poem as identifying with language (a displacement of the centrality of the human subject) accords with Hill's emphasis on mining or sculpting language and the pervasive reflexivity of his poetry (reference, not to the poet's 'self' but to the poem itself as language).[40]

Overall, then, the significance of *The Waste Land* as model, for Hill as for other poets working in a late modernist mode, is less a matter of specific stylistic influences than the inheritance of a conception of the long poem

---

[37] John Haffenden, *Viewpoints: Poets in Conversation with John Haffenden* (London: Faber, 1981), 93.

[38] Hill, *Collected Critical Writings*, 701.

[39] Noel-Tod, 'In Different Voices' 112.

[40] 'That commonplace image, founded upon the unfinished statues of Michaelangelo, "mighty figures straining to free themselves from the imprisoning marble" ... seems ... to embody the nature and condition of those arts which are composed of words.' Hill, *Collected Critical Writings*, 3.

or poetic sequence characterized by a range of distinctive features: putative unification or connection at the level of idea and symbol (without narrative coherence and often lacking stylistic consistency); a combination of lyric and dramatic elements, perhaps with fragments of narrative; and the juxtaposition of historical and cultural reference or commentary with personal and emotional expression. The result of these methods is that the work is susceptible to a range of formal hermeneutic strategies, involving a 'reading' of the work through the lens of various formal conceptions (none of which comes to seem definitive): as collage or 'spatial form', as stream of consciousness, as performance, as palimpsest, as a speaking/hearing of voices; even as chaotic or semi-random impingement of material from multiple contexts and media (when the work is read as 'postmodernist').[41] In Hill's earlier work this model is relevant to poems such as 'Metamorphoses' and 'Of Commerce and Society', but it comes to sustained fruition in later book-length poems (with a certain cross-fertilization by American models such as John Berryman), such as *Speech! Speech!*, *The Triumph of Love* and the posthumously-published *The Book of Baruch by the Gnostic Justin*. Such works are distinguished from other sequences by Hill, such as 'Funeral Music' and *Orchards of Syon*, which are marked by greater stylistic consistency and continuity; even if the latter is no less dense with allusion and dizzying leaps of register than Hill's other book-length sequences, there is a stronger sense of a persistent consciousness. *Mercian Hymns* is an interesting marginal case: it might be seen as Wordsworth's *Prelude* through a modernist filter, thus combining Romantic and Modernist elements. The dualism of child poet and Anglo-Saxon king has elements of the mythic structures of *The Waste Land*, but there is a unity of context and a degree of consistency of tone which produces a very different effect. Underlying the *Waste Land* model is some implicit sense of the poet as having a public role, whether as prophet (an inheritance from Romanticism) or as social commentator (from the Augustan satirical tradition). It need not exclude elements of the 'personal' (such as the traces of Eliot's marriage, or of Hill's self-representations), but it subdues or displaces them by incorporating them into a wider social or historical vision by its ability to shift register, voice and discursive level. As Peter Robinson puts it:

> *The Waste Land* ... a collage of selves suffering from and, some of them, seeking a way out of imprisoning situations, helped sponsor the poet's imper-

---

[41]   Alastair Fowler comments that '[i]nstead of the spoken voice's sequentiality in time ... [*The Waste Land*] aims at spatial form, in which parts relate simultaneously as in visual art. What related the pieces of Eliot's collage is not syntax but juxtaposition'. See his *A History of English Literature* (Oxford: Blackwell, 1987), 345.

sonality theory of individual talent and its relation to a tradition, as well as his notion of an objective correlative. Both of these ideas are attempts to manage the relations of a learnedly troubled self to a complex cultural and historical situation.[42]

The poet is not obliged to attribute historical importance to their own experience, because the collage-like form enables the personal and historical to be juxtaposed while the nature of the relationship between them remains suggestive rather than determined.

Roy Fisher

Roy Fisher's poetry could also be termed 'late modernist' and, like Hill, he inherits aspects of Eliotic modernist form and thematics. Fisher makes extensive use of poetic sequences and, to a greater extent than Hill, deploys collage-like forms. Fisher follows the Eliot of *The Waste Land* in making the city central to his imaginative world and representation of culture. Fisher is also, in his own distinctive manner, a social critic, as when he aligns the harsh urban 'regeneration' of Birmingham with earlier models of power and tyranny:

> Seven hundred years ago
> an earlier model of the idea, set up
> on land above the Bull Ring by the proprietors,
> did business as an Enterprise Park
> for freed serfs. Similar rules apply.
> [...]
> The Forum of Augustus, sitting firm and new,
> drawing centrality to itself,
> had to have its back to a massive
> curtain wall, set there to mask
> slum tenements behind. That sort of place.[43]

The way in which historical parallels and overlays function here owes something to the mythic-historical palimpsests of 'The Burial of the Dead', in which the post-war crowd flowing over London Bridge is also the crowd

---

[42]   Peter Robinson, *Twentieth Century Poetry: Selves and Situations* (Oxford: Oxford University Press, 2005), 2.

[43]   Roy Fisher, 'Six Texts for a Film', in *Birmingham River* (Oxford: Oxford University Press, 1994), 11–23; collected as 'Texts for A Film', in *The Long and the Short of It* (Tarsent: Bloodaxe, 2005), 285–94 (289).

of Baudelaire's nineteenth-century Paris and that of Dante's *Inferno*, and Stetson is both Eliot's contemporary and a survivor of the Punic War. A further link between the two poets is found in the theme of death and deathliness. Peter Robinson has considered in detail 'the theme of death and the relationships between the living and the dead in the poetry and prose of Roy Fisher', and interprets the theme of death as crucial to a 'stop-start aesthetics' which shaped Fisher's longer works.[44] As Robinson's account implies, in Fisher's poetry death is both metaphorical and real (in historical and existential senses), and this duality of reference is shared with Eliot. The sense of deathliness and the occurrence of death on thematic and symbolic levels which we find in *The Waste Land* are historically symptomatic of the period just after the First World War, when the loss of much of a generation of men informs lines such as 'I had not thought death had undone so many'. Fisher, like Geoffrey Hill, was a child during the Second World War, and the fact of civilian war deaths from bombing figures in his key early collage sequence, *City*:

> I saw the garden where my aunt had died
> And her two children and a woman from next door
> It was like a burst pod filled with clay.
> A mile away I had heard the bombs
> [...]
> The last of them crushed the four bodies into the ground,
> Scattered the shelter, and blasted my uncle's corpse
> Over the housetop and into the street beyond.[45]

Fisher himself commented that this 'simple narrative poem' (which became the section of *City* entitled 'The Entertainment of War') was 'the thing most untypical of anything I believe about poetry that I ever wrote'.[46] Corpse, garden, ground are there as in Eliot's 'The Burial of the Dead', but the mode here seems confessional and anecdotal rather than symbolic: the poem goes on to reflect on the child poet's apparent lack of trauma as well as the strangeness of such obliteration: 'Never have people seemed so absent from their own deaths'. Other sections of *City*, however, have a surreal, sinister urban atmosphere which has affinities with *The Waste Land* (as well as the Eliot of 'Preludes' and 'Prufrock'):

[44]   Robinson, *Twentieth Century Poetry*, 236.
[45]   Fisher, *The Long and the Short of It*, 33.
[46]   Jed Rasula and Mike Erwin, 'An Interview with Roy Fisher', in *Nineteen Poems and an Interview* (Pensnett: Grosseteste, 1975), 20.

The wind drives itself mad with messages,
Clattering train wheels over the roofs,
Collapsing streets of sound until
Far towers, daubed with swollen light,
Lunge closer to abuse it,[47]

Robinson finds some echoes of *The Waste Land* in Fisher's 1959 short poetic sequence, 'Five Morning Poems from a Picture by Manet'; in the fourth section the dead speak, recalling 'What the Thunder Said' in the line 'Then I heard what the corpses said'.[48] Michael O'Neill finds the 'symbolic plot' of 'What the Thunder Said' recalled in Fisher's 1975 poem, 'Of the Empirical Self and for Me': 'Sudden rain / Thunder burst across the mountain'; he observes that, '[l]ike Eliot, Fisher proposes a symbolic plot without committing himself to it'.[49] In a 1997 interview, Fisher refers to *A Furnace* (1986), and imagines his role as poet as 'this evangelist who's at your elbow ... "talking about death ... and the burial of the dead"'.[50]

City forms the first part of what Peter Barry has characterized as 'a "composite epic" of urban material, a sequence which has its own overall structural logic and coherence'; the epic comprises *City* (1961), 'Handsworth Liberties' (1978), *A Furnace* (1986) and 'Six Texts for a Film' (1994).[51] Barry also notes a parallel with the developmental process of *The Waste Land*:

> the interaction between Shayer and Fisher ... is itself a 'cross-fertilising' scenario which seems to reproduce that of the production and publication of *The Waste Land*, for Shayer acted as the Ezra Pound figure who, Fisher says in interview, took in hand 'my great heaving mass of odds and ends that I was writing about Birmingham ... and saw that this material could be used as a kind of collage work ... So he shook it around a bit and produced the first draft of *City*'.[52]

[47]   Fisher, *The Long and the Short of It*, 41.
[48]   Ibid., 325.
[49]   Michael O'Neill, '"Exhibiting Unpreparedness": Self, World and Poetry', in *The Thing about Roy Fisher: Critical Studies*, edited by John Kerrigan and Peter Robinson (Liverpool: Liverpool University Press, 2000), 209–30 (222).
[50]   'John Tranter interviews Roy Fisher', *Jacket* 1 (1997), http://jacketmagazine.com/01/fisher-iv.html.
[51]   Peter Barry, *Contemporary British Poetry and the City* (Manchester: Manchester University Press, 2000), 196–201.
[52]   Ibid., 195.

'Handsworth Liberties', described by Barry as a 'minimalist' 'late coda' to *City*, is a reflection on space, place, perception and self-inhabiting, with notes of alienation and loss ('A mild blight, a sterility'), but also of freedom ('Open – and away // in all directions: room at last for the sky / and a horizon').[53] *A Furnace*, however, is an urban poem persistently concerned with death and the relation of the living and dead; as Clair Wills writes: 'The poem is haunted by ghosts'.[54] However, Fisher's loose, at times discursive, but oblique style and his democratic or egalitarian values mark a distance from Eliot. Wills gives a judicious assessment of the similarities and differences between *A Furnace* and *The Waste Land*:

> *A Furnace* belongs to the modernist tradition of meditation on the state of a civilization and social world which begins with ... *The Waste Land*. We find in both Eliot and Fisher the same impersonal treatment of cultural cycles, the same 'masculine' avoidance of sentimentalism ... The difference between the ways the two poets operate in this genre lies in the contrast between Eliot's cultural pessimism ... and Fisher's more defiant targeting of social and political shibboleths. Whereas in Eliot ... the working-class voices are expressions of the same nihilism and despair that typifies modern urban society as a whole, Fisher's aim is to restore a sense of the dignity of buried, occluded lives ... overshadowed by the immense material presence of the city itself.[55]

I would add the suggestion that some of Fisher's ambivalence about moral or didactic elements in his own poetry may have been a response to Eliot's prominent example; Fisher was clearly interested in elements of social critique, but very wary of seeming to moralise.[56] He has also observed that 'the British forum of articulate culture-bearers is a self-deluding group' – a comment which in context refers to later thinkers such as Richard Hoggart, F.R. Leavis and Raymond Williams, but could be applied easily enough to the Eliot of the later essays in particular. Fisher's interviews, of which a number have been collected, are in fact notable for a paucity of allusions to Eliot

---

[53] Ibid., 199, 198; Fisher, *The Long and the Short of It*, 273, 270.

[54] Clair Wills, '*A Furnace* and the Life of the Dead', in *The Thing about Roy Fisher*, 257–74 (262).

[55] Ibid., 259.

[56] Fisher talks of his poetry at certain points in terms of didacticism, political intention and ethics, but also objects to the tendency to moralise poetry or images and expresses suspicion of his own moralizing tendencies. See, for example, Roy Fisher, *Interviews through Time and Selected Prose* (Kentisbeare: Shearsman Books, 2000), 60, 80. In his poem 'It is Writing', we read: 'I mistrust the poem in its hour of success / a thing capable of being / tempted into ethics by the wonderful.' Fisher, *The Long and the Short of It*, 221.

(even by way of distancing himself).[57] This despite the fact that he reflects on the influence (or otherwise) of numerous poets and artists, describes *A Furnace* as 'a collage of various sorts of experience ... an examination of that whole cultural era' and is at pains to downplay any connection of that poem to Ezra Pound's poetic: 'all I could think of to do in this poem was not to pitch against Pound, but to make, in a similar way to all the books of *Paterson* ... an accretive work'.[58] The only significant mention of *The Waste Land* in *Interviews Through Time and Selected Prose* compares it (along with other long poems) unfavourably with *Briggflatts*:

> [Bunting] was the only poet I've known personally who was capable of undertaking a work on that scale and bringing it off ... you only have to start running the tally of the century's attempts to see how that factor was surren-dered or abandoned ... *The Waste Land* – filleted and collapsed; *The Bridge* – hysterically overpitched; *The Cantos* and *Maximus* left to run themselves into the sand or expanding cosmic space, respectively, and *Paterson* likewise left with nowhere to go.[59]

In their different ways, Fisher and Geoffrey Hill show signs of a need to hold *The Waste Land* at a distance, and this inclination may be in itself sympto-matic of the inescapability of Eliot's poem as a literary-historical presence.

Paul Muldoon

Paul Muldoon's work exemplifies a certain form of postmodernism: playful, ironic, allusive, self-referential, pervaded by parodic and pastiche elements, in a relationship of both connection to and reaction against what had come to be termed 'modernism', for which *The Waste Land* offers an obvious exem-plar. Muldoon's differing uses of Eliot's poem can be seen in his sequences 'Immram' from *Why Brownlee Left* (1980) and 'American Standard' (2019–21). In both of these poems, Muldoon in effect revisits and revises (to very different ends) three questions which dominated critical discussion of *The Waste Land*: its 'unity' or lack of it, how it can or should be interpreted,

---

[57]   With typical dry humour, however, Fisher responds to a review which queried some hints of the mystical in *A Furnace* by commenting that the reviewer 'was alarmed in case I was about to commit *Ash Wednesday*'. *News for the Ear: A Homage to Roy Fisher*, edited by Peter Robinson and Robert Sheppard (Exeter: Stryde, 2000), 111–12.

[58]   Fisher, *Interviews through Time*, 94–5.

[59]   Ibid., 113–4.

and its allusiveness together with the alleged obscurity or limited readership which that allusiveness is sometimes held to involve.

'Immram', as the poet explained in interview, is a contemporary (1980) 'version' of the medieval Irish genre of 'voyage tale' ('Immram'), a form which was often given a 'Christian veneer'.[60] The indebtedness of 'Immram' to *The Waste Land* is most apparent in its tongue-in-cheek evocation of the quest narrative, its symbolism of water and baptism ('Shall we Gather at the River?'; 'A pint of lukewarm water'; 'I did a breast-stroke through the carpet'; 'that old Deep Water Baptist mission'), and of snow and thaw ('snow from the slopes of the Andes, so pure / it would never melt in spring'), its address to the reader ('And done myself, and you, a favour'; 'I already told you his name'), Biblical and Shakespearean allusions (John the Baptist and Salome; Ariel and Prospero), a dream-like vision of a corpse, pseudo-religiosity ('The Way of the One Wave') and a reimagining of the grail as a drug-mule's 'wooden statue ... The Christ of the Andes'. Also the skeletal Howard Hughes-like figure, who suggests Tiresias, and the concluding 'steady stream of people / That flowed in one direction', recalling Eliot's crowd on London Bridge. On a formal level, the underlying idea of some form of structuring through mythic patterns (the quest) and earlier historical models (the Irish voyage tale) are indebted to Eliot's work. However, the actual structure of 'Immram' is very different from *The Waste Land*, involving a series of ten-line stanzas, with an intermittent rhyme scheme (and many half-rhymes), and a Chandleresque plot which follows something like the standard detective story heuristic, in which a mystery is unravelled even if there are, in typical Chandler fashion, significant loose ends.[61] Muldoon combines the teleology of the detective narrative (from mystery to resolution) with the circularity of the existential situation (a series of events and experiences which are emotionally inconclusive). The idea of a heroic epic given a 'Christian veneer', together with a structure which offers an ambivalent resolution, reflect an oblique light back onto *The Waste Land*, refracting its concerns through a late-twentieth-century and American medium as well as the filmic. To echo the questions which I posed in relation to *The Waste Land*: to what extent is the eighth or ninth-century Irish voyage tale *Immram Máele Dúin* (and its later manifestations in Christian and literary form) a framework

60   Haffenden, *Viewpoints*, 139.
61   Alison Muri writes that 'at the poem's end we have discovered nothing', but this seems an overstatement; the narrator does discover why his father disappeared in a narrative beginning 'This is how it was'. Alison Muri, 'A Pilgrim's Progress: Paul Muldoon's "Immram" as a Journey of Discovery', *Canadian Journal of Irish Studies/ Revue Canadienne d'Etudes Irlandaises* 21.2 (1995), 44–51.

which orders or structures the meanings of Muldoon's poem, and to what extent is that connection rather one of ironic distance and postmodernist anti-structure? (Is the point that the narrator's experience of Los Angeles conspicuously fails to match up to the meanings and values of the quest and journey model?) Muldoon's comment in interview, that '[t]he quest is the powerful and important centre of the poem', somewhat like Eliot's note on Tiresias, makes the poem sound more centred and resolved than it may feel to the reader.

'American Standard' appeared almost forty years later, after the arrival of the internet and associated resources such as online maps and social media. The later poem is much more explicit than 'Immram' in its allusions to *The Waste Land* (as well as occasionally to 'The Love Song of J. Alfred Prufrock'), to the point where it hovers between pastiche or parody of Eliot's poem, and a form of poetic critical commentary on it. Formally it is also more akin, although by no means closely parallel. 'American Standard' is irregular in line and stanza length (with some quite complex, though intermittent, use of rhyme, often comic in effect).[62] Whereas 'Immram' had a pseudo detective-fiction plot dotted with allusions, 'American Standard' resembles a collage of allusions to Eliot, with traces of a quest plot (in the form of the quest to rescue a brother from an immigration centre). Whereas 'Immram' ends with a gesture of circularity (the narrator's return to the pool hall where the poem began), which reflexively and ironically comments on the uncertain herme-neutics of the detective genre, 'American Standard' ends with a sustained spray of allusions, echoing but also upping the scale of Eliot's concluding lines, and again reflexive in announcing its own poetic technique:

> When it comes to a finale it's hard to beat the combined forces of Buddy Bolden,
> Captain Beefheart, the recently cashiered Cap n' Crunch,
> Charlemagne and his twelve Paladins,
> William Tell, William Holden
> and the Wild Bunch, ...[63]

The list of names continues for most of another twelve stanzas, with a mixture of historical, contemporary, pop-cultural, high-cultural, religious and mythi-cal figures, upping the ante and broadening the range on Eliot's concluding

---

[62] For example, section 3 uses a twelve-line stanza, and initially rhymes the second and eighth lines and the third and twelfth lines, but the fourth stanza breaks into a more sustained pattern: aa bb cc aa ca (some half-rhymes).

[63] Muldoon, *Howdie-Skelp*, 38.

of the Fisher King myth via popular song, Dante, *Pervigilium Veneris*, Gerard de Nerval, Thomas Kyd and the Upanishads; and though Eliot ends with quotations, Muldoon does so with allusions (mostly names). It is rather as if Muldoon is acting up to the hostile terms applied to *The Waste Land* by some early reviews, as a 'mad medley ... a smoke-screen of anthropological and literary erudition', 'parodying without taste or skill', decorated with 'borrowed jewels [which] ... do not make Mr Eliot's toad the more prepossessing'.[64] Reflexivity, here in part an inheritance from Eliot's 'These fragments I have shored against my ruins' (taken as a reflexive statement about the poem's form), is one of the keynotes of Muldoon's poetry, as it is of much postmodern writing. Reflexivity runs through 'American Standard', in references to the interpretation of allusions ('One likeable, if unlikely, theory / is that Trent Razor's band-name, Nine-Inch Nails, / refers to the crucifixion of Christ'); to the influence of Eliot and Pound (Ezra and Tom in section 4); word-play on techniques such as allegory ('Pardon, *Senor*, but do you have any food allegories?'). Reflexivity enables a layering of ironies, as when 'Ezra said that he was a great believer in less / being more', a reference to Pound's editing down of the draft of *The Waste Land*: it is advice which Muldoon himself can hardly be said to have followed in 'American Standard', which deploys a poetic of excess rather than restraint.[65]

'American Standard' is also a specifically Trump-era poem and appeared on the website of the *Times Literary Supplement* with a photograph of Trump at its head.[66] When referencing Donald Trump, Muldoon's habitual irony and playfulness give way to something more like plain anger and accusation:

> As the first deaths from Hurricane Florence are being reported,
> President Donald Trump claims
> Hurricane Maria's death toll of near 3,000 in Puerto Rico
> was inflated to cause him political harm.[67]

These lines are followed by the first occurrence of one of a number of variable onomatopoetic refrains, here as 'Co co rico Puerto co co rico', which echo Eliot's several sound-based lines: 'O O O O that Shakespeherian Rag'; 'Twit twit twit / Jug jug jug jug jug jug'; 'Weialala leia / Wallala leialala'.

---

64   Cox and Hinchcliffe, eds., *A Casebook*, 29, 32, 37.
65   Muldoon, *Howdie-Skelp*, 11, 25, 4.
66   Paul Muldoon, 'American Standard: A New Poem by Paul Muldoon read by Lisa Dwan, *Times Literary Supplement*, 1 February 2019, https://www.the-tls.co.uk/articles/american-standard-paul-muldoon-poem/. Accessed 5 October 2021.
67   Muldoon, *Howdie-Skelp*, 7.

Muldoon's 'Co co' refrain alternates in places with another one-line refrain which more specifically references *The Waste Land*: versions of Eliot's concluding message of transcendence and reconciliation, 'Shantih shantih shantih', which Muldoon reproduces with transformations of the word into 'Shanty', 'Chantey', 'Santee', 'Shandy', 'Shinto', 'Shantee' and 'Cento' in a form of phonetic deconstruction of Eliot's invocation. Other lines on Trump include the direct 'Vis-à-vis Trump, we have only ourselves to blame for giving ourselves over to pablum', and a sequence of satirical comments in Section 14 on various US presidents, one of which begins 'Some Presidents' attempts to make America great / are less than gratifying ... Some are plain ol' lying.' Section 6 is a pretty explicit commentary on partisan manipulations of Texas elections ('Uncle Jim says we need no help from the Russians when it comes to rigging elections').[68] If *The Waste Land* is, as sometimes claimed, an analysis of a degenerate or decaying civilization, it is not hard to see why Muldoon might find it a suitable model for a Trump poem. The source for Muldoon's title is stated at the end of Section 6 – 'The toilet she is wiping down is an American Standard' – recalling many satirical images and news stories linking Trump with toilets, such as Steve Bell's cartoons in *The Guardian*.[69] The toilet in 'American Standard', like the hollow statue in 'Immram', may figure as a parodic version of the grail symbol in *The Waste Land*. Readers are likely to hear echoes of *The Waste Land* in the fragmented voices, displaced classical characters ('My name is Virgil and I'll be your waiter'), and water imagery ('May I start you off with a little water?') but, in case they do not, Muldoon makes the connection explicit by taking lines from Eliot's poem and subjecting them to repetition with variation. In Section 3 'Come in / Come in under / Come in under the shadow / Of the Red Rock amphitheatre' recalls Eliot's parenthesized '(Come in under the shadow of this red rock)', and then recurs in each stanza with a different fourth line ('under the shadow / of the fossil ...'; 'under the shadow / cast by *Lost Highway* ...', etc.).[70]

One of the general impressions generated by Muldoon's poem, with its extensive use of echo and variation, is of the almost infinite malleability of symbol and intertextuality: a postmodern or internet-saturated environment in which almost anything might refer to anything else. If *The Waste Land* was informed by the technology of the gramophone (the distanced 'recording' of

---

68   Ibid., 7–8, 27–8, 32, 36, 17.
69   See, for example: https://www.theguardian.com/commentisfree/picture/2017/nov/29/steve-bell-on-donald-trump-and-britain-first-cartoon. Accessed 5 October, 2021.
70   Muldoon, *Howdie-Skelp*, 6, 9–11.

personal yet depersonalized 'voices'), Muldoon's work may echo structural elements of digital technology such as the hypertext link. Online it can seem as if anything potentially leads to anything else, so that everything is connected in ways which are both motivated (commercially and ideologically) yet seemingly chaotic. In Muldoon's poem, a surreal logic echoes but subverts such motivation, as a carton of eggs in a store leads to a dinosaur or *Zorro* to *zecchino*.[71] 'American Standard' represents a form of parodic apotheosis or *reductio ad absurdum* of Eliot's methods in *The Waste Land*. Muldoon's poem feels almost as if it is mutating into its own (potential) footnotes (or hyperlinks). Muldoon has always been responsive, in his poetry, to the formal and hermeneutic aspects of other media: 'Immram' has filmic qualities, in its jump cuts, dream sequence and flash-backs. There seems to be no adjective akin to 'filmic' to indicate responsiveness to the internet, but, if there were, it would apply to 'American Standard'. The notorious allusiveness of *The Waste Land* was long a subject of debate concerning its address to readers; an early review suggested that it was not for everyone, and it continued to be seen as excluding readers without the appropriate background in opera, the classics and the like.[72] In 'Immram', Muldoon used contemporary, American and pop cultural references, although Tennyson, *The Tempest* and medieval Irish literature also play a role. This made his poem less likely to be stigmatised as 'elitist', although by the 1990s Blind Lemon Jefferson or even the work of Raymond Chandler were not necessarily familiar to younger readers. By the time of 'American Standard', however, Muldoon is writing in an internet-saturated culture and hardly needs to worry about whether readers will be pre-informed about the history of civil rights campaigning in the USA, the music group Nine Inch Nails, a line from the Irish song 'Harrigan' or what a 'lariat' might be (although the oblique allusions to Doubting Thomas from the New Testament might be missed by some). In this sense Muldoon's work seems to reflect the transformation of the status of Eliot's poem (and of allusion, recognition and interpretation in general) by the ready availability of internet searches. This is one of the ways in which *The Waste Land* has arguably 'become' postmodern, in that the equalizing and intensification of sources of information by the internet and the spreading of once-arcane sources of allusion across multiple media have resulted in a form of the weakening or disappearance of the high/low culture divide.

There is another dimension in which 'American Standard' follows *The Waste Land*: that of what Peter Barry terms the 'urban-specific' (as dis-

---

[71]   Ibid., 11, 22.
[72]   'This poem ... with a page of notes to every three pages of text is not for the ordinary reader'. Cox and Hinchcliffe, eds., *A Casebook*, 29.

tinct from the 'urban generic').[73] Eliot's poem mentions London Bridge (pretty universally known), but also London locations such as 'the Cannon Street Hotel', Lower Thames Street, Moorgate, Richmond as well as other locations in England such as Margate Sands. Muldoon, similarly, names numerous very specific locations, mostly in San Antonio, Texas. Again, the internet defines a new condition of such reception: a reader who can be bothered can easily discover that Luby's Cafeteria, Mudslingers Drive-Thru, or the corner 'where Escort Drive runs into Sunup' are real places, and can look at them on Google Street View for a sense of place and appearance. Most of the place references are to Texas; The Red Rock Amphitheatre, however, is in Colorado and feels chosen because of its serendipitous echo of *The Waste Land*. Like obscure borrowings, such references to specific locations, which once seemed to define a particular audience, now address merely an audience with an internet connection. Lyotard sees allusion as indispensable to the modern 'aesthetic of the sublime' because allusion is to 'something which does not allow itself to be made present' – the unpresentable as 'missing contents'.[74] But the internet allows the target of allusions to be made present – or to *seem* present.

The possibility of performance, and the ways in which both poems might invite or require it, in particular by their use of voices, is another connection. Fiona Shaw's filmed performance of *The Waste Land* (as well as the live performances of it which she has given) emphasize and bring to life its dramatic qualities, so it is interesting that the publication of 'American Standard' in the *Times Literary Supplement* took the form of a text accompanied (on the web page) by a recorded reading or performance of the poem by Lisa Dwan which, like Shaw's reading, is quite actorly and 'performed'. For both poems, actual performance recalibrates the connotations of voice, by incorporating the imagined textual presence of a narrator's or characters' voice or voices within an actual live or recorded voice.[75]

Within what framework can Muldoon's relationship to Eliot and, specifically, to *The Waste Land* then be best considered? Neither friendship nor oedipal rivalry seems quite right; where Muldoon exhibits such relations, Seamus Heaney is his primary object, being an older poet with whom Muldoon has shared experience and social-professional contexts. Pastiche, a

---

[73]   The urban-specific involves naming (of streets, areas, buildings, etc.), whereas the urban-generic involves non-specified places (such as 'the hospital') or a generalised urban scene. Barry, *Contemporary British Poetry and the City*, 6.

[74]   Lyotard, 'What is Postmodernism?', 80–1.

[75]   Fiona Shaw gave live performances of *The Waste Land*, in Wilton's Music Hall London, in a 1997 production directed by Deborah Warner, reprised in 2009–10.

broad and tricky term, seems appropriate to 'Immram'; although the stylistic pastiche is primarily of Chandler not Eliot, there is something like a pastiche of the techniques and themes of *The Waste Land*. Fredric Jameson's idea of pastiche as 'blank parody', 'the imitation of dead styles, speech through all the masks and voices stored up in the imaginary museum of a now global culture', existing after the loss of any sense of 'some healthy linguistic normality' is suggestive in this context, but depends upon a historical teleology (a trajectory from modernist parody to postmodernist pastiche) which is not responsive to the variety, detail and co-existence of such modes.[76] Muldoon's work is certainly not, as Jameson prescribes, 'amputated of the satiric impulse, devoid of laughter'. There is tribute, appreciation and mockery in the stance which 'Immram' takes up towards Chandler's style and Eliot's mythic-symbolic technique and form; the ironies are not, in Jameson's terms, 'stable', but nor are they 'blank'. Arising in part from the integration of disparate literatures and genres (American detective fiction; American-British high modernist poetry), the ironies float: mocking the quest for 'origins' ('Your old man was an ass-hole / That makes an ass-hole out of you') but they also bite ('She told me how his empire / Ran a little more than halfway to Hell / But began on the top floor of the Park Hotel'). In *The Waste Land*, origins are evoked ('Bin gar keine Russin, stamm' aus Litauen, echt deutsch'), but are far from stable. While the application of the iconography of Hell to contemporary life is clearly tragic in Eliot, Muldoon's tongue-in-cheek, wise-cracking style diffuses but does not efface the possibility of tragedy. With 'American Standard' we are closer at times to straight parody ('Shandy. Shandy. Shandy') and the satiric impulse is out in full force ('Some presidents love a big-ass motorcade').

Twenty-first Century Fragments

Hill and Fisher both belonged to the generation born before the Second World War and began to write at a time when Eliot remained a dominant figure of the English literary establishment (as poet and literary critic but also as editor and director at Faber & Faber until 1965); both can be described in certain respects as late modernist poets. Muldoon, born in 1951, came to prominence when postmodernism was an established mode, and his work in some ways fits such a term, as we have seen in 'Immram',

---

[76]   Fredric Jameson, 'Postmodernism, or The Cultural Logic of Late Capitalism', in *Postmodernism: A Reader*, edited Thomas Docherty (Hemel Hempstead: Harvester Wheatsheaf, 1993), 69–92 (74).

while 'American Standard' carries forward elements of postmodern techniques and mood into an alienated and satirical twenty-first century consciousness. Denise Riley (born in 1948) similarly spans that period: an
influential figure in the experimental poetry world of the 1980s and 90s,
her 2016 volume *Say Something Back* has elements of her earlier innovative engagement with lyric traditions, but in the context of an impassioned
personal elegy, which involves a certain consistency of subject position. The
central sequence of that volume, 'A Part Song' certainly does not resemble
The Waste Land in theme or style, using on the whole metaphor rather than
symbol and being overtly autobiographical, although informed by Riley's
self-conscious interrogation of the lyric tradition and its ways of forming the
human subject. Is her use of the line 'She do the bereaved in different voices'
(alluding to Eliot's original title for *The Waste Land*, 'He do the police in
different voices', drawn from *Our Mutual Friend*), as the first line of the
penultimate section, merely an isolated echo or parodic allusion, without
wider significance for her poem? The lines which follow, addressed to the
lost son, relate to hearing and replying:

> She do the bereaved in different voices
> For the point of this address is to prod
> And shepherd you back within range
> Of my strained ears; extort your reply.[77]

A wider connection with *The Waste Land*, then, is the thematic of voice and
ear, speaking and listening. Crucially, in Riley's poem this speaking and listening takes place in the emotive and 'impossible' context of elegy: speaking and
listening to the dead. There is an elegiac strand in *The Waste Land*, hinted at
most clearly in the opening lines ('mixing / memory and desire'), but largely
submerged in its broader symbolic project of communication with the past
and the dead. As a result, echoes of the poem have a habit of surfacing in the
context of reflections on meanings which the dead might hold for the living.
Tom Sastry's 'Underground' recycles elements of the London Underground
as metaphorical 'place of disaffection' in *Burnt Norton*, combined with hints
of the 'dead' crowd on London Bridge from *The Waste Land*: 'The dead pass
through turnstiles into the earth, / ... They stand on the jetty / bothered by
hot winds / and stare into the dark mouth of time'.[78] Gareth Prior, in 'The

---

[77]   Denise Riley, 'A Part-Song', in *Say Something Back* (London: Picador, 2016),
2–14 (14).
[78]   Tom Sastry, 'Underground', in *A Man's House Catches Fire* (Rugby: Nine
Arches Press, 2019), 16.

Idea of the Memory Theatre', makes a more knowing, reflexive use of allusion to both Eliot and Dante in a fragmented collage sequence (using some visual form including a graph):

> halfway
> in a dark wood
> DON'T STRAY FROM THE PATH
> & shush about the
> wasteland
> *[trigger warning]*
> bitter & grave but
> to translate the benefits I'll
> tell the worst of it[79]

The influence of *The Waste Land* continues to be perceptible, although often in intermittent form, in poetry understood to be continuing the modernist project, as represented in an anthology such as *Vanishing Points: New Modernist Poems* (2004). Lee Ann Brown's poem 'My Uncruel April, My Totally Equal Unforetold April Unfolded' uses Eliot's famous opening line as a point of reference for a radically dislocated series of phrases and images, some of which might be read as comments on Eliot's 'Tradition and the Individual Talent' ('As with all good (real) poetry movements we splice the past') and the emotional undertones of *The Waste Land* ('Aprils, walking near himself before there, her pleated heart, heated'). Ulli Frear's 'fragmento', the title of which appears with a strike-through, thereby positions itself as a collection of ironically fragmentary anti-fragments, with some echoes of Eliot ('plants glisten fresh dust'). Marjorie Welish's 'Detained by Rest' has a thread of reflexivity directed at poetics: 'And "lyricism" / [...] into carp'; 'An ambulance to give a close reading and apply / instrumentality'. It ends with a sequence of lines in which one might find traces of the imagery (rocks, snow in the mountains, corpses), address to the reader and critical reception of *The Waste Land*:

> Off these rocks,
>
> sincerity did escort authenticity once; once, sincerity did shoulder
> mountains in snow. Then later. Literary torsos placed there cope with their
> being prior
> When you say 'public' which public? When? Why? Or alternatively,

[79]   Gareth Prior, 'The Idea of the Memory Theatre', in *Ibant Obscuri* (Newton-le-Willows: Knives Forks and Spoons Press, 2019), 20–33 (26).

>deputy literary critics translate business listings into beauty: heavily again,
>her own criteria list
>>lend
>regularities
>>stipulating this rock, these discursive rocks.

The 'regularities' or otherwise of poetry, the question of its readership, the debatable role of literary critics and the poet's 'own criteria' all register the 'being prior' of 'Literary torsos' such as Eliot.[80]

As *The Waste Land* reaches its centenary, how far will it continue to be a significant influence? Its status as cultural icon and canonical instance of modernism would seem to assure it a certain role. Its formal devices, such as fragmentation and multiple voices, are perhaps coming to seem of less significance; in part because they have been so thoroughly absorbed into the canon of poetic techniques since modernism, and in part because, for a technology-saturated and globalised culture, they no longer seem surprising or disruptive. However, there is evidence that Eliot's work continues to resonate with younger poets. Caleb Femi, a poet, photographer and film-maker who was born in Nigeria in 1990 and brought up from the age of seven on the North Peckham Estate in London (which figures in much of his work), has said that he 'discovered a reflection of his own experience in T.S. Eliot's description of Margate in *The Waste Land*'.[81] Eliot has come to be seen in some quarters as a figure of conservative, even 'elitist' authority, on the basis in particular of aspects of his later career and prose writing. That Femi relates to his work so directly may have been enabled by the place of Eliot in the university curriculum (Femi studied English Literature at university), but his statement indicates something more than just exposure. It may also be the case that Eliot's cultural pessimism in *The Waste Land*, which had come to seem regressive and conservative to many by the 1960s, can strike more sympathetic echoes in the 2020s, in a civilization which is manifestly in crisis (with water and its absence being material threats rather than symbols).

---

[80] *Vanishing Points: New Modernist Poems*, edited by Rod Mengham and John Kinsella (Cambridge: Salt, 2004), 20, 82, 275, 277.
[81] Interview with Claire Armistead, *The Guardian*, 31 October 2020, 17–19 (19).

7

Compositional Process and Critical Product

PETER ROBINSON

The history of *The Waste Land* at its centenary divides almost exactly around the publication in 1971 of *The Waste Land: A Facsimile & Transcript of the Original Drafts*, edited by Valerie Eliot. In his review of the publication, 'My God man there's bears on it', William Empson questions the book's authorial epigraph which calls his poem 'only the relief of a personal and wholly insignificant grouse against life' and 'just a piece of rhythmical grumbling.'[1] The reviewer notes that a 'sheer page is given to a reported assertion by the poet, of unknown date and uncertain accuracy (surely, Eliot would never *talk* this kind of formal irony to Ted Spencer)'. Nevertheless, though the 'placing of this remark gives it too much importance', Empson was 'sure [Eliot] did at some time say such things and believe them,'[2] elsewhere adding that Eliot 'seems to have said this kind of thing when irritated by some particularly sanctimonious interpretation'.[3] 'What then was the grouse about?', Empson asks, and responds by ingeniously leading biographical material from the editor's introduction back into the representations of 'the contemporary world' for which the poem remains both famous and notorious.

The Waste Land's first reception took it for a criticism of western culture whose account, in the first three parts, was understood to be underlined by values asserted in the final one. This interpretation was buttressed by authorial Impersonality, sustained by use of the Objective Correlative, and reinforced by the Mind of Europe via the Dissociation of Sensibility. The publication of the drafts made the poet's 'personal ... grudge' and 'rhythmical grumbling' only too prominent. It pointed towards readings in which the first three sections were not so much about what was wrong with society, as what was amiss with Eliot – a reading Empson helped sketch in his review. These contrasting critical accounts (each figured by the uncertain intona-

[1] T.S. Eliot, *The Waste Land: A Facsimile & Transcript of the Original Drafts Including the Annotations of Ezra Pound*, edited by Valerie Eliot (London: Faber & Faber, 1971), 1.

[2] William Empson, *Using Biography* (London: Chatto & Windus, 1984), 192.

[3] William Empson, 'Eliot and Politics', in *Argufying: Essays on Literature and Culture*, edited by John Haffenden (London: Chatto & Windus, 1987), 367.

tional implications of 'my' in 'Shall I at least set my lands in order?')[4] invite the question how *The Waste Land* could be both impersonal critique *and* personal complaint, and thus how the first three parts relate to the last. For, read personally, the poem appears broken backed: if it does affirm the spiritual values of the fifth part, then it really oughtn't to characterise the people of the first three as it does. Also, if it characterises them thus, then the values in 'What the Thunder Said' do not respond sufficiently to predicaments expressed, either for the criticised society or for poet and his grudge.

These issues arise if *The Waste Land* is considered as critical product, and may be usefully addressed by considering the compositional process revealed by the *Facsimile & Transcript*. What follows is an attempt to take Eliot's poem back to its becoming, its approaches to meaning, and away from the monumental edifice of its afterlife. This may help highlight the successes of its artistry by lowering expectations regarding either the coherence of its cultural criticism cum societal panacea, or self-diagnosis and medication.

Eliot was not the only poet irritated by how it had been interpreted. Donald Davie observed at the half-century that 'even today *The Waste Land* as a whole lives in my mind' as 'a famous challenge and ordeal, a sphinx's riddle; which is to say, not (strictly speaking) a poem at all.' Of the *Facsimile & Transcript*'s reception, Davie finds reviewers complaining 'of Eliot, or of Eliot and Pound together, for having made a frustrating tease out of what should have been complete and satisfying.' Davie finds on 'the other hand it may be that what seems unsatisfying about *The Waste Land* is nothing intrinsic to the poem', but with its 'reputation' – with how that reputation 'was first made and has been sustained ever since, in large part as an excitingly advanced exercise for the Modern Sixth.'[5] Pausing momentarily before the likelihood that reputation and intrinsic nature are not neatly separable, I recognise such an educational context as how Eliot's poem first came into this reader's biography, and recall the baffling impression it made five years after its author's death.

An upbringing in an inner-city vicarage gave access to the first of the themes enunciated in the author's Note to 'What the Thunder Said', namely 'the journey to Emmaus'. I could guess at what 'the approach to the Chapel Perilous' involved and apply knowledge of the Great War and the Russian Revolution to 'the present decay of eastern Europe'. These three themes,

---

[4]   T.S. Eliot, *The Poems of T.S. Eliot: The Annotated Text*, edited by Christopher Ricks and Jim McCue (New York: Farrar, Straus and Giroux, 2015), Volume 1, 71.
[5]   Donald Davie, 'Eliot in One Poet's Life', in *"The Waste Land" in Different Voices: The Revised Versions of Lectures Given at the University of York in the Fiftieth Year of "The Waste Land"*, edited by A.D. Moody (London: Edward Arnold, 1974), 222.

the Note said, 'are employed': but how do Gospel miracle, Grail quest and eastern European politics relate to each other? The poem is presented as a mysterious whole under the auspices of Frazer's *Golden Bough* and writings by Jessie L. Weston, and was somehow what Tiresias saw, though the figure appears fore-suffering all in only part of one section. But if the poem was daunting, its Notes were more so. While its rhythms and language could move, the authorial exegesis was more sublime in its producing awe and fear. In short, this 'sphinx without a secret'[6] encountered at the end of my teenage years resembled the object William Carlos Williams complained of when writing that Eliot 'gave the poem back to the academics'.[7] Yet still present were its mysteriously unattributed voices, its animus towards aspects of urban and sexual experience, its unarticulated transitions of metric and location, audibly interrelated by a music both haunted and troubled.[8]

I was on my way to studying at the University of York when *The Waste Land: A Facsimile & Transcript of the Original Drafts* appeared, and my first year overlapped with the half-century celebrations. There was a series of public lectures, including Davie's. Modernism's legacy was in the air, and scepticism about *The Waste Land* as critical edifice could be heard at the opening to David Moody's essay in the volume that collected those lectures:

> While the poem compels, the received criticism ceases to convince. That it is a poem about a crisis or breakdown of European culture, and that it seriously invokes primitive fertility myths – such accounts, for so long found persuasive, now seem out of touch with the actual experience.[9]

Moody's editorial preface had cleared the ground: 'It was time to ask, what does Eliot's work mean to us, now, in the next age? For we read him with different minds from the readers of fifty years ago; and we discover a different

---

[6]   Maud Ellmann, *The Poetics of Impersonality: T.S. Eliot and Ezra Pound* (Brighton: Harvester, 1987), 91. Nevertheless, Ellmann interrogates the sphinx for its misogyny.

[7]   William Carlos Williams, *The Autobiography* (New York: New Directions, 1967), 146. For further explanations, see 174–5. See also Peter Middleton, 'The Academic Development of *The Waste Land*', in *Demarcating the Disciplines: Philosophy, Literature, Art*, Glyph Textural Studies 1, edited by Samuel Weber (Minneapolis: University of Minnesota Press, 1986), 153–80.

[8]   Writing when Williams's view had appeared to triumph in the academy, Louise Glück caught Eliot's lasting appeal, not least to a teenage reader. His 'speakers either can't speak or can't be heard, their persistence makes the poems urgent.' Louise Glück, *Proofs and Theories: Essays on Poetry* (Manchester: Carcanet Press, 1999), 22.

[9]   A.D. Moody, 'To fill all the desert with inviolable voice', in Moody, ed. *"The Waste Land" in Different Voices*, 47.

poetry.' Another half-century on, is mine a different mind from the one that attended those lectures with their 'new look at the poem'? Did we then, and do we now 'discover a different poetry'?[10]

Basil Bunting described Pound's *Cantos* as like the Alps: 'There they are, you will have to go a long way round / if you want to avoid them.'[11] Eliot's poem can't easily be got round either. Yet the Alps may be better understood by learning what they are made of and what forces pushed them up; appreciating *The Waste Land* better may be helped by looking again at how the poem emerges from the process of composition and revision, and how its meanings arise from acts of reading, interpretation and judgment first performed by the poet himself with his first wife, Vivien, and Pound in attendance. Looking again at Ezra Pound's pencil marks and marginalia, and observing Eliot's responses, finds readerly imagination engaged by uncertainties of a work in progress. The poem's living in our minds remains a measure of its dwelling in uncertainty.

If my initial encounter was unsatisfactory, I am glad of it before exposure to *The Waste Land* drafts. In that pre-creative-writing-course era, aside from reading poetry, I didn't know where to look for help with how to write it, clutching at such straws as Mayakovsky's *How Are Verses Made?*[12] But in the *Facsimile & Transcript* you could glimpse it being done, both in the local adjustments, and large-scale shaping. This includes an entire opening deleted by Eliot,[13] or Pound's reducing the fourth part from epical narrative to lyric fragment. The drafts showed distinctiveness being produced not by deleting and replacing lines with horizontal or vertical substitutions, but by butting together passages which had suffered deletions. They try to integrate fluency with critical and editorial acumen, considering every fragmentary inspiration, including lines from discarded poems, as potentially part of a work whose ramifications would build to more than the sum of those parts. Yet I knew it couldn't be imitated, and noticed *The Waste Land* grazing Roy Fisher's

[10] Moody, ed., *"The Waste Land" in Different Voices*, ix.
[11] Basil Bunting, *The Poems*, edited by Don Share (London: Faber & Faber, 2016), 117.
[12] Vladimir Mayakovsky, *How Are Verses Made?*, translated by G.M. Hyde (London: Jonathan Cape, 1970).
[13] Lawrence Rainey demonstrates that the Boston opening was a late addition to the Spring 1921 work on section I, but reports it as cancelled by Pound in *Revisiting "The Waste Land"* (New Haven, CT: Yale University Press, 2007), 20. Colour-coding and the note on page five of the *Facsimile & Transcript* attribute it to Eliot. Pound did not annotate the first typed page, suggesting that for him the poem already began on the second with 'April is the cruellest month'. His first intervention is to ring 'forgetful' on page six.

City when 'What are the roots that clutch, what branches grow / Out of this stony rubbish?'[14] echoes behind 'What steps descend, what rails conduct?'[15]

My first supervisor at York was the same David Moody who edited those lectures published in the year I graduated. His Appendix on 'The drafts of "The Waste Land"' in *Thomas Stearns Eliot: Poet* evokes that educational ambience. He concludes that the 'major lesson is in the correspondence of Pound's critical method to Eliot's creative process'. But his belief in that 'critical method', centred on its technicism, leaves more to explore and explain:

> His test of the genuine was directly technical: a weak word or rhythm, a facile or false effect, was evidence of insincerity or of inadequately realised feeling. Applying this test he discovered the poem within the drafts. There is nothing to suggest that he tried to understand the poem, in the sense of seeking an interpretation or explanation of its meaning. Eliot, on the contrary, would seem to have been wanting to preserve the invalid parts just because he did have conscious ideas of what he was after. Pound's contribution was to elicit what he had actually achieved – the poem in itself.[16]

Moody's passage channels Pound's assertion that 'technique is the only gauge and test of a man's lasting sincerity'.[17] Yet in creating art, sincerity may be necessary but is by no means sufficient, and technique alone is not enough either. Ignoring what an author may have intended to concentrate on what's written is a good principle for critical engagement, including with attempts of your own. If the publication of the *Facsimile & Transcript* would result in chips to the monolith encountered at school, its adoption on creative writing courses would not be how that was achieved.

Moody idealises Pound's interventions: 'to watch him going through the shipwreck passage is an education in his own verse principles; his work on parts II and III is a demonstration of practical criticism at its best.' This derives from an exaggerated premise: 'Pound's criticism treats the poetry not as something to be explained but as immediate experience. Its axiom is that "technical" rightness will be the enactment or creation of right feeling and perception – that the perfect song is a well-ordered mind.'[18] The contrast of

---

[14]   *The Poems of T.S. Eliot*, vol. 1, 55.
[15]   Roy Fisher, *The Long and the Short of It: Poems 1955–2005* (Tarset: Bloodaxe Books, 2005), 30.
[16]   A. David Moody, *Thomas Stearns Eliot: Poet* (Cambridge: Cambridge University Press, 1979; second edition, 1994), 317.
[17]   Ezra Pound, *Selected Prose 1909–1965*, edited by William Cookson (London: Faber & Faber, 1973), 34.
[18]   Moody, *Thomas Stearns Eliot*, 318.

'something to be explained' with 'immediate experience' misleads by valoris-
ing unmediated encounter. However much, in F.H. Bradley's words, 'the
mediated and complex should appear immediate',[19] reading poetry requires
acculturation in its art and practice, something Moody and his colleagues
were helping effect in me at the time. A profoundly unfounded cultural opti-
mism assumes that technique alone will produce 'perfect song' and exemplify
a 'well-ordered mind'. Pound's later career is a painful illustration of how sincerity is not enough, and how confidence in technique can lead to anything
but a well-ordered mind.

Moody states that with 'the water-dripping song' Eliot 'found what he
most deeply needed to say: what his life really meant to him and how he
must live it. Such saying, to paraphrase Rilke, is a mode of being – the lyric
is knowledge become power.'[20] But it's not only in politics that power may
corrupt. Nor do Moody's comments on Pound's excisions and marginalia to
The Waste Land characterise someone not interpreting the poem or understanding poetic technique as inextricable from implications of meaning. The
critic's account of why 'The Fire Sermon' needed to be cut from two hundred
lines to seventy-five convinces in its noting that the draft

> was hopelessly given over to the kind of satire which indulged the poet's sick-
> ness of soul without doing anything to observe and cure it in himself. There
> was no centre of intense personal experience here; instead there was the idea
> of correlating contemporary decadence with the myth of a decay of English
> sensibility since the seventeenth century.

Eliot is found to be merely illustrating his own 'Metaphysical Poets' essay in
this reading, and Moody concludes: 'But no idea could save the bad writing
and bad feeling from Pound's justly savage attack.'[21]

Alluding to the Dissociation of Sensibility in his criticism of the original
version of 'The Fire Sermon', Moody has Eliot's contemporaneous critical
writings contributing to the poem as critical product, and finds them shifting
in light of the *Facsimile & Transcript*'s publication. Empson had touched on
the Objective Correlative as means to Impersonality:

---

[19]   Cited from Bradley's *Collected Essays*, Volume 1, 15, in Christopher Ricks, *T.S.
Eliot and Prejudice* (London: Faber & Faber, 1988), 214, n. 1.
[20]   Moody, *Thomas Stearns Eliot*, 315. This derives from 'Gesang ist Dasein' in
Rilke's *Sonette an Orpheus*, I. 3, which is used as epigraph for his 'To fill all the desert
with inviolable voice' in Moody, ed., *"The Waste Land" in Different Voices*, 47.
[21]   Moody, *Thomas Stearns Eliot*, 313.

An author needs to find an 'objective correlative' for his emotion – this phrase assumes that the outside of his writing can never simply belong with the inside, because he must never write about the things that really matter to him. One ought to have realized at the time that only some great personal distraction could account for so bizarre a judgement.[22]

Such a displacement method explains how *The Waste Land* might be 'an important bit of social criticism' when 'it was only the relief of a personal and wholly insignificant grouse against life'. It also explains why 'The white-armed Fresca blinks, and yawns, and gapes, / Aroused from dreams of love and pleasant rapes' offers an outside that doesn't belong with its inside.[23] Hapless subjectivity leaks out though Eliot's correlatives across his poem, both muted and sharpened by Pound's interventions, as when beside the lines 'One of those simple loiterers whom we say / We may have seen in any public place / At almost any hour of night or day' he writes: 'Personal'.[24] Yet without the animus behind that evidence of something wrong in the first three parts of the poem, *The Waste Land* would not have caught the psycho-social phenomena of its immediate post-war world which were taken to be representative in the first place.[25]

Empson reconsiders Eliot on *Hamlet* and its problems in a knock-down paraphrase: 'the play is a failure because Shakespeare thought he could express this feeling through an old plot about murder, incest and suchlike trivialities, so that we feel Hamlet is making a fuss about nothing.'[26] The *Facsimile & Typescript* reveal Eliot's criticism of Shakespeare's play to better characterize *The Waste Land*'s disjunctions between symptomatic vignettes, 'emotion' disco-ordinated from its objects, and the implications of its whole. Vivien wrote, with justification, beside the opening twenty-five lines of 'The Game of Chess': 'Don't see what you had in mind here'.[27] The mention of the Menorah, for instance, the 'seven-branched candelabra', which is hyphenated in the drafts, insinuates a gratuitous racial profiling to the lady in her Chair.[28]

---

22   Empson, *Using Biography*, 198.
23   *The Waste Land: a facsimile and transcript*, 1, 39.
24   Ibid., 45.
25   Empson found Eliot evoking Dickens and scolding, but without benefit of a plot to explain why, challenging thus the practice of image-based poetry. See Empson, *Using Biography*, 191.
26   Ibid., 198.
27   *The Waste Land: a facsimile and transcript*, 11.
28   Eliot's imputed anti-Semitism was intensified by the *Facsimile & Transcript*. For Empson's relation of it to familial conflicts, see *Using Biography*, 196–7. Ricks

Moody's acceptance of Poundian 'absolute' technical standards meets an inconsistency when he gives interpretive reasons for why the less-than-'*echt*' parts are weak, offering judgments about how words, phrases, lines, and passages might be unsatisfactory also because of what they say. Pound, for instance, rings 'closed carriage' and comments 'Why this Blot on the Scutchen between 1922 & Lil', writing '1880' in the right margin. He guides Eliot away from aping Joyce's *Ulysses*, deleting 'yes!' after 'those are pearls that were his eyes', writing 'Penelope J. J.'[29] Pound is not an obstetric nurse helping deliver Eliot's baby by caesarean section (as the metaphor in their correspondence had it)[30] because he aided in its conception. Nor is he simply *il miglior fabbro*, but rather a poet with divergent agenda altering the poem's still and perpetually uncertain meanings. Nor is his confidence in editorial intervention always in sympathy with Eliot's creative impulses.

Moody implied that Pound's 'justly savage attack' on 'The Fire Sermon' was motivated by more than technique, that he understood how the satire didn't bite because, out of focus both in verse form and cultural detail, the one implicated in the other. Pound's crossings out of the elegiac quatrains relating the encounter of the clerk and typist are similarly accompanied by multiple objections: 'inversions not warranted by any real exegience [*sic*] of metre' addresses the intersection of natural syntax and metrical structure; 'not in that lodging house' questions the accuracy of class-coordinated detail; 'Too easy' beside Tiresias's 'Knowing the manner of these crawling bugs' criticises this disparagement of the clerk and typist partly prompted by the obligation to rhyme on 'wrinkled dugs'; 'Personal' criticises the introduction in that stanza of the floating 'we say' and 'We may' grounding comment in restricted class sensibility; 'Perhaps be damned' reacts against tentative presentation, while 'alternate nights' may comment on the stanza's sexual implication in the clerk's flitting 'from flat to flat' for his day job, and 'mix up of the couplet and grishkin not good' combines a criticism of form with reference to mate-

---

explored it in *T.S. Eliot and Prejudice*, 25–76. Anthony Julius, *T.S. Eliot, Anti-Semitism and Literary Form* (Cambridge: Cambridge University Press, 1995) gave it fresh impetus. Bryan Cheyette carefully reviewed the case in 'Eliot and "Race": Jews, Irish and Blacks', in *A Companion to T.S. Eliot* edited by David E. Chinitz (Oxford: Wiley-Blackwell, 2009), 335–49. For comment on its relation to finance, see Peter Robinson, *Poetry & Money: A Speculation* (Liverpool: Liverpool University Press, 2020), 158–61.

[29] *The Waste Land: a facsimile and transcript*, 13. Pound is alluding to Browning's play to indicate datedness of idiom. Not able to use 'taxi' again, Eliot changed 'carriage' to 'car'.

[30] See 'Ezra performed the caesarean' in 'Sage Homme', *The Selected Letters of Ezra Pound 1907–1941*, edited by D.D. Paige (New York: New Directions, 1950), 170.

rial already used by Eliot in 'Whispers of Immortality'. Pound comments on the implausibility of the typist having a 'false / Japanese print, purchased in Oxford Street' and questions whether the clerk could have 'been with Nevinson today'. This sexual opportunist might be boastfully lying about meeting the Futurist painter C.R.W. Nevinson, but, even if intended, this is also implausible 'in that lodging house'. Not all of Pound's deletions were followed. The entire 'Bradford millionaire' stanza is deleted, but Eliot keeps the war profiteer image in his second two lines. Moody is right that the 'major lesson is in the correspondence of Pound's critical method to Eliot's creative process', though not because Arnaut ignores what Dante meant to mean.

Moody accuses the poet of being 'unreal' when composing the pub scene in 'The Game of Chess',[31] but he doesn't discuss its evocations of back-street abortion, lack of contraception, the imposition of male conjugal rights, of sexual rivalry, any relevance of Ophelia's madness and death by water, or how these might trouble and confuse the poem's themes. *The Waste Land* as published is rarely thought sensitive to the predicaments of women at the time. Moody's Appendix on the drafts defends his critical interpretation of the finished product by drawing upon a theory of Poundian technique that clears away the excesses of the diseased Eliotian sensibility. Thereby he creates a more direct path through the falsely-identified diagnosis (not of European civilisation but the poet's subjectivity) towards a healthy relationship with life and sexuality. Yet Pound understood and interpreted the poem enough to know that this is not what it meant at all, for the personal solution sketched out in the fifth part is a disjunctive withdrawal towards transcendence from the diagnostics in the first three parts, barely attached to them via the inverted baptism of the lyric remnant that is 'Death by Water', or by the recidivism of the final passage's citational collage before the work's last, resigning line.

Eliot's described rape scene in 'He Do the Police in Different Voices: Part II' began with 'so lively' a glimpse of sexual violence:

> Above the antique mantel was displayed
> In pigment, but so lively, you had thought
> A window gave upon the sylvan scene,
> The change of Philomel, by the barbarous king
> So rudely forced, yet there the nightingale
> Filled all the desert with inviolable voice,
> And still she cried (and still the world pursues)
> Jug Jug, into the dirty ears of death; lust;
> And other tales, from the old stumps and bloody ends of time

---

[31] Moody, *Thomas Stearns Eliot*, 88.

Were told upon the walls, where staring forms
Leaned out, and hushed the room and closed it in.[32]

Pound deleted most of the second line ('but so lively, you had thought'),
ringing the words 'you had thought' which he describes as 'the weakest part'.
He circles the word 'inviolable', suggesting the rhythm is 'too penty' (too
routinely iambic pentameter); he cuts 'of death', rings and crosses out 'lust',
brackets the next line and removes 'and other tales, from the'; he also cuts
'the' before 'dirty ears', then 'where' two lines later and 'and', twice, in the
last line. Proposing changes of this sort inevitably alters meaning, producing
a 'change of Philomel' as the poem itself changes.

When Eliot revised, he accepted Pound's deletions to his second line, but
did not remove the word 'inviolable'; he followed the lopping off of 'death;
lust; / And other tales' but revised the remainder of that line, muting the
image of time ('stumps and bloody ends') which recalls not so much the body
of Philomel as Lavinia's in *Titus Andronicus*. The final version tones down
the scene and increases the distance by emphasizing that, while the picture
may be thought real, we're not to confuse act and representation, for now it
is 'as though':

> Above the antique mantel was displayed
> As though a window gave upon the sylvan scene
> The change of Philomel, by the barbarous king
> So rudely forced; yet there the nightingale
> Filled all the desert with inviolable voice
> And still she cried, and still the world pursues,
> 'Jug Jug' to dirty ears.
> And other withered stumps of time
> Were told upon the walls; staring forms
> Leaned out, leaning, hushing the room enclosed.[33]

Both passages are representations of an imagined painting, itself a representation of a tale told in a Latin poem, and retold in translations such as Arthur
Golding's *Metamorphoses*, read by Shakespeare, and (as Eliot's lines insinuate
by allusion) in many other versions or adaptations such as the aggravated
copycat crimes perpetrated on Lavinia.

Eliot describes the nightingale's voice, of Philomel turned into a bird,
as 'inviolable' – a word too crucial to remove or alter. 'Inviolable' speaks

---

[32]   *The Waste Land: a facsimile and transcript*, 11.
[33]   *The Poems of T.S. Eliot*, vol. 1, 58.

for the transforming work of art, and of representation, able to make the violated inviolable through metamorphosis. It turns pain into art as a form of remembrance and warns with the much-noted alteration of tense: 'And still she cried, and still the world pursues'. Yet the process by which this inviolable representation came to be made involved chopping and changing by two poets. W.H. Auden put the thought succinctly when observing that 'in the process of arriving at the finished work, the artist has continually to employ violence.'[34] His mimetic fallacy produces a misleading analogy, tendentiously associating the 'barbarous king' and revising poet. Both 'employ violence', as if they had equally 'rudely forced' the objects of attention to change and be changed. Moody's phrase characterising Pound's 'justly savage attack' evokes a deep-rooted aggression in admiration for cultural work, though we don't hope for savagery in midwives.

The following Pound-deleted quatrain from the encounter between typist and clerk receives similarly 'savage' treatment:

> Pride has not fired him with ambitious rage,
> His hair is thick with grease, and thick with scurf,
> Perhaps his inclinations touch the stage –
> Not sharp enough to associate with the turf.

Pound deletes the first and last lines and circles the word 'Perhaps'. In the margin he writes 'Perhaps be damned' and emphasises the intensifier with a short underline. In the quatrain leading into the Goldsmith parody, Eliot had written: 'Across her brain one half-formed thought may pass: / "Well now that's done, and I am glad it's over".' Pound cuts the 'may', rings it, and writes: 'make up yr. mind'. Then he adds, commenting on more than the tentative modal: 'you Tiresias if you know know damn well or else you don't.' He isn't universally in favour of knowing and telling. Immediately above he had scored through the second half of the clerk's parting verse: 'And at the corner where the stable is, / Delays only to urinate, and spit', writing 'probaly [sic] over the mark'.[35] There's nothing tentative about Eliot's picturing the clerk's post-coital behaviour. It's Pound who considers readers' sensitivities here – which Eliot accepts, leaving the two remaining lines from the quatrain unrhymed.

---

[34] W.H. Auden, 'The Poet & the City', in *The Dyer's Hand* (London: Faber & Faber, 1963), 293. For a criticism of Auden's view of poetic revision, see Peter Robinson, *In the Circumstances: About Poems and Poets* (Oxford: Oxford University Press, 1992), 24–8.

[35] *The Waste Land: facsimile and transcript*, 47.

Pound's marginalia regarding what Eliot knows or doesn't know has an affinity with the poet's Note to line 218:

> Tiresias, although a mere spectator and not a 'character', is yet the most important personage in the poem, uniting all the rest. Just as the one-eyed merchant, seller of currants, melts into the Phoenician Sailor, and the latter is not wholly distinct from Ferdinand Prince of Naples, so all the women are one woman, and the two sexes meet in Tiresias. What Tiresias *sees*, in fact, is the substance of the poem.[36]

Is Eliot attempting to say whether he knows or doesn't? The wording is hardly decisive, when one figure is 'not wholly distinct from' another, and thus the logical connective 'so all' means that the women are also 'not wholly distinct from' one another, even if the formula has now sharpened into 'all the women are one woman'. And what's the difference between the poem and 'the substance of the poem'? If I had to choose between Pound's options, I would plump for 'he doesn't know.' The poet is not Tiresias, as is implied by calling him a 'personage', so he doesn't have the mythological figure's access to both sexual sides now, which is why he is tempted by the iambic pulse to speculate about what might be going through the typist's mind. He cannot be inside her mind, which prompts further questions because he knows well enough to denigrate the thought as 'half-formed' – his poem fully forming it in its pentameters. The equivocation of such writing is a more honest expression of the poet's relationship to this imagined encounter than the definitiveness and fictive cohesion that *il miglior fabbro* advocates.

Pound's comment about Tiresias goes to the heart of the problem. The experience of sexuality is inevitably one of difference, a difference experienced through uncertainty, because in the strictest sense we can never be sure what other people are feeling. The citation from F.H. Bradley in the Notes confirms Eliot's knowledge and experience of this, making his comment on Tiresias literally superhuman, something his lines are not.[37] The 'substance of the poem' cannot be what Tiresias sees, but rather what he doesn't, not least because *The Waste Land* at no point endorses the personage's findings according to Ovid and cited by Eliot in the Notes. There is nothing in the poem to suggest that men enjoy sexual pleasure more than women, something the wife of Jove, God of thunder, in any case contests. What Eliot represents does not coincide with Tiresias's report on his experiences, and the

---

[36]   *The Poems of T.S. Eliot*, vol. 1, 74.
[37]   Ibid., 76–7.

poet's Note then haplessly misleads, shying before the wide-ranging implications of what he has shown.

This supports the direction the poem takes in its fourth and fifth sections, both as composed in Lausanne and when edited by Pound. From the end of 'The Fire Sermon' until the last 11 lines of 'What the Thunder Said', except for 'London / Unreal' and stray echoes from earlier sections, the capital of the British Empire falls away. The original 'Death by Water' collaged a long narrative about a failed fishing expedition off the New England coast with the 'Phlebas the Phoenician' lyric. These were followed by the final section's indeterminate allegorical scenes with their ever more Eastern setting, from the original 'Polish plains', where Eliot vertically substitutes first 'perished' then 'endless', to 'Himavant' in the Himalayas. London and its problems are converted into further objective correlatives through association with feared migrating hordes and European collapse. These are then figuratively counteracted with suggestions of the Resurrection (the journey to Emmaus), the Grail quest, and injunctions from Hindu philosophy. But the poem's Sphinx-like problem lies in its diagnosis and cure being incompatible, 'yoked by violence together', as Dr Johnson described the Metaphysical conceit. Had the poet subscribed to the values said by the Thunder in the last part, he would not have presented the disturbances of the first three sections in such terms. This, conversely, implies that the three recommendations are not solutions growing out of or answering directly to those disturbances, whether of individual sensibility or socio-cultural conditions.

Of all the instances of 'perhaps' that Eliot removed responding to Pound's interventions, that from the encounter with Mr Eugenides seems the greatest loss, because it is not an authorial timidity but a nuanced imagining of the tacit sexual proposal being made:

> Unreal City, I have seen and see
> Under the brown fog of your winter noon
> Mr. Eugenides, the Smyrna merchant,
> Unshaven, with a pocket full of currants
> (C.i.f. London: documents at sight),
> Who asked me, in abominable French,
> To luncheon at the Cannon Street Hotel,
> And perhaps a weekend at the Metropole.[38]

Pound annotated two typescripts of this passage. In both, he brackets out the subjectivity ('I have seen and see') governing this complex sentence. He rings

---

[38] *The Waste Land: facsimile & transcript*, 43.

and questions the vocative 'your', deletes 'abominable' and proposes first 'his vile' then 'demotic'; and he brackets the 'perhaps' with a question mark beneath it in one, and underlines it in the other, writing 'dam [*sic*] per'apsez' in the right margin. Eliot accepts these suggestions and removes the 'Who', so the merchant becomes the agent of the main verb 'asked'. But the 'perhaps' had characterised the circumspection in the proposed assignation.

The revision mutes the aversion in 'abominable', a word sonically better coordinated than Pound's alternatives. Removing the signalled risk and insinuation turns this into the reporting of a fact, his asking 'me' to have 'luncheon at the Cannon Street Hotel / Followed by a weekend at the Metropole.' Pound discouraged the caution for reasons not sympathetic to the originally unstable mixture of 'memory and desire'. The authority of Pound's 'technique' and Eliot's sensitive touch in the portrayal are at odds.

Julian Barnes has spoken up for the virtues of more than an occasional 'perhaps':

> Teasing out the delicate and confused relationship between the suicide by water of Magritte's mother, the manner in which it was reported to him, the manner in which he reported it to others, the effect it might have had, and the consequent emergence into his art of female figures, shrouded and naked, Sylvester rightly prefaced his remarks with 'perhaps'. Not once, but constantly: there is one paragraph where six consecutive propositions are preceded by six successive perhapses. Pound complained to Eliot that his first draft of *The Waste Land* was 'too damned perhasy'. Sylvester showed the merits – too rare in art criticism – of perhapsiness.[39]

This real death by water has prompted Barnes's offhand recall of *The Waste Land*. But in the margins to Eliot's lines on Fresca's literary activities ('She scribbles verse of such a gloomy tone / That cautious critics say, her style is quite her own'), Pound ringed 'cautious' and vented some spleen: 'surely as you are writing of London this adj. is tauto.'[40] That's to say, it is tautological to use the adjective 'cautious' of London critics, so that Barnes and David Sylvester are equally pre-dismissed by Pound's damning 'perhaps'. That all metropolitan critics are cautious is by no means true, then or now, and asserting it only goes to underline the animus Pound felt towards the city that had, for just over a decade, been his base of operations. Yet there are more substantial concerns in the vicinity of his aversion to uncertainty, his belief

---

[39]   Julian Barnes, *Keeping an Eye Open: Essays on Art*, updated edition (London: Jonathan Cape, 2020), 305.

[40]   *The Waste Land: facsimile and transcript*, 27.

that the artist must display an executive confidence, a view running counter to Eliot's tendency towards the judiciously nuanced.

Uncertainty is required for there to be the possibility of revision. Pound's critical acumen depends upon his imagining that what he is reading could read differently, if words, phrases, and passages were excised or adjusted. As the lines from 'Prufrock' imply, the 'visions and revisions' of creative practice require a doubling of possibilities in time, creating a state of uncertainty between options which can result in a further havering, for 'revisions that a minute will reverse.'[41] Yet while Eliot's passage may be about dithering, the verse itself only dithers in so far as it evokes and enacts the state of mind that it characterises in memorably well-formed cadences and rhymes. If this is the state to which writing and revising are aimed, it requires what Giorgio de Chirico called *The Uncertainty of the Poet* exploratively to generate possibilities and alternative materials for resolution into a definitive text. In composition, there is no progress without uncertainty, and nothing worse than being too sure too soon.[42]

The *Facsimile & Transcript* invites an imaginative condensation of the roles played by its three participants. An aspirant poet might hope to combine the driven writer acting on instinct with an early reader recommending better lines, both monitored by a detached critical intelligence listening for filler or false note. A sensibility aiming to combine the roles played by Eliot, Vivien and Pound will need a high degree of critical self-scepticism to appreciate that 'If you don't like it you can get on with it' is more rhythmically pointed and relevant about sexual submission than 'No, ma'am, you needn't look old-fashioned at me'. Or, in another example, that 'you want to keep him at home, I suppose' is nudgingly suggestive when compared with the rhythmically vigorous and crystal clear 'What you get married for if you don't want children'. Vivien's suggestion is painfully aligned with the fertility materials said to be shaping the cultural critique at this stage in Eliot's poem.[43]

The non-conversation between the couple in 'The Game of Chess' has the woman's words recorded as direct speech, and the 'replies' without quotation marks in an indeterminate space, whether thought or spoken in aside. Only readers may register how the interpolated poetical lines don't aid the situation, because not reaching to any acknowledging auditor, and surely not the speaking woman, within their imagined room. Vivien asked Eliot to remove

---

[41] *The Poems of T.S. Eliot*, vol. 1, 6.

[42] John Dixon Hunt discusses the poem, De Chirico's *The Uncertainty of the Poet* and paintings by Magritte in '"Broken images": T.S. Eliot and Modern Painting', in Moody, ed., *Different Voices*, 163–84.

[43] For Vivien's twice-added suggestions, see *The Waste Land: facsimile and transcript*, 12–21.

'The ivory men make company between us' and, because Eliot wrote it back into a number of copies, Ricks and McCue print it in parentheses as line 137a of their definitive text. What Eliot's first wife knew about this line and why she wanted it removed is not known, though Ricks implies it may relate to sexual infidelity in the represented relationship that Vivien must have taken personally.[44] Her two suggested and accepted lines for the pub scene take on additional resonance because, unlike in the earlier intersecting monologues, with the acceptance of those lines into the definitive poem the couple are collaborating on its artistry. Her appreciation of 'The Game of Chess' (writing 'WONDERFUL' alongside it) further adds to the complexity of how the poem's sponsoring hinterland leaves a trace in the *Facsimile & Transcript*.[45]

That there might be issues in how *The Waste Land* was presented and canonised had been aired a decade before the drafts appeared. In his Preface to the 1961 edition of Roy Fisher's *City*, Michael Shayer observed:

> *The Waste Land* is particularly difficult to absorb, because in it are traces of a genuine ordering, and it is easy to mistake the genuine for the bogus. According to Hugh Kenner what happened was that the poet found himself with a great deal of material in which he could not find inner coherence. Pound then made it cohere. What seems to have happened is that at the time Eliot was stumbling towards a way of allowing poetic material to order itself which he only gained control over later, when he wrote the poem 'Marina'. What genuine order there is in *The Waste Land* resembles that in 'Marina'. But the bluff at the genuine structure based on the Grail myth seems to be all Pound's. I do not blame Pound for the attempt – only the bluff.[46]

Though the *Facsimile & Typescript*'s publication reveals the Grail myth to be Eliot's bluff, if bluff it be, one perpetrated more in his Notes than the poem, perhaps Pound's marginalia *were* a prompt for the misleading Tiresias comments. More searching is the implication that the older poet's interventions, and the structure he mined from the mass of materials, is itself a bluff, that the editorial process imposed an appearance of cohesion on passages that did

---

[44]   The line had begun life as part of 'The Death of the Duchess', which Rainey dates to early 1916 (*Revisiting "The Waste Land"*, 15). For the line in *The Waste Land* and comments on it, see *The Poems of T.S. Eliot*, vol. 1, 60, 637 and Ricks, *T.S. Eliot and Prejudice*, 212.

[45]   Kevin Jackson thought so. See his *Invisible Forms: A Guide to Literary Curiosities* (London: Picador, 1999), 176.

[46]   Michael Shayer, Preface to Roy Fisher, *City* (Worcester: Migrant Press, 1961), 3–4.

not have an inner structure. This also implies that the presentation of the poem and addition of the Notes began the work of establishing its compensatory critical coherence independently of the responses that the collaged passages prompt when read. Did, then, the publication of the *Facsimile & Transcript* alter what the poem is understood to mean?

What had been presented as a highly self-aware structure marked with a compositional confidence is discovered to be, until the fifth section, more an improvised collage produced by the removal of extended passages and the adjustment of much that survived the cull. These changes might be adduced as evidence for Geoffrey Hill's assertion that *The Waste Land* before Pound edited it was an example of Eliot's discursive mode: 'we also have the distinction in Eliot himself between two major modes of his poetic comprehension. To the discursive intelligence belong *The Waste Land* in the form in which Eliot first presented it to Pound's scrutiny'. This implies that the final form illustrates the opposed mode, though Hill doesn't name it as such when continuing: 'With the way of apprehension, the syntax of becoming, we may associate *Ash Wednesday*, *Sweeney Agonistes*, *Marina* and – perhaps surprisingly – the two sections of the unfinished *Coriolan*.'[47] This dualism, the discursive denigrated in favour of the apprehensive, is correlated with Hill's criticism in his contrasting 'pitch' and 'tone', where the weakness of the discursive is manifested in its collusive deployment of 'tone', while 'the syntax of becoming' exemplifies the preferred mode characterised by 'pitch'. The aligning of *The Waste Land* before and after Pound's midwifery across this binary suggests that his editorial interventions exemplify, in Hill's terms, the conversion of a reliance on 'tone' to a commitment to 'pitch'. This technical issue turns out to be intimate with the relation of creative uncertainty to the reciprocal give-and-take in readerly engagement.

One concern with Hill's binary is that he employs the two complexly-interconnected descriptive terms to make a broadly evaluative discrimination. But the descriptive senses feed back into his judgment, and tacitly question whether the evidence supports the criticism.[48] He appears so intent on Eliot's work having fallen off, that neither the discursive and the apprehensive, nor tone and pitch, sufficiently nuance the evidence. Pound's cuts and recommendations do remove weak transitional pentametric filler, simultaneously producing better instances of rhythmic lineation. The new cadences focus

<hr/>

[47]   Geoffrey Hill, 'Word Value in Eliot and Bradley', in *Collected Critical Writings*, edited by Kenneth Haynes (Oxford: Oxford University Press, 2008), 534.
[48]   See entries for 'Pitch' and 'Tone', words both employed to characterise the other, in *The Princeton Encyclopedia of Poetry and Poetics*, edited by Ronald Greene et al., 4th edition (Princeton, NJ: Princeton University Press, 2012), 1039–40, 1441–2.

appropriate stress-pitch-contours generating relevant vocalic tones within the ranges possible for readers activating the lines. But when Hill criticised a passage in *Four Quartets* for its collusion, he doesn't so much point to the fixing of a tone for its ready reception, but rather evinces hapless ambiguity in uses of the pronoun 'you'. Hill's criticism implies without stating that Eliot's attempt to apply his later values and commitment to the Church of England and a Christian society put severe strain on the attempted inclusivity of his pronoun use. This perhaps indicates that Pound's editorial interventions contributed to breaking the back of *The Waste Land*. Its opening three parts became moored alongside a lyric which forms a *cordon sanitaire* between the curbed satires and the final section's distantly rumbling, muted sermon.

Ricks' chapter on 'Tone' in *T.S. Eliot and Prejudice*, a source perhaps for Hill's attack on the term, helps us to think about the technical issues of 'pitch' and 'tone' in that it minutely explores degrees of uncertainty in the interpretation of rhythmically-shaped voicings. Take, for example, the lines Ricks treats with an awe-inspired deftness:

> Unreal city,
> Under the brown fog of a winter dawn,
> A crowd flowed over London Bridge, so many,
> I had not thought death had undone so many.[49]

In their Editorial Composite of *The Waste Land*, Eliot's editors acknowledge that what they print from the original draft 'does not represent the poem at any particular moment':

> Terrible city, I have sometimes seen and see
> Under the brown fog of your winter dawn
> A crowd flow over London Bridge, so many,
> I had not thought death had undone so many.[50]

'Terrible' is terrible, but might be explained by Eliot's three-syllable adjective aspiring to Baudelaire's cadence in 'Fourmillante cité'.[51] The *Facsimile & Transcript* reveals that the adjective had been x-ed out on the typewriter and replaced above with 'Unreal' before it reached Pound's pencil. He bracketed out, but didn't cancel, the whole of the first line and ringed the word

---

[49]   *The Poems of T.S. Eliot*, vol. 1, 57.
[50]   Ibid., vol. 1., 321, 327.
[51]   Nicole Ward Jouve's course on the Symbolists initiated a lifetime's attempts by this writer to learn from modern French poetry. See her '"Fourmillante Cité": Baudelaire and "The Waste Land"', in Moody, ed., *Different Voices*, 87–104.

'your' in the second. His fierce slash deletes the comma. These annotations are illuminated by those on the variant lines recurring in 'The Fire Sermon'. Pound circles only the phrase 'I have seen and see', and again rings 'your', writing in the margin 'vocative?' The accepted deletion of 'I have seen and see', removing the perceiver, requires the revision of the verb in line three from the dependent 'flow' to the main verb 'flowed'. As well as attributing autonomous agency, paradoxically enough, to the crowd of dead, this revision adds prominence to the first-person pronoun in 'I had not thought'.

These revisions superficially support the idea that Pound deletes the 'discursive' connective clause here, and so increases the apprehensiveness of the last line, making the passage more a process of becoming than a reporting on a consciousness. Nevertheless, the great *Inferno*-derived line not only stays the same but remains complexly indeterminate in its vocalisation: both 'city' and 'many' with their weaker second syllables invite a degree of stress-promotion to both the first 'I', deleted by Pound, and the preserved second 'I'. In the latter case, adding stress to the first-person pronoun distinguishes the speaker from others who don't notice the deathly crowd, or haven't thought about it. The stress cluster of 'thought death' allows degrees of uncertainty around deciding whether this perception is a result of the subject's mental state (emphasising 'thought'), or a consequence of the horror accurately perceived (emphasising 'death'). Ricks is eloquent on the deadening effect of the *rime riche* 'so many / so many' whose poverty he underlines. But he doesn't note the change of vocal pitch implied by the move from 'many,' with that comma, to 'many' with a full stop. It's the dropping pitch, the sentence-dying fall, that helps inscribe tone into the lines – an instance of why dividing 'pitch' from 'tone' doesn't illuminate how technique reaches into the innermost recesses of sense implication. Hill's discrimination also underplays how definitive rhythms do not exclude all productively-indeterminate uncertainties of vocalisation.

In his discussion of 'Tone' and the 'English Accent' in *T.S. Eliot and Prejudice*, Ricks ventures into the interrelations of meter, rhythm, and intonation – by which pitched syllables contribute to the articulation of cadence, which then indicate tonal possibilities for a line. *The Waste Land* drafts' revision of syntax over line endings reveals how the connection and momentary disconnection of enjambment can introduce uncertainties of intonation that may be variously adjudged. The much-commented on 'Unguent, powdered, or liquid – troubled, confused / And drowned the sense' is perfectly attuned to shift the participles into simple past tenses without requiring a revoicing of the words in light of the new syntactical context. In the same section, 'Under the firelight, under the brush, her hair / Spread out in fiery points / Glowed into words' is less perfectly turned. The absence of a comma at 'points' means that 'Glowed' cannot be the second of two past-tense verbs in parallel, and so 'Spread' must be a participle. This means you may have mis-intonated it, and will have to go back to re-sound the sentence aright.[52]

This latter emerges from Eliot's adoption of Pound's edits. The grammatical ambiguity had not been present in the lines as originally composed:

> Under the firelight, under the brush, her hair
> Spread out in little fiery points of will,
> Glowed into words, then would be savagely still.[53]

Pound's cancelling is adopted to the letter. Unlike the red line through the word and over the comma in the transcript, the facsimile reveals Pound's pencil entirely obliterating 'of will' and the comma, annotating it with 'dogmatic deduction but wobbly as well'. This is a further instance of his edits not being motivated by technique independent of interpretation. By removing the 'little', Pound shortened a rhymed pentameter into an unrhymed trimeter enjambed directly into the main verb, reducing 'Spread' to a participial adjective. Eliot decided against the preservation of his two verbs in parallel, which could have been achieved by reinstating the comma. If anything, *pace* Hill, Pound's objection to the 'dogmatic' increases the discursive subordination of the lines, even as it ruffles the unfolding apprehension. Here are two instances of constitutive uncertainty in the unfolding of poetic syntax, one finessed and the other slightly bodged, one energising reader engagement, the other momentarily flummoxing it.

The Waste Land as a critical problem largely disappears if returned, thus, to its compositional process of becoming. Then the larger uncertainties between its parts, the detachment of its diagnosis from its prescription, ramify from the local adjustments, cuts, and fixes that left it as first published and, with the equivocal aid of the Notes, critically received. *The Waste Land* may best be understood as located at a point of emotional and spiritual transition. The *Facsimile & Transcript* offers a broader view of the tracts across which its poet was moving and being advised to move, though in directions not always compatible with the aspirant points of arrival represented either by the poetics of Pound's interventions, or the values emerging from 'What the Thunder Said'.

Christopher Ricks, who was at Cambridge during my years as a graduate student and peripatetic teacher, would later acknowledge a contribu-

---

[52] *The Poems of T.S. Eliot*, vol. 1, 58.
[53] *The Waste Land: facsimile and transcript*, 11. The comma is absent in 'The Death of the Duchess', 105.

tion made to the debate concerning Hill's distinction between 'pitch' and 'tone' and its relation to Eliot's supposed decline: 'Peter Robinson, with the patience that can accompany exasperation, attended closely to the sequence of Hill's reasoning or reasons here, and (for all his admiration of Hill) is unconvinced.'[54] I was particularly grateful for the parenthesis, whose truth I feared might have been lost on its subject. Yet in that review, I was not so much unconvinced regarding the poet's reasoning or reasons, as persuaded that his divided terms are necessarily interdependent in the complexities of poetic composition.

I questioned Hill's assertion that it 'was the pitch of *Prufrock and Other Observations* that disturbed and alienated readers; it was the tone of *Four Quartets* which assuaged and consoled them. That is to say, Eliot's poetry declines over thirty years from pitch into tone.'[55] I asked:

> Does the opening of 'Prufrock' have no tone? Hill's criticism of Eliot's 'success' takes tone to be a tactful selection of content and style to suit an audience. But 'Pitch is highness or lowness of tone' and 'tone' is the way something is said. Thus 'tone' characterizes phrases and sentences, while 'pitch' informs single syllables, such as pronouns. The composition of 'pitch' over words and lines in a poem, its 'pitch contour', produces 'tone'.[56]

That is where my thinking about these techniques had reached towards the end of the last century. Almost twenty years later, I attempted to combine those recognitions with awareness of the exigencies in metrical prediction (the way the binary options of an abstract template such as iambic tetrameter create expectations of stress-patterning) and how these expectations intersect uniquely with the contours of English speech rhythms (never binary, and generated employing pitch in creating stress to effect tone). The implications of those variables, composed together into unique amalgams in individual poems, resulted in the findings and ramifications laid out in *The Sound Sense of Poetry*, which I might have prefaced by again citing Eliot's observation that 'we cannot say at what point "technique" begins or where it ends'.[57] None

[54]   Christopher Ricks, *True Friendship: Geoffrey Hill, Anthony Hecht, and Robert Lowell Under the Sign of Eliot and Pound* (New Haven, CT: Yale University Press, 2010), 32.
[55]   Geoffrey Hill, 'Divided Legacies', in *Collected Critical Writings*, 377.
[56]   Peter Robinson, 'Toiling in a Pitch', *The Cambridge Quarterly* 26.3 (1997), 264–5.
[57]   See Peter Robinson, *Collected Poems 1976–2016* (Swindon: Shearsman Books, 2017); and Peter Robinson, *The Sound Sense of Poetry* (Cambridge: Cambridge University Press, 2018). Eliot's remark on technique is from 'Preface to the 1928 edition', in *The Sacred Wood* (London: Methuen, 1928), ix.

of these insights would have come if I hadn't gone on trying to write and publish poetry for over forty years. The part played in that by my mentoring, as regards *The Waste Land* and its *Facsimile & Transcript*, forms the burden of what you have been reading.

8

Hypocrisy and After:
Persons in The Waste Land

MICHAEL WOOD

From Time to Time

Italo Calvino's *If on a winter's night a traveler* opens with these words: 'You are about to begin reading Italo Calvino's new novel, *If on a winter's night a traveler*'. This is almost true. The book is not a novel, and we have already started. Various instructions follow, which may or may not apply. Perhaps there isn't a 'TV always on in the next room', and we may not have gone 'to the bookshop and bought the volume'. We could have borrowed it from a library or a friend. In any case, most of the possible truths soon disappear. 'You' becomes a male (still true for some of us) and a full-blown fictional character (not so true), meets a female reader, and by the end of the book is married to her. She says 'Aren't you tired of reading?' And you say, 'Just a moment, I've almost finished *If on a winter's night a traveler* by Italo Calvino.'[1]

There are plenty of fictions where a grammatical second person becomes a character within the story – I think of Michel Butor's *La Modification*, with its use of 'Vous', second-person, to refer to its middle-aged male protagonist.[2] Perhaps every 'you' in a text, whether novel or poem or newspaper article, combines an actual address with some sort of fantasy. But it's still hard to think of 'you' as the name of a character, and to keep ourselves disentangled from the conversation that is not quite taking place. This is why I am suggesting that Calvino may be quite a good guide to *The Waste Land*.[3]

---

[1]   Italo Calvino, *If on a Winter's Night a Traveler*, translated by William Weaver (New York: Harcourt Brace, 1981), 3, 260.

[2]   Michel Butor, *La Modification*, translated as *Second Thoughts* by Jean Stewart (London: Faber, 1958).

[3]   In an essay published in 1984, Calvino wrote that Eliot 'will remain the greatest poet of our century', and in other pieces spoke of 'the lightness of the irony' and 'his delightful rhymed irony'. Italo Calvino, *Saggi*, 2 volumes (Milan: Mondadori, 1995), Volume 1, 727, 1348, and Volume 2, 1684.

I'd like to call on two other helpers, though, before getting down to work. 'He imposes orders as he thinks of them', Wallace Stevens says of 'the maker of fictions'; 'It is a brave affair'.[4] I take it the irony in the last phrase suggests not that the affair is *not* brave, just that it is not as brave as it thinks it is. It is what poets and critics do. Or, to follow a distinction made by Frank Kermode, a great reader of Stevens, 'poets ... help us to make sense of our lives', while 'critics ... attempt the lesser feat of making sense of the ways we try to make sense of our lives'.[5] For a long time, from 1920 to 1980, say, this would have been a truism, complicated only by a quibble or two about whether the second feat was 'lesser' or not. Order and sense were indispensable, if only as failed dreams. Stevens also reminds us that 'to impose is not / To discover',[6] and many critics have felt they were in the business of discovery. Order and sense were there to be found. Or not.

The suggestion is more modest in *Our Mutual Friend*, where Mrs Higden praises her 'beautiful reader of a newspaper' for being able to 'do the Police in different voices'.[7] There is still an idea of order – what else are the police for? – but an interesting ambiguity has crept into the wording. Does the reader do the police differently from the way he does other speakers? Or does he represent different policemen differently? I'm sure Mrs Higden knew what she meant, but we are the readers of her view of reading, more precisely of how she hears what is read to her, and we need to decide what choice to make, or if we are to make any. How do we hear difference?

A recurring device in *The Waste Land* (as in many poems) is the belated correction of a meaning or a reference. Often it's a matter of a line break, the pause that is only a pause, not a stopping point. In Stéphane Mallarmé's 'L'après-midi d'un faune', we read 'Tu sais, ma passion, que, pourpre et déjà mûre', and we recognize the coherence of the phrase: the speaker's passion is purple and ripe. We're wrong, though, because the next line is 'Chaque grenade éclate et d'abeilles murmure', and we transfer the epithets. Pomegranates are even better candidates for ripeness and the colour purple than passions are.[8] But then we don't quite cancel out the first meaning, we shelve it, or hide it among meaning's ghosts.

[4]   Wallace Stevens, 'Notes towards a Supreme Fiction', in *Collected Poems* (New York: Vintage, 2015), 428.

[5]   Frank Kermode, *The Sense of an Ending* (New York: Oxford University Press, 2000), 3.

[6]   Stevens, 'Notes towards a Supreme Fiction', 468.

[7]   Charles Dickens, *Our Mutual Friend* (Harmondsworth: Penguin, 2008), 197–8.

[8]   Stéphane Mallarmé, 'L'après-midi d'un faune', *Oeuvres complètes* (Paris:

This result is even stronger in Yeats' couplet in 'Nineteen Hundred and Nineteen':

O what fine thought we had because we thought
That the worst rogues and rascals had died out.[9]

Here the 'error' can't even be shelved. The sentence closes perfectly at the end of the first line, where our mind supplies the missing full stop. Of course, our thoughts are fine while we are thinking them, and of course thinking is itself the problem. Just happening to land on the wrong thought seems rather trivial by comparison.

In *The Waste Land* Eliot tends to use grammar rather than metre for this effect, but it is also very powerful, and forms a sort of school for reading much of the rest of the poem. There may be a 'we' in its first lines, if we find ourselves agreeing with the proposition about April. And surely most of us, all but the very unlucky ones, will feel ready to sing along with 'winter kept us warm'. A very comfortable condition in its sleepy way – who wants to wake up to the annoying energies of spring? 'Summer surprised us' continues this thought, but then our collective enterprise as readers runs into trouble. Have we been anywhere near the Starnbergersee lately, or at all? And how many of us have a cousin who is an archduke? Our 'we' has become a 'they', a person in a narrative that is not ours.

We stopped in the colonnade,
And went on in sunlight, into the Hofgarten,
And drank coffee ...

This new 'we' then becomes an I, says (in German) that she is German and female, and she soon has a name: Marie. 'I feel frightened', she says. 'I read, much of the night'. And when she seems to address us she is perhaps talking to herself, and we are just eavesdropping: 'In the mountains, there you feel free'.[10] It's possible too, we now realize, that our relation to the opening lines of the poem may be the same. Perhaps we weren't supposed to read them as a statement calling for assent or denial; only ponder them as a symptom, a clue to a state of mind.

Gallimard, 1995), 163.
9   W.B. Yeats, 'Nineteen Hundred and Nineteen', *Collected Poems* (London: Macmillan, 2016), 283.
10   T.S. Eliot, *The Waste Land* (New York: Harcourt Brace, 1997), 3–4.

Another instance, less freighted but still instructive. We are reading a report of what a woman says she said:

> When Lil's husband got demobbed, I said –
> I didn't mince my words, I said to her myself,
> Hurry up please it's time

No, she didn't say that. Let's try again:

> When Lil's husband got demobbed, I said –
> I didn't mince my words, I said to her myself,
> HURRY UP PLEASE ITS TIME

We read the typographic signal, and then move to the next line.

> I didn't mince words, I said to her myself,
> Now Albert's coming back, make yourself a bit smart.
> He'll want to know what you done with that money he gave you
> To get yourself some teeth.[11]

None of this is difficult. Of course, the bartender or the landlord of an English pub calls time when the pub is about to close, and of course he's likely to interrupt all kinds of conversations. But the speaker is also, in her way, saying 'Hurry up, please, it's time'. She and her companions are at the end of a war, soldiers are returning home, a life supposed to be ordinary is supposedly beginning, and it's not good for a woman to 'look so antique', as the speaker later says.[12] Certainly 'it's time' may well mean, as it often does, 'it's too late', but that's just the beginning of the multiplication of times arising from the accidental meeting of two voices.

Sudden changes of voice in *The Waste Land* are not exactly corrections, but they often have the same effect, especially when the relevant pronoun remains the same. A voice says, or sings, 'Sweet Thames, run softly' three times and identifies a work as 'my song'. A note helps us to recognize Spenser's *Prothalamion* as the source. But are we to hear Spenser's voice, or the voice of someone quoting him? While we are thinking about this, between the first and the second addresses to the river, a quite different voice says: 'By the waters of Leman I sat down and wept'. Now we are simultaneously in Switzerland and the Hebrew Bible. For good measure this voice is usually

---

11   Ibid.,10.
12   Ibid., 11.

associated with Eliot himself, who wrote a portion of the poem in Lausanne. The problem here lies not with attributing a voice to the poet in person, but in understanding that all the voices are his, although none perhaps is uniquely his, or without disguise. This is true even when we accept the autobiographical reading of certain lines: they are borrowed from a picture of the poet's life, and he could have borrowed words from another day or another mood. Hugh Kenner's sense of the effects of quotation in the poem is very astute:

> If London had become a kind of jumbled quotation of former cities, he himself [Eliot] in his unfortunate marriage had become something like a quotation: a character in an overfamiliar play, which sometimes seemed to be *The Duchess of Malfi* and sometimes a French farce.[13]

Make yourself a bit smart

In an essay accompanying an edition of *The Waste Land* printed for its seventy-fifth anniversary, Christopher Ricks looked at some of its early reviews: by Edmund Wilson, Elinor Wylie, Conrad Aiken, John Crowe Ransom, Allen Tate and others. He found them alert and perceptive, even when they were making what were perhaps impossible demands. 'A better critical tour has never been given than Aiken's', Ricks writes, and suggests that Ransom's sense of the 'extreme disconnection' of the poem – 'there are something like fifty parts which offer no bridges the one to the other and which are quite distinct in time, place, action, persons, tone, and nearly all the unities to which art is accustomed' – can't really be denied, even if the notion of art being accustomed to anything doesn't sound quite right. But the key phrase in this essay is Ricks' own, when he speaks of the poem as a 'new deep diverse astonishment'.[14] The poem was an astonishment in 1922 and remains one now. What has changed quite a lot, though, is our attitude towards astonishment. To put it too crudely, early critics – of *The Waste Land* as of other modernist works, like *Ulysses* – sought to reduce their surprise, wanted to understand the poem according to accepted criteria, whereas recent critics virtually require continuing disorder. Many commentators in the first period wrote of the 'protagonist' or 'speaker' or 'narrator' of the poem, as if there was a single story beneath the mask of diversity. And even when, like Stephen Spender or Robert Langbaum, they considered different selves within the

---

[13]   Hugh Kenner, 'The Urban Apocalypse', in *Eliot in his Time*, edited by A. Walton Litz (Princeton, NJ: Princeton Unversity Press, 2016), 37.
[14]   Christopher Ricks, 'Afterword', in *The Waste Land*, 43, 41, 38.

poem, or different forms of consciousness, they wanted to subsume them into some sort of unity.[15] Hugh Kenner is again both funny and exact:

> There used to be a kind of conducted tour, in which the student was bidden to observe how checkpoints would align if he closed one eye and sighted in the proper direction. This or that feature ... entered one or another thematic system, depending on the part of the terrain you were visiting, and the poem seemed a great feat of civil engineering.[16]

We can compare this remark with Michael Coyle's assertion, made in 2009: 'There is no "story" to this poem; it sustains no one locational or temporal logic: there is no consistent speaker for this poem.' And again in 2015, the same writer says the poem is 'famously anti-narrative'.[17]

In fact, even Coyle acknowledges that there are 'numerous broken narratives' on offer,[18] and it's quite interesting to think of genre here as well as voice: memoir, prophetic injunction, song, short play, novel fragment, piece of gossip, recurring parody, revelation. And of Michael Levenson's interesting line-up of speech acts: interrogation, demand, wish, apology, testimony.[19] In all of these cases we as readers are doing at least three things at once. We do them readily, almost without thinking, even if they sound monstrously complicated when we try to turn them into any sort of analytic account. We identify the voice or the posture; we work out how we feel about what is being said; and we fold a sense of the tone of the speech into our interpretation – how much sarcasm or innocence do we hear in the assertion that Madame Sosostris 'is known to be the wisest woman in Europe'? By 'identify' I don't necessarily mean 'name'; it may be enough to register a difference we can use for contrast and connection.

There has been some very good work along these lines, and I couldn't even have begun this piece without its help. I am thinking especially of essays

---

[15]   Stephen Spender, *T.S. Eliot* (New York: Viking, 1976), 128; Robert Langbaum, 'New Modes of Characterization in *The Waste Land*', in Litz, ed., *Eliot in his Time*, 88–100.

[16]   Kenner, 'The Urban Apocalypse', 23.

[17]   Michael Coyle, '"Fishing, with the arid plain behind me": Difficulty, Deferral and Form in *The Waste Land*', in *A Companion to T.S. Eliot*, edited by David E. Chinitz (Oxford: Wiley-Blackwell, 2009), 158. And Michael Coyle, 'Doing Tradition in Different Voices', in *The Cambridge Companion to The Waste Land*, edited by Gabrielle McIntire (Cambridge: Cambridge University Press, 2015), 116.

[18]   Coyle, 'Doing Tradition in Different Voices', 120.

[19]   Michael Levenson, 'Form, Voice, and the Avant-Garde', in McIntire, ed., *The Cambridge Companion to The Waste Land*, 91.

by Paul La Chance and Michael Edwards, and a chapter by Maud Ellman. La Chance begins modestly: 'With the term "voice" in our critical arsenal, perhaps we can murder less by dissecting with a better tool; or at least our work as murderers will be easier.' He thinks there are 'about a dozen distinct voices' in the poem. He uses the word 'about', he says, 'because it seems impossible (and perhaps not worthwhile) to nail down every voice'.[20] La Chance distinguishes between the first and second voices as we have above, although he thinks the second voice starts later (at line 12). There is then 'the seer's' voice, followed by that of Madame Sosostris, interrupted briefly by that of 'the quester' who quotes from *The Tempest* ('Those are pearls that were his eyes. Look!'). La Chance jumps to the second part of the poem and describes the non-dialogue between the woman whose nerves are bad and her silent but readable partner. Of the latter's utterances, he says 'this voice ... is talking to itself or to no one; it is primarily a thinking voice'. Then we have 'the gossipy chatter of a lower-class woman', interrupted by the voice of the publican, which La Chance wants to associate, once we have taken in its local reference and moved on to a broader understanding of 'this cry to the awareness of time', with that of the prophet. 'This voice of a modern publican ... seems to be a parody of Ecclesiastes' calm celebration of God's diurnal cycle'.

La Chance insists on the need to 'isolate and identify the quester's voice', because it is where we find 'the ambiguous strain of hope in *The Waste Land*', before turning to what he calls a 'traditional narrative voice', which introduces other voices or is named as that of Tiresias. He also pauses over the voice of the quester 'which occurs again and again throughout the poem'. 'Because of its pensive, intimate, philosophical, meditative quality which is more a talking to itself, more thought than speech, it is fitting that it be called a quester's voice. ... It is also appropriate that the words of Dante's and Baudelaire's lamentations be uttered by this quester's voice'. The same voice, La Chance continues, draws on Chaucer, Spenser and the New Testament.[21]

'So many voices', Michael Edwards says. But they are speaking in the poem and inside us, so that 'it becomes difficult to hear the voice of the poem'.[22] This is an interesting claim because the voice of the poem may simply *be* the many voices we heard. What exactly would the alternative be? 'The poem continually probes the "I"', Edwards says.[23] Actually, it probes

---

[20]   Paul La Chance, 'The Function of Voice in *The Waste Land*', *Style*, 5.2 (Spring 1971), 112, 103.

[21]   Ibid., 106, 106–107, 111.

[22]   Michael Edwards, 'Hearing Eliot *Now*', *Études Anglaises*, 65.4 (October–December 2012), 401.

[23]   Ibid., 413.

all the personal pronouns, and any of them could live something of the life suggested by Calvino's fiction.

Maud Ellmann, with Hegel, thinks that the deep truth about the legend of the sphinx is that the creature herself did not know the answer to her riddle, and adds that '*The Waste Land* too, is a riddle to *itself*'. 'Caught in an infinite quotation,' Ellmann writes, 'the "I" is exposed as a grammatical position, rather than proof of the presence of the author'. 'The first-person pronoun roams from voice to voice. ... The disembodied "I" glides in and out of stolen texts'. 'Writing, in the waste land, is the "wake" or voice – at once the after-image of the author and his obsequies'.[24]

There You Feel Free

I want to concentrate on 'you' for a while, because its use seems relatively unproblematic in *The Waste Land,* and because of its entire absence from the third part of the poem. The first 'you', as we have seen, is quite casual, implicitly includes an 'I", and means something like 'no doubt most of us'. The second is dramatically different. The reader (or some invisible person in the poem) is addressed as a 'Son of Man', and told what he knows and doesn't know. The voice is authoritative, but also curiously (suspiciously) helpful: 'Come in under the shadow of this red rock'. It offers to show the addressee something different from either one of two shadows, although what is to be shown is not all that heartening, indeed the verbal gesture sounds more like a threat: 'I will show you fear in a handful of dust'.[25]

The next 'you' is in German, and from a song in an opera. It is the object of a question: where are you, or where are you lingering? 'Wo weilest du?' And now there are two 'you's in rapid succession. A young woman says 'You gave me hyacinths first a year go', a man speaks in return of 'your arms' and 'your hair'. Madame Sosostris addresses a client as 'you' and indeed as someone who moves in the same circles as she does – 'If you see dear Mrs. Equitone'.[26]

At the end of this part of the poem a speaker catches sight of 'one I knew', calls him by his name and reminds him who he is: 'You who were

---

[24]   Maud Ellman, *The Poetics of Impersonality* (Edinburgh: Edinburgh University Press, 2013), 92, 96, 106. Louis Menand, writing in 1987, the year of the first publication of Ellman's book, suggested that '*The Waste Land* appears to be a poem designed to make trouble for the conceptual mechanics ... of *literary* reading'. See Louis Menand, *Discovering Modernism: T.S. Eliot and his Context* (Oxford: Oxford University Press, 2007), 90.

[25]   Eliot, *The Waste Land*, 4.

[26]   Ibid., 4, 6.

with me in the ships at Mylae'. He asks the man a question about the 'corpse you planted last year in your garden', warns him about the probability of dogs digging up anything we may have buried and then in an amazing conclusion to a flutter of times and places – modern London, the American West, ancient Sicily – takes us to France with a quotation from Baudelaire.[27] According to the poem's punctuation, the 'you' directly addressed is the friend, but the speech in question is a call across a street, and the more immediate, literal hypocritical reader is the one that we actually are, or may be, as at the beginning and end of Calvino's book. Another interesting 'you' lurks in the preceding line of Baudelaire's poem. The topic is 'the ugliest, meanest and most disgusting' of our vices, the 'delicate monster' known as Ennui – ordinarily translated as 'boredom', but meaning something like melancholy and despair, a terminal sense of the eternal sameness of things.[28] 'You know him', Baudelaire says, 'Tu le connais'. And then he names us 'hypocrite lecteur, – mon semblable, – mon frère'.[29]

The first 'you' in the second part of the poem is the silent partner in a dialogue, a person manifestly listening to the other but talking only to himself. The figure here is very close to the portrait biographers offer of Eliot's life, and the gender choice seems justified for this and other reasons. There is a 'you' implicit in the imperative 'Stay with me', and it becomes fully present in the next lines: 'Why do you never speak ... What are you thinking of ... I never know what you are thinking'. And then after the man has 'answered' these and three more questions, 'Do / You know nothing? Do you see nothing? Do you remember / Nothing?' A curious feature of this apparent non-dialogue is that the woman appears to have heard the non-response to one of her questions. She asks about a noise, the man 'says' it's the wind, and she asks a question about the wind. And then the woman asks the crucial question: 'Are you alive or not? Is there nothing in your head?' Of course he is alive, and there is plenty in his head. That is his problem. Still the query does produce one of the poem's great lines, calling on ragtime as a kind of mindless fun with a dash of Shakespeare thrown in. The man also mentions, in his head, the game of chess that provides the title of this part of the poem.[30]

Then we are in the pub, or being told what was said in the pub. The story presumably has an unnamed audience, we are reading an imaginary

[27]   Ibid., 6.
[28]   See Richard Scholar, *Émigrés: French Words That Turned English* (Princeton, NJ: Princeton University Press, 2020), passim.
[29]   Charles Baudelaire, *Les Fleurs du mal/The Flowers of Evil*, translated by James McGowan (Oxford: Oxford University Press, 2008), 6.
[30]   Eliot, *The Waste Land*, 8–10.

transcript. 'You' is Lil, addressed by a storyteller (and by Albert within the story), who records what seems to be a loss of patience with the unfortunate woman: 'You are a proper fool ... if Albert won't leave you alone, there it is ... What you get married for if you don't want children?' Of course there may be an implicit 'you' in the landlord's repeated instruction. Are we among those being asked to hurry up? We are quite remote here, though, there is no *hypocrite lecteur*, just a world of eavesdroppers. There was also at one point a sort of critical agreement about 'our' distance from the storyteller in terms of class: we don't talk like that. I think we need to speak for ourselves here. I don't talk like that now, but the storyteller sounds like several of my relatives.

And then we have the end of this part of the poem, the whole of the next part, and the beginning of another part – 155 lines – without any address to us or a surrogate, except for the 'thou' St Augustine uses (in English) to address his God. There are many ways of responding to this silence. We may feel troubled that the poem thinks it can manage without us. We may feel a certain comfort in being left alone. We may feel too comfortable, or too lonely. And then as if to compensate for this long exclusion, the poem addresses us directly as sailors, literal or metaphorical (mainly metaphorical, I would guess):

> O you who turn the wheel and look to windward,
> Consider Phlebas, who was once handsome and tall as you.

Phlebas is a Phoenician, two weeks dead at the time of the poem's speaking, and the sea has 'picked his bones in whispers'. Are we (or were we) handsome and tall? If not, it will be hard to 'consider Phlebas' in a comparison. But then we have learned that in death he went backwards through his life, and that is certainly worth thinking about.[31]

When we are addressed again, we are simultaneously on the road to Emmaus with the person we do not recognize as Jesus Christ and at the South Pole with Shackleton in the early years of the twentieth century. We are being questioned:

> Who is the third who walks always beside you?
> When I count there are only you and I together
> But when I look ahead up the white road
> There is always another one walking beside you ...

---

[31]   Ibid., 20.

The stanza ends 'But who us that on the other side of you?'[32] Eliot's Note mentions 'the constant delusion' of 'the party of explorers', but the wording in the poem is more delicate. The speaker sees three persons but counts only two, and you/we are being asked not whether there is a third, but who it is. The relevant point from the Emmaus story is that it takes place on the day of Christ's rising from the dead. The King James Bible tells us that the eyes of his disciples 'were holden that they should not know him', and then rather eerily has him disappear as soon as they recognize him: 'And their eyes were opened, and they knew him; and he vanished out of their sight'. Presumably the explorers see or imagine they see one of their dead companions.

There is an implied 'you' in the address 'my friend', as the poem begins to interpret what the thunder is saying, and a little later we read that 'your heart would have responded' to the idea of control, the third item in the thunder's instructions. The last instance of 'you' in the poem pulls us into a quotation again, and we become members of the group taunting Hieronimo, in *The Spanish Tragedy*, after his son's death.[33]

We could perhaps include in this set of voices the type of 'we' that seems to fold a 'you' into itself, make us part of a team, players of a double, generalized role. I'm thinking of the we-figures in 'winter kept us warm'; Madame Sosostris saying 'one'; 'we who were living'; 'no one'; those who have (or haven't) 'given', and who 'think of the key'.[34]

What sense do we make of this series? This is where La Chance's taxonomy is extremely useful, although for the moment I am seeking something a little more tentative, and with a greater suspension of belief. Among the open addresses to a second person there are only two that are generalized, and notionally include us, whoever we are: 'there you feel free' and 'handsome and tall as you'. We might call this Calvino's 'you', and connect it to the 'you/ we's I have just listed. There are some targeted 'you's that are quite close to this one: the 'hypocrite lecteur', 'my friend', 'your heart'.[35] All the rest are 'you's who in principle are not us, who are caught up in a quotation or a story that we are remotely sitting in on: the person addressed by the prophet, the figure in *Tristan und Isolde*, the hyacinth couple, the fortune teller's client, Stetson, another couple, Lil and husband, characters in the Emmaus/South Pole story and in *The Spanish Tragedy*.

---

[32] Ibid., 22.
[33] Ibid., 24–25.
[34] Ibid., 3, 6, 20, 24, 25.
[35] Ibid., 6, 24, 25.

I Will Show You Something Different

Counterpoint or cacophony? Or both? Maud Ellman writes of a 'cacophony beyond control',[36] and this is certainly what the poem suggests, and something we need to register before we start to analyse it. But of course a suggested lack of control is not itself a lack. It is an arrangement of sounds (and in this case script). I want to explore this construction a little further by looking at two passages in the poem where the vocal traffic is relatively quiet, but still present, and essential to the more discreet forms of our astonishment; and then at a passage full of noise.

The first section of Part II opens with invocation of a 'she', but the focus is on the splendour of her quarters. We have candlelight, a couple of Cupids carved into the candelabra, and the pronoun becomes a possessive: 'her jewels', 'her strange synthetic perfumes'. The smoke from the candles reaches a ceiling imported from Virgil, where 'the flames defeat the night'/'noctem flammis vincunt', as Dido presides over a banquet she is giving for Aeneas. This scene might give a different meaning to a later line in the poem: 'to Carthage then I came' – although St Augustine was no doubt not in such a festive mood. None of this tells us anything about whoever 'she' is, though it does seem that luxury can be oppressive. The only verb 'she' gets is 'sat', while her chair glows, glitter rises, jewels are poured, perfumes lurk (and trouble and confuse and drown the senses), odours ascend, a fire burns and a dolphin swims.[37]

Do we now return to the woman, and the narrative we were half-expecting? No, now we look at the walls. Above the fireplace is a representation of the story of Philomela, raped by Tereus, and converted by the gods into a nightingale after she and her sister had fed Tereus his own son for his supper. At this point, the narrator gets mildly excited. The nightingale not only sang, she 'filled all the desert with inviolable voice' – good to know the inviolable still exists – and the world hears her even now. Some figures in whatever world that is no doubt like the idea of rape, but the suggestion that no one is indifferent ('the world pursues') is encouraging. And then the narrator loses interest in the rest of the stories illustrated on the walls of the room, or perhaps is frightened by having come too close to reality, and offers what may be the strangest lines in the poem.

---

[36]   Ellmann, *The Poetics of Impersonality*, 100.
[37]   Eliot, *The Waste Land*, 7.

And other withered stumps of time
Were told upon the walls ...[38]

Oh yes, those other stumps. The throwaway effect is stunning. Perhaps that's what ancient mythology was. All rape and domestic cannibalism. Or is this just a way of not thinking of time's brutal collection of horrors?

Eliot told Ford Madox Ford he thought there were 'about 30 *good* lines in *The Waste Land*', inviting his correspondent to find them, and then giving the game away: 'you need not scratch your head over them. They are the 29 lines of the water-dripping song in the last part'.[39] The lines are preceded by an evocation of violence whose most obvious point of reference would be the arrest and execution of Christ, but of course arrests and executions occur everywhere in history, and the narrative voice here is cautiously talking about an aftermath: 'After the torchlight ... After the frosty silence ... After the agony ...'. The main item of information is double. 'He who was living is now dead', and – this is a wonderful use of the hesitating line-break effect I described earlier – 'We who were living are now dying / With a little patience'.[40]

The first forty lines of this part of the poem provoke no Notes from Eliot except the archly comic identification of the ornithologist's name for the hermit-thrush, and the information that Eliot himself heard the bird in Canada. It's tempting to assume that Eliot thinks these are the only good lines in the poem because there are no quotations, and because the voice is single. This wouldn't mean they *are* the only good lines, but it would suggest a gap between the voice he was seeking and the 'so many voices' that he found – to the poem's benefit, most of us would say. It is instructive therefore to listen to this voice, not as definitive or personal, but as a version of quiet, a home for low-intensity voice work.

It certainly doesn't 'say' anything – except that 'there is no water'. The absent water figures in 11 out of the 29 lines, an excellent example of apophasis. In this waterless place there is 'only rock' and a 'sandy road ... winding among the mountains'. And in case we might think this scenery may offer a version of the Romantic sublime, we are told that 'there is not even silence in the mountains' (there is 'thunder without rain'), and 'not even solitude in the mountains' (because 'red sullen faces sneer and snarl / From doors of mudcracked houses'). Just the sound of water would be something, the poem suggests, and this is where the 'water-dripping song' of the hermit thrush

---

[38]   Ibid., 8.
[39]   Quoted in T.S. Eliot, *The Waste Land* (London: Faber and Faber, 1971 edition), 129.
[40]   Eliot, *The Waste Land*, 20.

comes in.[41] But there is no such sound. And still less is there any actual water. We can see why Eliot liked this concentrated emblem of the waste land, and of *The Waste Land*.

But the emblem works so well because of its setting among other voices, so many other voices. The combined thought of counterpoint and cacophony becomes helpful here. Let's listen to the end of the poem, where the cacophony is carefully designed and extreme. The visual effect of the different languages is already noisy:

> I sat upon the shore
> Fishing, with the arid plain behind me
> Shall I at least set my lands in order?
> London Bridge is falling down falling down falling down
> *Poi s'ascose nel foco che gli affina*
> *Quando fiam ceu chelidon* – O swallow swallow
> *Le Prince d'Aquitaine à la tour abolie*
> These fragments I have shored against my ruins
> Why then Ile fit you. Hieronymo's mad againe.
> Datta. Dayadhvam. Damyata.
>   Shantih   shantih   shantih[42]

The shift from 'sat' to 'set' is intriguing, both for the similarity of the words and the shift of tense. When did he sit fishing, and where is he now, thinking of 'at least' setting his lands in order? His lands? So this is the Fisher King borrowed from Jessie Weston, and not just a possessive London fisherman? In this context, the gliding movement of the next line becomes another instance of the device of 'correction' – we read the words as the fisherman's comment on a local disaster, until the repetition of the phrase reminds us of the nursery rhyme and suggests we are hearing a quite different voice.

Before this voice and its associations can settle, we encounter six languages and four new persons: Dante's description (in Italian) of the Provençal poet Arnaut Daniel's disappearance into the refining fires of Purgatory, a memory of being a swallow in Latin, a sudden English echo from Tennyson, and a line from a poem by Gérard de Nerval, written (and quoted) in French, but possessing for good measure a Spanish title, 'El Desdichado'. A phrase follows that sounds even more like a quotation than these quotations – 'These fragments I have shored against my ruins' – and we plunge finally

---

[41]   Ibid., 20–22.
[42]   Ibid., 25.

into Elizabethan tragedy and the Upanishads. We are to be 'fitted', and to receive some kind of blessing.

This welter of languages makes us think of many things, and Eliot's suggestion that 'Shantih' finds an 'equivalent' in 'the Peace which passeth all understanding' is both helpful and curiously wishful. But then what we wish for is also part of who we are, and in this context I think of Mallarmé's sly remark about translation, defining languages as 'imperfect because there is more than one of them' ('imparfaites en cela que plusieurs').[43] The only perfect language would be the one that preceded the construction of the Tower of Babel, and that idiom would not really resemble anything we know as language. 'The true paradises are the ones we have lost', as another French writer said.[44] Imperfections may be repaired, but that doesn't make perfection a reality, or peace a possibility just because we need it.

The difference of one language from another plays a large part in the creation of its character, and there is no single story that will collect the personages here: a disappearing poet, two birds and a figure who calls himself dark, widowed and unconsoled – Nerval's poem opens with the words 'Je suis le tenebreux, le veuf, l'inconsole'.[45] The personages make, in this context, a remarkable portrait of disarray, linguistic and otherwise. But that is not all they do, and this portrait is not a version of the mimetic fallacy.

The poets and the birds are connected as well as separable, and it is especially revealing that Eliot should want us to think of Philomela (and Part II of the poem) as we read these lines, since she became a nightingale and not (like her sister Procne) a swallow. It is possible that Eliot is inviting us to see all the birds in the poem as one bird, since 'all the women are one woman', but we don't have to follow his invitation in this direction. In fact, the mixture of sameness and difference is precisely what seems to matter most. We may even want to think about why different versions of the myth reverse the allocation of the roles of swallow and nightingale. What if each of those 'withered stumps of time' has its own inviolable story, as it probably does?

We are caught between an espousal of disarray as a sort of meaning, and a sustained attention to a set of complex encounters and departures we can't properly arrange. This is not firm ground but it is real territory, and we have to make our own way across it. For myself, although I like La Chance's notion of the quester, I find myself turning, whenever (which is not often) I need a surrogate within the poem, not to Parsifal but to Amfortas, and it

[43]   Mallarmé, *Oeuvres complètes*, 363.
[44]   Marcel Proust, *À La Recherche du Temps Perdu*, Volume 4: *Le temps retrouvé* (Paris: Gallimard, 1989), 449.
[45]   Gérard de Nerval, *Selected Writings* (London: Penguin, 1999), 363.

is the voice of the wounded king that I hear in the contemplation of 'stony rubbish', 'dry ground', a 'dull canal', various wrecks, the 'rat's foot', the arid mountains and the falling cities. Only in this version the king is not cured and spring does not come. It could come, but I would have to be a different reader to believe it will.

Even this loose account is too constricted, I think, and many other interpretations remain possible, need to remain possible. This is where our hypocrisy as readers plays a role. Most of us, unlike Lil, want to make ourselves a bit smarter than we are, and consequently rob the poem of much of its own fragmented smartness, underrate what I have called its design. The cacophony is unmistakable but the design is active. There it is, as the lady in the pub says. Or there we are. No, there 'we' are.

Index